PRAISE FOR *REPUTATION INTELLIGENCE*

"For decades, business leaders have struggled with a critical question: how do I understand where my customers are going, not just where they've been? Traditional metrics like C-Sat and NPS are retrospective — they tell us about past experiences, not future needs. *Reputation Intelligence* provides a practical guide to get ahead of the pace of change. Dr. Escobedo's book gives us a unique look into the power of this forward-looking approach."

— **Rick Hamilton**, CEO, Infovista

"Every CCO I know has struggled with the same question: how do I prove that what we're doing actually moves the needle on reputation and ultimately valuation? Evan's book finally answers that. He's built a methodology that connects media signals to business outcomes in a way that's rigorous, practical, and most importantly, earns credibility at the C-level."

— **Nicole Vogrin**, Chief Communications Officer, Waterdrop (formerly Western Union)

"*Reputation Intelligence* is the rare book that turns measurement from a reporting function into a strategic advantage. Dr. Escobedo gives practitioners a clear, actionable system for detecting signals early and shaping executive decisions before crises unfold. A must-read for anyone serious about elevating communications into true strategic advisory."

— **Philippe Barillon**, Corporate Affairs Executive Director, Novartis

"What stands out about *Reputation Intelligence* is that the analyst-to-advisor evolution isn't positioned as just better analytics — it's operational. Building the right cadence, mapping decision-makers, and having a system that consistently converts signals into action and outcomes. This is a must-read for measurement professionals ready to make that shift."

— Elena Viveiros Rung,
Vice President – Analytics, RUTH (Edelman)

"This book captures a shift many of us in data and insight roles have been pushing for years. Evan Escobedo shows how reputation measurement can move beyond monitoring and reporting to provide the early signals and judgement leaders actually need. It is a practical guide for anyone responsible for turning complex data into clear advice that shapes decisions at the top table."

— Filipe Zuluaga,
Director of Data, Analytics and Insights, DGA Group

"This is how you earn a permanent seat at the table. By replacing vague sentiment with 'proof chains' and actionable signals, this guide turns reputation management into a validated business driver."

— Mathieu Trepanier, PhD, CEO, PharosGraph

"As communications continues to evolve, the ability to correlate measurement to business impact and reputation is absolutely critical. Evan's book gives communications professionals the framework to connect measurement to decisions — and decisions to business value."

— Brad Jones,
Corporate Communications, Edward Jones

"*Reputation Intelligence* reframes communications measurement in a way that senior leaders can actually act on. Evan brings deep practitioner experience to a discipline that often struggles to connect data to decisions, offering a clear path to greater strategic relevance. A timely guide for teams navigating both executive expectations and rapid technological change."

— Karen Santos,
Corporate Communications, Eaton

"Evan brought something communications had long needed — a science-based discipline for getting the right message to the right audience, through the right channels, at the right moment. Working together at Western Union, that rigour transformed how we engaged the C-suite: programs got funded because we could anticipate outcomes, not just tally what the world had already decided. *Reputation Intelligence* puts that same discipline within reach of every communications professional."

— Pia De Lima,
Global Reputation Strategist |
Former Global Head of Communications at Western Union

"Dr. Escobedo gets right to the point: measurement isn't the job, but what you do with it is. *Reputation Intelligence* is clear, practical, and written for the real world, where leaders crave insightful and actionable information. The ideas and examples in this book land because they're grounded in experience, not theory, and you can see how to apply them immediately. If you want reputation work to matter in the boardroom, read this book."

— Cameron Lawrence, Ph.D., Professor Emeritus,
University of Montana

"In *Reputation Intelligence*, Dr. Evan Escobedo tackles a problem I see every day in my practice as a data storyteller: data that reports activity and outputs, but fails to change decisions or measure genuine impact. I love this book's relentless focus on recognizing meaningful signals and using data to inform judgment, demonstrating how comms professionals can progress from measurement to meaning, from dashboards to influence. This practical, disciplined guide is a must-read for anyone who wants data to earn its place at the top table, not just describe what we already see in the rearview mirror. It also correctly positions AI in measuring reputational impact. What a breath of fresh air!"

— **Dr. Sam Knowles**, Creator and Host,
Data Malarkey podcast

REPUTATION INTELLIGENCE

A COMMUNICATIONS LEADER'S GUIDE: FROM DATA PROVIDER TO STRATEGIC ADVISOR

DR. EVAN D. ESCOBEDO

Founder, measuredIO

REPUTATION INTELLIGENCE
A Communications Leader's Guide: From Data Provider to Strategic Advisor

For permission requests, contact:
measuredIO Press
An imprint of measuredIO LLC
www.measurediopress.com

Author Photo by Peter Eklund | eklundphotography.com
Editing by Dave Plank
Design by Transcendent Publishing | TranscendentPublishing.com

Limit of Liability/Disclaimer of Warranty:
While the author has used best efforts in preparing this book, the author makes no representations or warranties with respect to the accuracy or completeness of the contents. The advice and strategies contained herein may not be suitable for your situation. Consult with a professional where appropriate.

Note on Case Studies:
TechFinance, QuickServe, and EcoGear are composite case studies drawn from multiple real-world implementations. While company names are fictitious, the signals, patterns, challenges, and outcomes reflect actual experiences across organizations implementing reputation intelligence programs.

Trademarks:
Media Reputation Score (MRS), Persona-Based Insights (PBI), and Brand Equity Score (BES) are trademarks of measuredIO. All other trademarks are the property of their respective owners.

ISBN: 979-8-9954412-0-5 (Paperback)
ISBN: 979-8-9954412-1-2 (Hardback)
ISBN: 979-8-9954412-2-9 (Digital)

First Edition: 2026
Printed in the United States of America
10 9 8 7 6 5 4 3 2 1

DEDICATION

For Robin
Through the years, my one and only.

For Jessica, Jonathan, Jonas, Jacob, and Juliana
You are my inspiration.

For Mom, who taught me to never stop learning.
And for Pops, who I know is still watching.

Everything in Pursuit of Better—because of you.

FOREWORD

Every year, I talk to hundreds of communications leaders around the world. They run teams at Fortune 500 companies, global agencies, and fast-growing startups. They're smart, strategic, and deeply committed to their craft.

Nearly all of them tell me the same thing: they're drowning in data but starving for impact.

It's a paradox that defines our industry. Teams have never had more information about what's being said about their organizations — more mentions, more sentiment scores, more dashboards, more alerts.

The data is there. But data isn't intelligence. And intelligence isn't impact.

The gap between having data and driving decisions is where most measurement professionals get stuck. They can tell you what happened, but they struggle to explain how, why or what to do about it.

This is the challenge Evan Escobedo has spent his career solving.

I've had the privilege of watching Evan's work evolve over the past several years — first as a Meltwater power user at Western Union, where he developed the Media Reputation Score methodology that forms the backbone of this book, and more recently, when he helped the Meltwater team build the Data-Driven Communications Research Lab, a special unit within Meltwater created to help communications professionals transform into strategic business partners by proving ROI.

Meltwater's Communications Maturity Model, which assessed over 500 communications professionals, confirmed what Evan had observed in the field: the difference between teams that struggle and teams that thrive isn't the sophistication of their tools. It's the methodology they apply to those tools.

When we look at measurement maturity, having the right tools only adds two points to a team's maturity score. But having the right skills adds twenty. It's this finding that informs everything in the pages that follow.

Evan isn't selling you a new platform or a proprietary dataset. He's teaching you a system, a way of thinking about reputation signals, stakeholder needs, and executive communication that transforms how your work is perceived and valued.

The frameworks here — Persona-Based Insights, Media Reputation Score, the SIGNAL methodology — are practical and proven. They've been tested across industries, from financial services to biotech to consumer brands. They work because they're built on a simple insight that too many measurement professionals miss: you cannot build effective measurement until you understand who you're serving and what they actually need.

This book arrives at a critical moment for the PR and Communications industry. Artificial intelligence is automating the manual work that used to define measurement roles — the counting, the summarizing, the basic sentiment analysis. The professionals who thrive in this new environment won't be those who resist that change. They'll be those who rise above it, providing the strategic judgment, contextual understanding, and executive advisory that no algorithm can replicate.

That's the transformation Evan is offering. Not just better measurement, but a complete evolution in how you create and communicate value.

At Meltwater, we've always believed that data should drive decisions, not just fill dashboards. This book shows you exactly how to make that happen.

The signals are there. The tools are there. What's been missing is the system to connect them to business outcomes.

Now you have it.

John Box,
CEO, Meltwater

CONTENTS

Preface: The Crisis You Didn't See Coming . . . . **xvii**

PART I: THE FRAMEWORK

Chapter 1: The Activation Gap **1**

The Monday Morning Test. 3

The Four Levels of Measurement Maturity. 11

The Path Forward: From Data Provider to Strategic Advisor . 18

Chapter 2: The Evolution of Measurement **23**

Generation 1: Output Metrics (1900s-2010s) 29

Generation 2: Survey-Based Reputation Models
(2000s-present) 36

Generation 3: Signal-Based Reputation Intelligence (2020s+). 46

The Barcelona Principles: Progress, but not Transformation. . 51

Chapter 3: Decoding Signals **63**

Section 1: What Is a Reputation Signal? 65

Section 2: Defining Your Reputation Pillars 69

Section 3: From Signals to Intelligence Layers 83

Section 4: Building the Capability 88

Section 5: The Evolution—Where This Is Headed 90

Chapter 4: Persona-Based Insights (PBI) 97

The Problem: One Report Serves No One 99

The Breakthrough: Borrowing from Agile 102

Why This Builds Trust 110

How These Tools Became the Foundation for MRS 111

Chapter 5: Media Reputation Score 123

Why Traditional Metrics Fail 125

Mapping Coverage to Reputation Drivers 132

From "So What?" to "Now What?" 136

Building Your MRS Scorecard 142

PART II: THE IMPLEMENTATION

Chapter 6: Executive Storytelling 159

The Solution: The SIGNAL Framework 162

The Six Components of SIGNAL 164

How SIGNAL Components Work Together 166

A Second Example: The CFO and Trust Erosion 169

SIGNAL ALERT: Trust Erosion Detected 169

Chapter 7: AI + Human Intelligence 183

The Hybrid Model: AI Detection + Human Interpretation . 190

Why Human Judgment Remains Essential 193

The Efficiency Math 197

The Critical Discipline: Tuning as You Go 198

Common Implementation Mistakes to Avoid 202

Chapter 8: Building Reputation Intelligence Culture **207**

Why Organizations Stay Stuck 210

The Shift: From Output to Input 211

The Operating Cadence: Making Intelligence Habitual 217

The Five-Stage Action System 219

The One-Year Transformation: What Changes 225

PART III: PROGRAM EVOLUTION

Chapter 9: Build Your Playbook **231**

The Implementation Phases 234

Phase 1: Foundation (Months 1-3) 234

Phase 2: Proof of Concept (Months 4-6) 236

Phase 3: Enterprise Expansion (Months 7-12) 237

Critical Decisions Along the Way 239

Chapter 10: The Future of Reputation Intelligence **255**

Persona-Based Insights: Delivering What Each
Stakeholder Needs. 260

Media Reputation Score: Making Measurement
Meaningful 260

Acknowledgments 275

About the Author 277

Appendix 281

Index 293

THE CRISIS YOU DIDN'T SEE COMING

February 14, 2025: The communications team at TechFinance watched the company's Trust score drop from 75 to 68 in just two weeks. Governance concerns were spreading through financial media.

The team had built a historical database of similar situations. SoFi. LendingClub. Robinhood. Affirm. In each case, this type of Trust erosion preceded stock drops, regulatory scrutiny, and customer churn.

If the pattern held, TechFinance had a narrow window of time to respond.

Most communications teams wouldn't have seen the warning signs this early. They'd be tracking quarterly reputation surveys, monitoring media mention volumes, or waiting for social media sentiment to shift. And even if they saw the data, they wouldn't know whom to alert or what action to recommend.

But TechFinance had done something different. A year earlier, Sophia, their measurement lead, had done the discovery work you'll learn in Chapter 4. She'd identified her key executive sponsors—including Henrik, a Regional President worried about digital transformation in his markets; and the CFO, who cared most about Trust and Performance.

She'd documented their priorities. She'd built measurement around what they actually needed.

So when Trust dropped seven points, Sophia didn't just see a metric change. She saw a signal that mattered to the people who mattered. Within an hour, the CFO had a SIGNAL brief on her desk. Within a day, Henrik knew how the Trust erosion was playing out in his specific markets.

A note on TechFinance, Henrik, and Sophia: These are composite case studies drawn from multiple real-world implementations. While the company name is fictitious, the signals, patterns, and challenges reflect actual experiences across many organizations. Financial projections and ROI calculations presented here represent realistic scenarios based on the methodology—not documented results from any specific organization.

Throughout this book, I'll share the methodology through two lenses: the frameworks and tools themselves, and the story of implementing them with executives. We'll follow TechFinance's communications team—and the people at the center of that story.

__Henrik__ is a Regional President whose questions, skepticism, and ultimately transformation from polite dismissal to active partnership illustrate what becomes possible when measurement professionals shift from data providers to strategic advisors. He represents the executive persona whose needs shaped how I learned to deliver intelligence that drives action.

__Sophia__ is the measurement analyst who builds the intelligence capability and makes it work. She's the one processing metrics, developing SIGNALs, securing executive sponsorship, and transforming methodology into organizational change. She represents the practitioners who do this work—perhaps someone like you.

And if Sophia's starting position feels familiar—if you recognize the experience of doing careful, rigorous work that somehow never quite breaks through—then her story is yours to claim too. The gap she closed wasn't just methodological. It was professional.

Both characters are composites drawn from years of experience across multiple organizations. Their story illustrates not just what reputation intelligence looks like, but how it gets built.

Also, specific dollar figures (such as projected market value or ROI calculations) represent illustrative projections based on the methodology—not documented results from any specific organization. These estimates demonstrate the type of value calculation the methodology enables. Your actual results will depend on your organization's context, implementation quality, and market conditions.

KEY CONCEPT

THE CORE PREMISE

This book is built on a simple truth: You cannot build effective measurement until you understand whom you're serving and what they actually need. Every framework in these pages—MRS, PBI, SIGNAL—flows from this principle.

Before you measure anything, discover what matters to the people who will act on your intelligence.

The Measurement Challenge

Reputation issues rarely announce themselves in measurement dashboards. They build quietly—hidden in the noise of daily media coverage, lost in sentiment averages, obscured by volume metrics that look healthy until they suddenly don't.

As communications measurement professionals, we hear the same frustrations: "Our metrics show we're doing well, but the C-suite doesn't see it that way." "How did this narrative take hold without our metrics flagging it?""Why does our measurement feel reactive when the business needs foresight?"

The root issue is that most reputation measurement tools weren't designed for early detection. They were designed for reporting. They tell you how you're perceived today, not what patterns are forming that could reshape perception next month.

In a world where trust shifts in days and narratives crystallize in hours, historical reporting isn't enough. You need signal recognition.

What's Actually at Stake

Let's be clear about the business implications of reputation measurement that comes too late.

Market Impact. Analyst downgrades triggered by reputation issues can significantly affect market capitalization. For public companies, perception becomes valuation.

Competitive Positioning. Enterprise buyers increasingly cite governance and trust factors in purchasing decisions. A weak reputation score costs deals the sales team will never hear about.

Talent Considerations. Top candidates research employer reputation across multiple sources before accepting offers. Negative perception patterns affect talent acquisition in ways traditional HR metrics can't capture.

Executive Credibility. When reputation issues surface without warning, the question inevitably arises: "Why didn't our measurement systems catch this earlier?" Your professional credibility is directly tied to your measurement framework's ability to detect patterns.

As measurement professionals, our job isn't just to report what happened. It's to help the organization see what's forming—while there's still time to shape the outcome.

QUICK CHECK

> **IS THIS BOOK FOR YOU?**
>
> Ask yourself: When was the last time your measurement changed an executive decision? If you struggle to answer—or if your honest answer is "never"—this book provides the framework to change that. If your intelligence already drives action, this book will help you systematize and scale what you're doing.

A Different Approach to Reputation Intelligence

This book introduces a measurement framework built on signal recognition rather than historical reporting. The framework integrates three foundational components:

Persona-Based Insights (PBI) is a methodology for understanding the specific information needs, decision-making patterns, and reputation priorities of key business stakeholders—from C-suite executives to board members to strategic internal stakeholders. PBI ensures that measurement intelligence is structured around the questions that actually drive strategic decisions. Before you measure anything, you must discover what matters to the people who will act on your intelligence.

Media Reputation Score (MRS) quantifies reputation against the priorities discovered through PBI. Rather than tracking generic mentions or sentiment averages, MRS scores coverage across multiple dimensions—source authority, prominence, sentiment, key message alignment, and voice—mapped to the specific reputation pillars your organization cares about. Whether those pillars are Trust and Innovation, Digital Leadership and Platform Excellence, or Product and Workplace depends on your business context. The methodology is consistent; the pillars are yours to define.

SIGNAL is the communication framework that transforms measurement into executive action. The format structures insights around decision-making needs: Signal detected; Implication for business; Gap analysis; Narrative recommendation; Action required; and Lift expected. SIGNAL ensures that intelligence doesn't sit in dashboards—it drives decisions.

Together, these components enable organizations to track strategic signals rather than activity metrics, build pattern libraries from precedent, deliver insights executives act on, and validate the methodology with proof chains—where every insight becomes trackable from signal delivered to action taken to outcome observed to value demonstrated.

Back to TechFinance: The communications team used this framework to brief the CFO with specific pattern recognition, historical precedent, and a recommended response. The company invested in a governance transparency program. The anticipated negative outcomes didn't materialize. The proof chain validated the approach. More importantly, the communications team demonstrated strategic value by providing early detection, not just crisis response.

But What About AI?

This new approach to reputation intelligence combines AI for theme analysis and summarization with human expertise. But human judgment isn't optional—it's required. Required to understand context. Required to interpret nuance. Required to translate signals into strategic action.

AI Is Coming—But You're Still the Strategist

Make no mistake: AI will transform communications measurement. It's already automating sentiment analysis, summarizing media coverage, and generating reports that once took days to produce. Many tactical analysis tasks will be AI-driven within months, not years. Jobs focused purely on data aggregation and basic reporting will evolve or disappear.

But here's what AI cannot do: AI cannot be your strategist.

AI can process thousands of articles and identify patterns. It cannot understand the nuanced context of your industry, your competitive dynamics, or your organizational culture. It cannot grasp why a governance issue that barely registers in another company might be existential for yours. It cannot connect seemingly unrelated signals into a strategic narrative that changes executive decision-making.

The measurement professionals who thrive in the AI era won't be those who resist automation—they'll be those who understand how to leverage AI for speed while providing the irreplaceable strategic layer: human judgment, contextual understanding, and business acumen.

Whether you're just starting out in the field, trying to keep current, or looking for a mid-career shakeup or reinvention because you're feeling stalled where you are, this book positions you to become that strategic advisor—not just a data provider. The signal-based reputation intelligence framework gives you the methodology to deliver insights that neither humans nor AI can produce alone: insights grounded in pattern recognition, validated by precedent, structured for executive action, and proven through outcome tracking.

This book tells you how to make AI a tool and a partner—instead of a threat.

KEY CONCEPT

AI + HUMAN: THE FORMULA

AI provides scale. Humans provide judgment. Neither is sufficient alone. Throughout this book, you'll learn to leverage AI for what it does well (processing thousands of mentions, detecting patterns, flagging anomalies) while preserving human judgment for what only humans can do (interpreting context, navigating politics, building relationships, recommending action).

What This Book Provides

This is a practitioner's guide, not an academic theory text. By the time you finish reading, you'll have both the conceptual framework and the practical tools to implement signal-based reputation intelligence at your organization.

Part I: The Framework (Chapters 1-5). Learn the conceptual foundation of signal-based intelligence: what signals are and how to detect them (Chapter 3); how to discover your stakeholders' priorities through Persona-Based Insights (Chapter 4); and how to quantify reputation with Media Reputation Score against those priorities (Chapter 5).

Part II: The Implementation (Chapters 6-8). Follow TechFinance's 90-day pilot implementation: from securing executive buy-in and establishing the measurement framework through delivering the first SIGNAL to validating the proof chain. Every step is documented with real decisions, real challenges, and real results.

Part III: Program Evolution (Chapters 9-10). Learn how to evolve from pilot to sustained program: scaling to multiple personas and markets; establishing measurement rigor through validated success metrics; and building credibility with executive stakeholders through validated proof chains.

Appendix: The Reputation Intelligence Toolkit. This is where framework becomes practice. The appendix includes nine ready-to-use implementation tools mapped to the core workflow: Discover → Measure → Communicate → Prove.

The toolkit begins with the Persona-Based Insights™ Builder — a guided, interactive application for capturing your Henrik's priorities, KPIs, and decision triggers, and producing your Agile Persona Statement. From there, the Priority Markets Map, Media Weighting Matrix, and Competitor Influence Scorecard focus your intelligence resources on what actually matters to your stakeholder. The MRS Scoring Guide provides complete rubrics for article-level scoring, while the MRS Roll-up Calculator aggregates those scores into the pillar MRS, overall MRS, and competitive benchmarks that go in your executive briefings. The SIGNAL Brief Template structures your intelligence for action. The Proof Chain Builder documents the signal-to-decision-to-outcome sequence that proves your program's ROI. And the 90-Day Implementation Roadmap translates the entire methodology into a week-by-week plan with Go/No-Go checkpoints.

Every tool connects to the methodology in the chapters. All nine are available as free interactive applications at measuredio.com/book/tools — no software required.

This is an implementation system designed for communications measurement professionals.

Whom This Book Serves

This book is written for anyone who believes reputation deserves strategic management, not just quarterly reports.

Communications Leaders (CCO, VP Corporate Communications, Corporate Affairs) are accountable for reputation but often lack the intelligence infrastructure to manage it proactively. This framework shows you how to build a function that detects threats early, quantifies impact credibly, and earns a permanent seat at the strategic table.

Measurement and Intelligence Professionals are responsible for demonstrating the value of communications programs. This book helps you move beyond vanity metrics to deliver intelligence that executives actually use—pattern recognition, validated business outcomes, and recommendations that drive decisions.

Marketing and Brand Leaders (CMO, VP Brand) know that brand perception shapes business results but struggle to connect media signals to market outcomes. The Media Reputation Score provides a systematic way to measure drivers of perception change and benchmark against competitors.

Functional Executives (CFO, CPO, CHRO) make decisions that depend on reputation intelligence—investor confidence, competitive positioning, employer brand. This book shows you what to expect from your communications partners and how to use reputation signals in your own decision-making.

Strategy and Corporate Development Leaders evaluate markets, assess acquisition targets, and advise on market entry. Reputation intelligence provides an external signal layer that complements traditional financial and operational analysis.

Anyone Building Measurement Capability for their organization will find in this book both the conceptual framework and the practical templates to implement signal-based reputation intelligence from scratch.

If, whatever your role, you've ever thought:

- *"Why didn't anyone see this coming?"*
- *"What does this coverage actually mean for the business?"*
- *"We have dashboards, but I'm still looking for the action."*

This book will give you the framework and tools to answer those questions—before the next crisis forces you to.

Before We Go Further

A word for those of you who may be reading this from a harder place.

Not everyone picking up this book is looking to level up from a position of stability. Some of you are already marginalized—sidelined by leadership that stopped listening years ago, stuck in a role where your budget keeps shrinking and your seat at the table keeps moving closer to the door. Maybe you've been delivering solid work for years and still can't get a meeting with your own CCO. Maybe you've watched a peer with half your experience get the VP title because they told a better story. Maybe you're genuinely worried that AI is coming for your job—not as a distant abstraction, but as something you feel every time you open your inbox.

This book is especially for you.

The methodology here isn't just a system for building smarter measurement programs. It's a pathway back to relevance—and forward to a career you didn't think was still possible. The skills in these chapters don't belong to your organization. They belong to you. Every framework you build, every executive relationship you cultivate using PBI, every SIGNAL brief that earns a second look—that's yours. You take it with you. In a moment when AI is automating the tactical work that used to define our value, the strategic judgment this book develops is exactly what can't be replaced.

If you're starting from zero credibility, that's okay. So did Sophia.

The Implementation Path

By the end of this book, you'll have a clear implementation roadmap.

Phase 1: Foundation (Weeks 1-4): Conduct persona interviews to understand executive information needs. Build your Media Weighting Matrix to classify sources by influence. Calculate baseline MRS scores across business priority signals and establish your competitive benchmarking framework.

Phase 2: Signal Recognition (Weeks 5-6): Identify your first signal using the pattern library approach. Structure the insight using the SIGNAL format. Brief executive stakeholders with specific precedent analysis and recommended actions.

Phase 3: Validation (Weeks 7-12): Track action implementation and outcome development. Document the proof chain from signal to result. Measure whether the pattern recognition framework successfully identified a developing situation early enough to enable a response.

Phase 4: Program Evolution (Week 13+): Present validated results showing signal detection → executive action → business outcome. Use the proof chain to build credibility for expanding the measurement framework to additional personas, markets, or use cases.

This is a 90-day pilot with clear milestones and measurement validation points. You're not implementing a multi-year transformation. You're testing a measurement approach with a defined proof point. Instead of pitching an expensive, ongoing new program without any hard proof it will work, you're offering to "bootstrap" a new approach, keeping the stakes low if it doesn't work out.

Why Signal-Based Reputation Intelligence Matters Now

The window for reactive reputation measurement is closing—these days, information propagates too quickly. Stakeholder expectations for organizational transparency have accelerated. A single social media post, one headline, or one employee comment can trigger seismic perception shifts—and once trust erodes, rebuilding requires significantly more effort than early intervention would have.

The measurement professionals who demonstrate strategic value in this environment aren't the ones with the biggest monitoring budgets or the most sophisticated sentiment analysis. They're the ones who help organizations see patterns forming. They identify signals while response is still possible. They demonstrate value through validated proof chains, not just dashboard exports.

TechFinance's communications team saw the pattern early. They structured the insight effectively. They validated the approach with a documented proof chain. That's the measurement capability this book helps you build.

Let's Build Better Measurement

Signal-based reputation intelligence through Persona-Based Insights, Media Reputation Score and other proven methods provided in this book isn't just about avoiding negative outcomes—though signal recognition certainly helps with early detection. It's about evolving communications measurement from historical reporting to strategic foresight. It's about building professional credibility by demonstrating that your measurement framework helps the organization respond to reputation dynamics while response is still possible.

It's also about securing your professional relevance in an AI-driven future. The tactical work is being automated. The strategic work—contextual understanding, pattern interpretation, executive advisory—is becoming more valuable than ever. That's you. This book shows you how to position yourself as the strategist, not the data provider, now and into whatever future is coming.

This book will show you how to build this measurement capability, for your company and yourself. The framework has been tested through implementation. The tools are ready for practical use. The only question is: are you ready to shift from reporting what happened to helping your organization see what's coming?

Turn the page. Let's build signal recognition into your measurement practice.

— **Evan Escobedo**, March 2026

CHAPTER 1

THE ACTIVATION GAP

Why Measurement Professionals Are Drowning in Data but Starving for Impact

If you're a measurement professional in PR or corporate communications, your job has fundamentally changed.

Not long ago, your role was clear: count the clips, calculate reach, track sentiment, and report it when your CCO asked. Those skills still matter—but they're no longer enough.

Today, you're not just expected to measure what happened. You're expected to decode what it means, predict what comes next, and shape what your organization does. You're expected to walk into leadership meetings and answer the question every CCO dreads:

"So what?"

The measurement professionals who can answer that question are becoming strategic advisors. The ones who can't are being replaced—by cheaper tools, junior analysts, or worse, by AI.

This isn't about working harder. It's about working at a different altitude.

Why I Wrote This Book

I've spent two decades building measurement frameworks for Fortune 500 companies, helping communications teams move from reporting outputs to proving business impact. I've sat in hundreds of budget meetings where measurement teams defended their existence with dashboards full of metrics that executives didn't understand, let alone care about.

I watched talented analysts—people who could decode media narratives in their sleep—get dismissed because they couldn't translate their insights into executive language. I saw CCOs lose influence because their teams couldn't connect reputation shifts to revenue, retention, or risk.

The problem wasn't the quality of the work. It was the measurement model.

For years, we measured what brands said about themselves (owned media, campaigns, messaging). Some sophisticated teams also measured what others said about them (earned media, social discourse, analyst reports). But almost nobody measured what stakeholders did as a result—the behavior changes, the business outcomes, the ROI.

That gap—between reputation data and business impact—is what I call the activation layer. And it's where most measurement professionals lose the thread.

This book is the system for closing that gap. It offers you the frameworks, tools, and methodologies that transform you from a data provider into a strategic advisor. From someone who reports what happened to someone who shapes what's next.

The New Reality

We live in a moment of permanent scrutiny. Everyone is a broadcaster. Information moves faster than corporate response cycles. Stakeholders expect transparency, and they expect it now.

In this environment, brand equity has become one of the most valuable—and vulnerable—assets on the balance sheet. It's not just about visibility. It's about whether your brand is trusted, seen as innovative, credibly positioned, and resilient in the face of change.

As a measurement professional, you're positioned at the intersection of data and decision-making. You see the signals before they become headlines. You can connect reputation shifts to business outcomes. You have the potential to be the most valuable advisor in the room.

But only if you have the right system.

The Monday Morning Test

Let's make this concrete:

It's Monday morning, 9:47 AM. Your phone buzzes.

Your CCO has been forwarded a competitor's press release by the CEO. Your CCO messages you: "CEO wants thoughts. Meeting in 20 min. What do I say?"

You have 20 minutes. What do you send?

Choice 1: The Data Provider Response

You open your monitoring platform (Meltwater, Cision, Muck Rack—doesn't matter which). You copy the mention count. Pull the reach numbers. Paste them into a message:

"The announcement generated 11,327 mentions with 108.2M reach. Sentiment is 68% positive. Competitor was mentioned in WSJ, Bloomberg, and TechCrunch."

You hit send. Your CCO forwards it to the CEO with no additional context. The CEO doesn't respond. The meeting happens without your CCO having anything strategic to say.

You keep your $95,000 salary. You've been at this level for three years. Your CCO is wondering if they could just give a junior analyst access to the dashboard and get the same result.

You're a data provider. You measure outputs. You can't answer that "so what?" from the CEO. And you're one AI upgrade away from being replaceable.

Choice 2: The Planner Response

You pull the coverage. Read through it. Write a two-paragraph summary:

"Competitor announced a new product feature targeting our enterprise segment. Coverage was strong in tier-1 business media. Key messages focused on innovation and customer ROI. No direct comparison to our offering. Total reach: 108.2M. Sentiment: 68% positive."

Your CCO forwards it. The CEO replies: "Thanks." That's it. The meeting happens. Your CCO is there but doesn't have much to contribute beyond summarizing what you sent.

You're making $125,000. You've been stuck at this level for two years. You add context to data, but you still can't answer "what should we do?"

You're a planner. You connect inputs to outputs. But you're still descriptive, not predictive. You don't drive decisions.

Choice 3: The Strategic Advisor Response

You pull the coverage. But you don't stop at counting or summarizing. You analyze the signal. In 15 minutes, you send a one-page intelligence brief:

> SIGNAL: Competitor X launched narrative around "AI-powered automation for mid-market."

> IMPLICATION: They're claiming the innovation position we need for our Q2 product launch. If this narrative sticks,

we'll be seen as "catching up" instead of leading. Our innovation perception score could drop 8-12 points in the next 30 days.

GAP: We have no counter-narrative in market. Our last innovation story was six weeks ago. In competitive coverage over the past 90 days, they're mentioned 3:1 vs. us on "innovation." We're invisible in this conversation.

NARRATIVE: They're owning "AI innovation for mid-market." We're being positioned as "enterprise legacy." This is the narrative that lost IBM market share to AWS in 2015-2017.

ACTION: Launch counter-narrative by Friday. Target Forbes, TechCrunch, and VentureBeat with an exclusive customer story. Lead with measurable ROI proof points (our AI already delivers results). Position as "proven innovation vs. vaporware." Pursue a CEO interview or contributed article, not a press release.

LIFT: Projected 8-point recovery in Innovation signal within 30 days. Prevents 15-point competitive perception gap. Protects Q2 launch positioning.

BUDGET: $15K (freelance writer, media relations support)

ROI: Prevent significant launch marketing waste if we have to reposition later.

Your CCO reads it in 90 seconds. Forwards it to the CEO with one line: "Recommend we discuss in today's meeting. Analysis attached."

The CEO responds immediately: "Yes. Have [your name] present this. I want to move on it."

Your CCO calls you: "Can you join the meeting? CEO wants to discuss your recommendation."

You just got your CCO invited to the strategy table—and got yourself invited as the expert. Welcome to $180,000. Next year, you'll be at $220,000. In 18 months, you'll be Director. In three years, VP.

You're a strategic advisor. You deliver intelligence that shapes decisions. Your CCO depends on you. The CEO knows your name.

The difference between Choice 1 and Choice 3 isn't talent. Talent is common. It's not access to better data. Every measurement pro has access to the same platforms.

The difference is the system.

Choice 1 measures outputs: mentions, reach, sentiment. These are lagging indicators. They tell you what happened after it already happened. They can't answer "so what?" or "now what?"

Choice 2 adds context: what was said, who said it, where it appeared. This is better. But it's still descriptive, not predictive. It doesn't drive decisions.

Choice 3 delivers intelligence: what changed, why it matters, what's at risk, what to do, and what it will cost vs. what it will save. This is strategic. This is what gets budgets approved and careers accelerated.

The gap between Choice 1 and Choice 3? That's the activation layer. The system that turns signals into narratives. Narratives into recommendations. Recommendations into executive action. And executive action into career advancement.

KEY CONCEPT

THE THREE RESPONSE LEVELS

Choice 1 (Data Provider): "Here's what happened." Reports metrics. Choice 2 (Planner): "Here's what it means." Adds interpretation. Choice 3 (Strategic Advisor): "Here's what to do about it." Recommends action with expected ROI.

The gap between Choice 1 and Choice 3 isn't talent—it's system. This book gives you that system.

Here's the Uncomfortable Truth

If you can't deliver Choice 3-level intelligence in 15 minutes, you're not indispensable—you're replaceable by ChatGPT.

AI can count mentions. AI can summarize articles. AI can even detect sentiment. But AI can't decode competitive narratives, predict strategic risk, recommend specific actions, or calculate ROI in the context of your company's business priorities.

That's where you become the strategist. That's where you add value. That's where you become indispensable.

This book is the system for getting there.

When Reputation Reshapes in Hours, Not Quarters

A few years ago, a senior communications leader at a global fintech company put it bluntly: "We used to worry about making headlines. Now we worry about making memes."

It was a joke. Kind of. But it captured a larger truth: Today's brand risks don't come just from journalists or shareholder letters—they come from screenshots, Slack leaks, and viral Reddit threads.

The media landscape has fractured. Authority is decentralized. And everyone is now a broadcaster with an audience, whether they're an employee, a creator, or an activist with a camera phone and a sharp opinion.

Management research has increasingly characterized this as an era of stakeholder capitalism, in which business success is tied to broader societal outcomes. Employees want companies to take stands. Customers expect shared values. Investors want ESG transparency. Regulators watch everything.

Your job as a measurement professional has become exponentially more complex.

Case in Point: The 24-Hour Reputation Collapse

In December 2024, YesMadam—an India-based at-home beauty services startup featured on Shark Tank India—became a global case study in how quickly reputation can be destroyed when weak signals are ignored.

The company conducted an internal survey asking employees about workplace stress. Then, an email surfaced on LinkedIn appearing to announce that employees who reported feeling "significant stress" were being fired. The email read: "To ensure that no one remains stressed at work, we have made the difficult decision to part ways with employees who indicated significant stress."

The post went viral within hours. Social media exploded. Former employees claimed 100 people had been terminated. Business media worldwide covered it. The hashtag #BoycottYesMadam trended globally.

Within 24 hours, YesMadam went from a success story to a symbol of toxic workplace culture.

The company quickly claimed the email was part of a "planned awareness campaign" to announce a new mental health leave policy. They insisted no one was actually fired.

But the damage was done.

The numbers tell the story: 162 million reach across news, social, and online platforms; coverage in Fortune, Business Standard, and dozens of international outlets; trust in the brand collapsed; narrative shifted from "innovative wellness startup" to "tone-deaf employer;" damage persists months later.

COMMON MISTAKE

VOLUME ≠ VALUE

YesMadam generated 162 million impressions in 24 hours. By traditional metrics, that's "success." In reality, it destroyed the brand. High visibility during a crisis isn't a KPI—it's a catastrophe.

Never confuse being talked about with being valued.

The lesson for measurement professionals: Traditional measurement would have tracked the volume and reach after the crisis exploded. That's reactive. That's too late.

Signal-based intelligence would have detected the risk before the email went viral through employee sentiment signals (the stress survey itself was a red flag); cultural context signals (India was debating toxic work culture after a high-profile death at Ernst & Young); stakeholder expectations (audiences expect empathy, not gimmicks, around mental health); and narrative risk assessment (layoffs + mental health = explosive combination).

A measurement professional operating at the strategic advisor level would have flagged this campaign as high-risk and recommended against it. Or at minimum, provided crisis response planning before launch.

This is where you add value. Not by counting mentions after the explosion. But by detecting the weak signals that predict the explosion—and giving leadership the intelligence they need to avoid it.

The Career Stakes: Two Types of Measurement Professionals

Let me be direct about what's coming: By 2027, two distinct types of measurement professionals will exist.

The first type—Signal Decoders—will serve as strategic advisors. They use AI tools but add human strategic judgment. They decode weak signals before they become crises, translate reputation data into business intelligence, and advise the C-suite on risk and opportunity. Their salaries range from $180K to $300K or higher. Their job security is high, and their career trajectory runs from Director to VP to the C-suite track.

The second type—Report Generators—will remain data providers. They rely on dashboards and automation. They report what happened after the fact and can't answer "so what?" without prompting. Their salaries range from $80K to $120K—if they still have jobs. Their job security is low, and their career trajectory ends when they're replaced by AI and junior analysts.

Which will you be?

The tools are commoditizing. ChatGPT can summarize articles. Monitoring platforms have AI sentiment built in. Dashboards auto-generate reports.

What can't be automated is strategic judgment: detecting weak signals in noisy data, understanding competitive narrative dynamics, predicting which signals will compound into crises, recommending specific actions with ROI justification, and translating reputation intelligence into business strategy.

That's where you add value. That's where you become indispensable.

The Four Levels of Measurement Maturity (And Where You Are)

Most measurement professionals get stuck at one of four levels. The difference isn't about how hard you work—it's about which intelligence layers you've built.

Level 1: Consumer. At this level, you're a data provider earning $80K-$100K. You deliver "Here are our mentions" and have no meeting access. Your career is stuck. You measure outputs after the fact, report metrics when asked, and can't answer "so what?" or "what should we do?"

Level 2: Planner. At this level, you're a tactical tracker earning $100K-$140K. You deliver "We sent 20 pitches, got 12 placements" and attend tactical meetings only. Your career growth is slow. You track inputs and outputs, and you can connect cause and effect—but you still can't prove perception changed or predict what happens next.

Level 3: Storyteller. At this level, you're a strategic narrator earning $140K-$200K. You deliver "Our campaign moved perception eight points" and attend strategic meetings, sometimes speaking. Your career is advancing. You use research to inform strategy and measure perception shifts—but you still can't fully connect reputation to business outcomes.

Level 4: Visionary. At this level, you're a strategic advisor earning $200K-$300K or more. You deliver "Here's how reputation drives business outcomes—and the ROI." You're always invited to meetings and often lead them. Your career is on the VP/C-suite track. You have all three intelligence systems working together. You prove business impact. You detect crises early. You're indispensable.

The gap between levels isn't about working harder. It's about adding the missing intelligence layers. Moving from Level 1 to 2 requires adding evaluation discipline. Moving from Level 2 to 3 requires adding research discipline. Moving from Level 3 to 4 requires adding business outcome tracking.

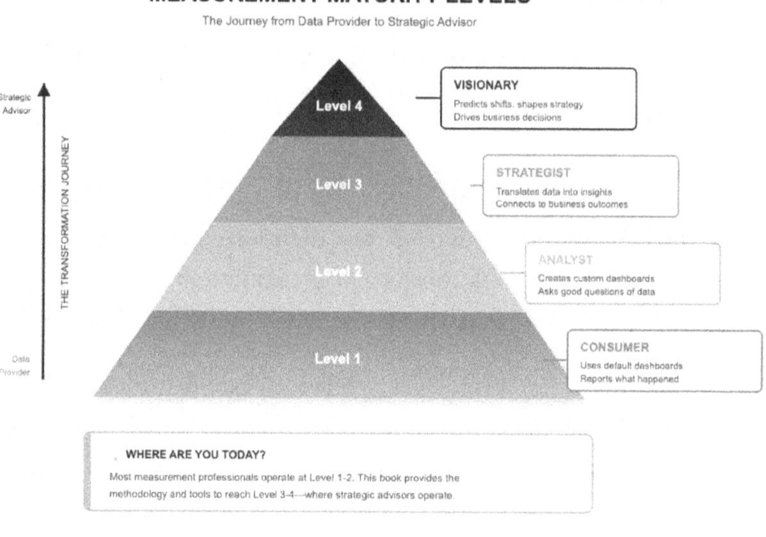

Figure 1.1: The Four Maturity Levels—Career Progression
from Consumer to Visionary

QUICK CHECK

WHERE ARE YOU TODAY?

Level 1 (Consumer): You deliver metrics when asked. No meeting access. Level 2 (Planner): You track inputs and outputs. Tactical meetings only. Level 3 (Storyteller): You measure perception shifts. Strategic meetings sometimes. Level 4 (Visionary): You prove business impact. Always invited, often lead. Be honest. The gap between levels isn't about working harder—it's about adding the missing intelligence layers.

The Data Behind the Levels

These four maturity levels aren't theoretical. They're based on assessments of 500+ communications professionals across industries, regions, and team sizes, conducted by Meltwater as part of their Data-Driven Communications (DDC) research initiative.

As Dino Delic, Head of The Data-Driven Communications Research Lab, observes: "The gap between what communications teams measure and what business leaders need isn't a technology problem—it's a methodology problem. Most teams have access to more data than ever, but they're using 20th-century frameworks to analyze 21st-century challenges."

The findings validate what many measurement professionals suspect but couldn't prove:

The average team scores 46 out of 100—firmly at the Planner level (Level 2). Nearly half of all communications teams (49%) operate here. They track metrics systematically but struggle to connect their work to business outcomes.

Only 8% reach Visionary status (Level 4), where they serve as trusted advisors with proven business impact.

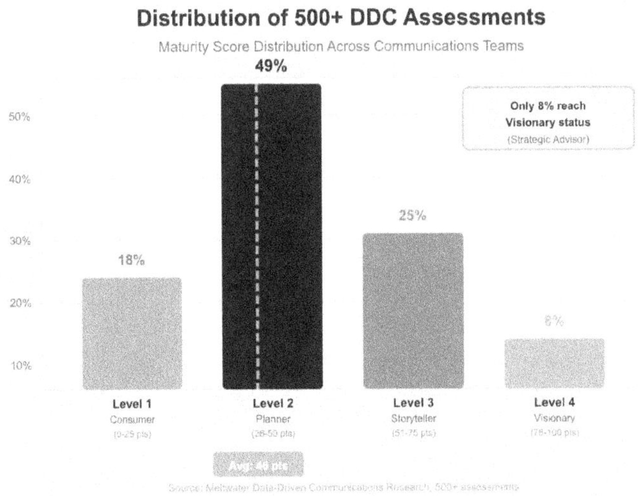

Figure 1.2: Distribution of 500+ DDC Assessments—Nearly Half of Teams Stuck at Level 2

Here's what separates the 8% from everyone else: It's not better tools.

When researchers analyzed maturity scores across three domains—Tools, Skills, and Resources—a clear pattern emerged: Teams that invest in sophisticated technology without building the skills to use it plateau early.

The numbers tell the story. Having a media monitoring platform adds just +2 points above average. Integrating business data (CRM, sales, web analytics) into comms insights adds +12 points above average. Having defined and regularly using leading/lagging indicators adds +19 points above average.

The tools aren't the problem. How you use them is.

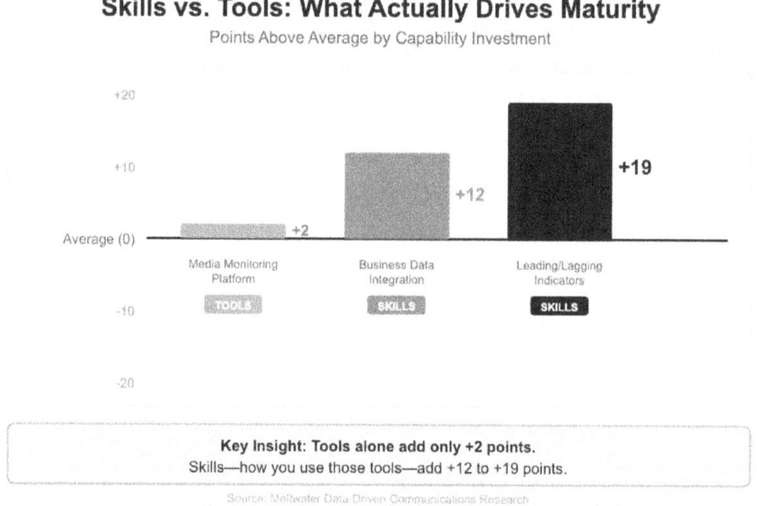

Figure 1.3: Skills vs. Tools Impact—Tools Add +2 Points, Skills Add +12 to +19 Points

The breakthrough to Visionary level comes from building three core capabilities:

Aligning to business outcomes. Teams whose communications strategy is strongly aligned to corporate objectives score nine points above average. Teams that use significant data to inform strategy design score 18 points above. Combined swing: 30 points.

Building intelligence systems. Teams that frequently include recommended actions in their reports score 11 points above average. Those that rarely or never do score 13 points below. Swing: 24 points.

Proving contribution. Teams that have defined and regularly use leading/lagging indicators to demonstrate impact score 19 points above average. Swing: 25 points.

This book gives you all three systems—with the frameworks, tools, and templates to build them yourself.

THE SKILLS VS. TOOLS GAP

Having a media monitoring platform adds just +2 points above average maturity. Integrating business data adds +12 points. Using leading/lagging indicators adds +19 points.

The tools aren't the problem. How you use them is.

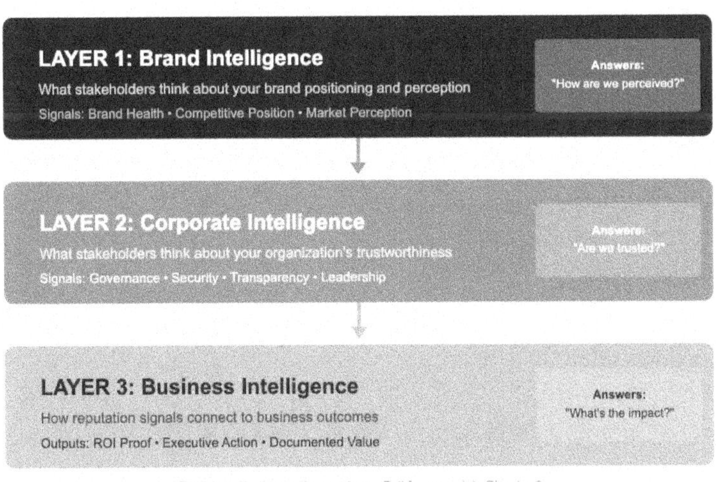

Figure 1.4: The Three Intelligence Layers—Preview
(Full Framework Detailed in Chapter 3)

(The complete DDC research findings and how they inform the signal-based framework are also detailed in Chapter 3.)

What This Book Delivers: Your Complete Transformation System

By the time you finish this book, you'll have a complete framework for becoming a Level 4 strategic advisor.

The Core Frameworks

This book provides four interconnected frameworks that build on each other in sequence. The Measurement Maturity Model establishes where you are today and what advancement looks like — so you can set a realistic starting point and measure progress. Persona-Based Insights (PBI) ensures you understand exactly who needs intelligence and what they care about before you build anything — because measurement without stakeholder alignment is just data. The Media Reputation Score (MRS) gives you a rigorous methodology to quantify reputation impact against the priorities you discovered through PBI — turning coverage into scores executives can act on. And the SIGNAL Framework teaches you how to write the kind of intelligence briefs that drive decisions — transforming scores into narratives, narratives into recommendations, and recommendations into documented outcomes.

Each framework feeds the next. PBI informs MRS. MRS feeds SIGNAL. SIGNAL generates the proof chains that justify expanding the program. The sequence is the system.

Ready-to-Use Tools

You'll get nine tools you can implement immediately, organized around the core workflow:

Discover: The Persona-Based Insights™ Builder guides you through the full PBI discovery process — from business priority to completed Agile Persona Statement. The Priority Markets Map tiers your geographies by strategic value. The Media Weighting Matrix translates your stakeholder's actual reading habits into source authority scores. The Competitor Influence Scorecard focuses your monitoring on rivals who actually threaten your narrative.

Measure: The MRS Scoring Guide provides complete rubrics, scoring dimensions, and tagging workflow for article-level analysis. The MRS Roll-up Calculator aggregates those scores into the pillar MRS, overall MRS, and competitive benchmarks that go to your executive.

Communicate: The SIGNAL Brief Template structures your intelligence for executive action — with urgency levels, live preview, and print-ready output.

Prove: The Proof Chain Builder documents every signal-to-decision-to-outcome sequence, building the ROI library you'll use in every budget conversation. The 90-Day Implementation Roadmap translates the entire methodology into a week-by-week plan with Go/No-Go checkpoints.

Every tool connects directly to the methodology in the chapters. All nine are available free at measuredio.com/book/tools — no software required, no account needed.

Your 90-Day Transformation Roadmap

Your transformation unfolds across three months.

Month 1: Foundation. Review the Four Maturity Levels in Chapter 1 to assess your current level. More importantly, you identify your Henrik—your executive sponsor, as Sophia did—and complete the Persona-Based Insights work from Chapter 4. Without this, everything else is guesswork.

Month 2: Breakthrough. You calculate your first MRS score using the pillars you identified in Month 1. You implement the SIGNAL brief format. Henrik receives his first intelligence brief tailored to his actual priorities—not generic metrics, but scores against the dimensions he told you matter.

Month 3: Expansion. You add competitive scoring to know where you stand versus competitors, refine your persona-based intelligence briefs based on Henrik's feedback, run a prioritization workshop to expand to additional stakeholders.

The Path Forward: From Data Provider to Strategic Advisor

Here's what separates measurement professionals who get promoted from those who get stuck.

Those stuck at $95K count outputs like mentions, reach, and sentiment. They report metrics when asked but can't answer "so what?" They wait for quarterly survey results and remain disconnected from strategy.

Those advancing to $180K and beyond decode signals before they become headlines. They deliver intelligence briefs that shape decisions, connect reputation shifts to business outcomes, spot competitive threats weeks early, and advise the C-suite on risk and opportunity.

The choice is yours. But the window is closing.

As AI gets better at counting, summarizing, and even basic sentiment analysis, the value you add must come from strategic judgment—the human ability to decode meaning, predict impact, and recommend action in the context of your specific business.

That's what this book teaches you. Not just better measurement—complete transformation. From someone who reports what happened to someone who shapes what's next. From a cost center defending budgets to a value driver getting promoted. From replaceable to indispensable.

What's Next: Understanding Why We're Here

The gap between data and decisions isn't a skills problem. It's a systems problem.

You have access to the same monitoring platforms as everyone else—Meltwater, Cision, Muck Rack, and others. The same data. The same dashboards. What you don't have yet is the activation layer—the system that turns signals into narratives, narratives into recommendations, and recommendations into executive action.

But before we build that system, you need to understand why traditional measurement approaches fail—why output metrics aren't enough, why even sophisticated survey models fall short, why the industry is evolving from Generation 1 (output metrics) to Generation 2 (survey models) to Generation 3 (signal-based intelligence).

Understanding this evolution isn't just academic—it's strategic. It positions your work as the natural next step, not a random departure. It gives you the language to explain to stakeholders why you're moving beyond traditional approaches and to defend budget increases and role expansions.

That's where we're headed in Chapter 2: "The Evolution of Measurement." You'll see why output metrics dominated for decades and why they're insufficient now; why survey-based models were important advances but can't keep pace with modern needs; and why signal-based reputation intelligence is emerging as Generation 3. We'll examine a $100 million crisis that proves traditional tools miss weak signals, explore how to integrate old and new approaches strategically, and revisit which lessons from the Barcelona Principles still apply.

By the end of Chapter 2, you'll understand exactly why measurement must evolve—and why your role is more critical than ever.

Ready?

Let's understand where we've been—so we can build where we're going.

References

Business Standard. (2024, December 10). YesMadam's 'Fired for Stress' Stunt Explodes, Company Faces Backlash. New Delhi, India: Business Standard. https://www.business-standard.com/companies/news/yesmadam-s-fired-for-stress-stunt-explodes-company-faces-backlash-124121000690_1.html

Fortune. (2024, December 10). Startup YesMadam Went Viral for 'Firing Stressed Employees' in Marketing Stunt. New York, NY: Fortune. https://fortune.com/2024/12/10/yesmadam-fires-stressed-employees-india-stunt/

Meltwater. (2025). Data-Driven Communications assessment findings (internal research, used with permission).

Snopes. (2024, December 10). *Home Salon Email That 'Fired' Stressed Employees Was PR Stunt.* https://www.snopes.com/fact-check/yes-madam-fired-employees-stress/

Note on Sources

The Monday Morning Test scenario and the three response choices (Data Provider, Planner, Strategic Advisor) are illustrative examples developed by the author to demonstrate the practical difference between measurement approaches. Salary ranges referenced throughout are directional estimates based on industry patterns and the author's professional experience; actual compensation varies by organization, market, and individual circumstances.

The Four Levels of Measurement Maturity framework and associated statistics (including the 8% Visionary finding and 46-point average score) are based on Meltwater's Data-Driven Communications (DDC) Research Lab, which assessed 500+ communications professionals. The Dino Delic quote is used with permission.

The YesMadam case study draws on contemporaneous reporting from multiple sources cited in the References.

CHAPTER 2

THE EVOLUTION OF MEASUREMENT

From Output Metrics to Reputation Intelligence—and Why Old Models Don't Work

In Chapter 1, you saw the problem: Measurement professionals are drowning in data but starving for impact. You saw the Monday Morning Test that separates data providers from strategic advisors. You saw what happens when reputation reshapes in 24 hours.

But here's the question: How did we get here?

Why are so many measurement teams still stuck counting mentions and calculating reach? Why do dashboards overflow with metrics that executives ignore? Why does the gap between data and decisions persist?

The answer lies in understanding the evolution of measurement itself— and why each generation of tools, while progressive for its time, ultimately failed to keep pace with business needs.

This chapter traces that evolution across three distinct generations. Generation 1: Output Metrics (1990s-2010s) encompasses press clippings, AVE, volume, and reach. Generation 2: Survey-Based Models (2000s-present) includes RepTrak, Harris Poll, Edelman, and others.

Generation 3: Signal-Based Intelligence (2020s+) is the framework presented in this book.

Note: Survey-based reputation models (Generation 2) emerged in the early 2000s, running in parallel with the late stages of Generation 1's digital transformation. These were complementary approaches, not strictly sequential.

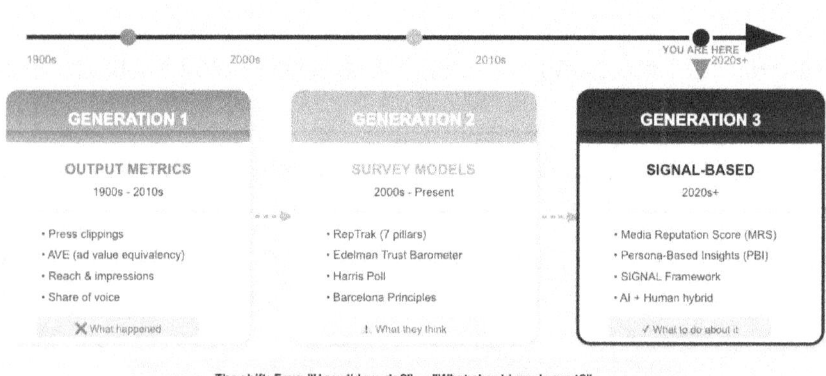

Figure 2.1: The Evolution of Measurement—From Output Metrics to Signal-Based Intelligence

Understanding this progression isn't just academic. It's strategic. It positions your work as the natural evolution, not a random departure. It helps you explain to stakeholders why you're moving beyond traditional approaches. And it gives you the language to defend budget increases and role expansions.

Let's start with why traditional measurement fails—using a $100 million example.

KEY CONCEPT

> ### THREE GENERATIONS OF MEASUREMENT
>
> Generation 1 (Output Metrics): Counts what happened. Press clippings, AVE, volume, reach. Generation 2 (Survey-Based): Measures perception. RepTrak, Harris Poll, Edelman. Generation 3 (Signal-Based): Predicts what's forming. Real-time detection, pattern recognition, actionable intelligence.
>
> You don't abandon earlier generations—you integrate them strategically. But if you only have one, get Generation 3.

The Problem with Traditional Measurement: A $100 Million Lesson

Before we trace the history, let's see why this matters. Here's what happens when measurement systems track outputs instead of signals.

The QuickServe Food Safety Crisis (Composite Case Study)

QuickServe is a composite case study representing patterns observed across multiple food safety incidents at global fast-food chains. While the company name is fictitious, the patterns, timelines, and outcomes reflect documented research on crisis management and food safety impacts. We use this composite to illustrate signal-based principles without referencing any specific company.

In late 2024, a global fast-food chain—let's call it QuickServe—faced a food contamination outbreak linked to a supplier issue. The pattern is tragically common in the industry.

The typical damage profile for major food safety incidents is severe: 75-150 people infected across multiple states, 25-40 hospitalizations, stock price drops of 5-10% in the immediate aftermath, and foot traffic declines of 10-15% nationally (30% or more in affected regions). Same-store sales impact typically lasts 2-4 quarters, with recovery investments ranging from $75-150 million.

Academic research confirms these patterns. A 2020 study published in the *Journal of Hospitality & Tourism Research* found that food safety events cause immediate negative stock market reactions, with the severity depending on firm size, past crisis history, and media attention (Jeon & Baeck, 2020). The researchers noted that even a one-time event can generate disastrous results, citing cases where restaurant chains closed operations entirely due to tainted brand image and negative publicity following contamination incidents.

The recovery investment: $100 million.

This figure—documented across multiple industry crises—typically breaks down to $30-40 million in marketing campaigns to rebuild trust, $50-70 million in franchisee support and operational improvements, plus implementation of enhanced monitoring systems and real-time signal detection capabilities. The cruel irony: Those detection capabilities are almost always added *after* the crisis.

Here's the Critical Question

Could signal-based reputation intelligence have detected this 2-3 weeks earlier?

The answer, supported by crisis management research, is yes. Igor Ansoff's foundational work on "weak signals" (1975) established that organizations can detect early warning indicators before crises fully materialize—if they have the right detection systems in place. Paraskevas (2006), writing in the *International Journal of Hospitality Management*, found that "with appropriate signal detection mechanisms in place, crisis signals can be picked up in time and then, some—if not all—crises can be averted before they happen."

Early warning signals typically precede food safety crises: social media threads about food safety concerns at specific locations; local health department mentions in regional media (below national radar); upticks in "food safety" and "quality concern" language from monitoring sources; source authority shifts in which mentions move from consumer reviews to health and regulatory sources; and geographic clustering of negative safety mentions.

These were weak signals. Not loud enough to trigger traditional monitoring alerts. Not negative enough to show up in basic sentiment dashboards.

What would traditional measurement have shown?

Generic dashboards would have displayed "Brand mentioned 25,000 times this week," "Reach: 22 million," and "Sentiment: 85% neutral, 10% positive, 5% negative." Nothing alarming. Nothing actionable. Just business as usual.

What would signal-based intelligence have flagged?

A very different picture: Trust signal declining in food safety and health authority sources; regional health language upticking with specific terminology associated with investigations; social discourse shifting from product quality to safety concerns; source authority changing from consumer reviews to regulatory and medical voices; geographic clustering of safety mentions; and thematic pattern recognition showing similar language across disconnected sources.

These signals don't show up in volume, reach, or basic sentiment scoring. They require a different measurement lens—one that tracks prominence, source authority, thematic shifts, and trust erosion patterns.

The Opportunity Cost

If the QuickServe team had detected these signals 2-3 weeks early, they could have investigated the supply chain immediately, tested products from flagged regions, alerted executives to emerging risk, and potentially identified the contamination source before the outbreak spread. They could have saved lives and avoided $100 million in damage.

What's the ROI of a signal detection system that prevents a $100 million crisis? Even a modest investment in advanced reputation intelligence would have delivered substantial returns—turning early detection into protected value.

Why Traditional Measurement Failed

The company almost certainly had measurement systems in place. They likely tracked total mentions, sentiment scores, share of voice, reach and impressions, and tier-1 media coverage.

But those systems measured outputs (what happened) instead of signals (what's forming).

They counted volume—they didn't decode meaning. They tracked after-the-fact sentiment—they didn't detect trust erosion patterns. They measured reach—they didn't weight source authority.

This is why traditional measurement isn't just insufficient—it's dangerous. When your monitoring system can't detect a crisis forming three weeks early, it's not adding value. It's creating false confidence.

Now let's look at how we got here—and why two generations of measurement tools all fell short in different ways.

Generation 1: Output Metrics (1900s–2010s)

From Press Clippings to "Going Viral"—and Why Volume Never Equaled Value

For over a century, PR measurement was defined by a simple mandate: prove the work happened. Count the clips. Calculate the reach. Report it to leadership. Repeat.

This generation spanned more than 100 years, evolving through distinct phases—but always focused on the same core question: "Did we get coverage?" It never asked: "Did that coverage matter?"

Let's trace that evolution.

Phase 1: The Early Era—Publicity Over Proof (1900s–1960s)

During the early 20th century, public relations leaned heavily on artistry rather than science. PR professionals focused on obtaining media exposure, often overlooking the need to measure its effectiveness. Success was defined by visibility, not influence.

An effective PR campaign was one where the brand appeared frequently in newspapers, magazines, and radio broadcasts. But there was no consistent method for gauging audience reach, sentiment, or business impact.

Press Clippings: The Original Measurement Tool

The first approach to measuring public relations was the press clipping method. Organizations and agencies would collect newspaper and magazine articles mentioning their brand, organize them into physical reports for executives and clients, and present these collections as evidence of PR success.

Although press clippings documented media presence, they failed to measure whether coverage was positive, negative, or neutral, whether the target audience actually received the message, or whether coverage shaped brand perception or influenced business results.

Even with these limitations, press clippings remained a cornerstone of PR measurement for decades, reinforcing the notion that achieving publicity was the ultimate objective.

Edward Bernays and the Birth of Strategic PR

Edward Bernays stands out as a pivotal figure in early public relations, often called the "father of public relations." During the 1920s and 1930s, Bernays pioneered systematic approaches to media influence, employing strategies grounded in psychology and social science.

His key contributions transformed the field. Rather than just generating press, he used media to shape consumer behavior and mold public perception. He leveraged third-party endorsements, encouraging journalists, experts, and influencers to share brand messages rather than relying solely on corporate statements. And he applied psychological principles, understanding how public perceptions could be influenced through narrative framing and strategic placement.

Case in Point: The Lucky Strike "Torches of Freedom" Campaign (1929)

In the 1920s, Bernays led a groundbreaking PR campaign for Lucky Strike cigarettes, targeting women—a demographic largely ignored by tobacco companies at the time.

The strategy was audacious: Frame smoking as a symbol of women's liberation and independence; orchestrate a publicity stunt where prominent women smoked cigarettes in public during the Easter Sunday Parade in New York City; and position cigarettes as "Torches of Freedom"—a powerful metaphor connecting smoking to women's suffrage and empowerment.

The results were undeniable: massive media coverage, normalization of women smoking in public, and significant sales increases for Lucky Strike.

Bernays elevated PR from simple publicity-seeking to strategic perception management. Yet even with his sophisticated approach, measurement remained subjective. Success was still judged by visibility and media buzz, not by data or tangible business outcomes.

Why Measurement Was Ignored

Several factors contributed to the lack of structured measurement in early PR. There were no tools to monitor audience reactions—no engagement metrics, sentiment analysis, or conversion tracking. PR concentrated on securing story placements, often ignoring whether those stories actually influenced public opinion or consumer behavior. And there was no industry consensus on how to measure effectiveness. During this era, public relations was viewed as an extension of journalism rather than a strategic business discipline.

The Push for Accountability Begins

As corporate competition intensified in the mid-20th century, executives began demanding greater accountability for PR expenditures. The industry slowly started adopting structured evaluation methods—tracking press coverage frequency, estimating audience reach, and comparing media placements against competitors—though these comparisons remained rudimentary.

Despite these efforts, a disconnect persisted between PR activities and tangible business results. Companies could track media mentions but struggled to measure PR's impact on brand reputation, consumer behavior, or sales.

The stage was set for the next evolution: attempting to quantify PR's monetary value.

Phase 2: The Rise and Fall of AVE (1970s-2010)

As executives increasingly demanded ROI proof, the PR industry attempted to solve the measurement problem with a seemingly simple solution: Advertising Value Equivalency (AVE).

The concept was straightforward: quantify the financial value of earned media coverage by comparing it to the cost of purchasing equivalent advertising space. If your brand gets a quarter-page article in The New York Times, and a quarter-page ad costs $50,000, then your PR coverage equals $50,000 in "value."

Executives loved it. It provided a dollar figure they could understand, allowed comparison to paid advertising budgets, and looked scientific and quantifiable.

Then came the multiplier madness. Agencies began claiming that earned media was worth 3x, 5x, or even 10x the value of advertising because of its credibility advantage. The logic seemed sound—paid ads are seen as biased while earned media carries third-party validation. The problem: No empirical evidence supported any specific multiplier, and different agencies used different numbers, creating chaos.

Why AVE Was Fundamentally Flawed

As the industry matured, AVE's problems became impossible to ignore.

First, earned media is fundamentally different from advertising. Advertising provides complete message control, guaranteed placement, repeated exposure, and targeted audience selection. Earned media provides third-party credibility and editorial context—but no message control, no guaranteed placement, and usually one-time exposure. These are different value propositions, not interchangeable.

Second, AVE ignored sentiment and context. It treated all coverage equally: a positive feature article, a negative investigative exposé, and a brief mention all received proportional "value." But negative coverage destroys value—it doesn't create it. The 2017 United Airlines passenger removal incident generated massive AVE numbers. By AVE logic, the crisis was valuable because it generated so much "coverage worth." Obviously absurd.

Third, AVE assumed all mentions had equal impact. It didn't account for prominence (headline vs. paragraph 12), source authority (*Wall Street Journal* vs. unknown blog), audience relevance, or competitive framing.

Fourth, the circular logic problem: AVE compared earned media to advertising rates, but advertising rates are based on guaranteed audience delivery. Earned media doesn't guarantee anything.

The Industry Rejects AVE

By the late 2000s, the PR industry reached a consensus: AVE was misleading at best, fraudulent at worst. The turning point came in 2010 with the Barcelona Principles—landmark measurement standards created by the International Association for Measurement and Evaluation of Communication (AMEC). Barcelona Principle #5 explicitly stated: "AVEs are not the value of communication."

This was revolutionary. The industry's own standards body declared that its most widely-used metric was fundamentally flawed.

Despite industry-wide rejection, AVE persists in some quarters—driven by executive demand for ROI proof, lack of better alternatives, vendor pressure, and slower adoption of Barcelona Principles in some international markets. But make no mistake: Using AVE today signals that your measurement program is stuck in the past.

COMMON MISTAKE

> ### AVE IS DEAD—STOP USING IT
>
> Barcelona Principle #5 explicitly states: "AVEs are not the value of communication." AVE treats all coverage equally—positive, negative, or neutral. By AVE logic, the United Airlines passenger removal crisis was "valuable" because it generated coverage. Using AVE today signals your measurement program is stuck in the past.

Phase 3: Digital Disruption & Volume Metrics (2000s-2010s)

The 2000s brought an explosion of digital media: blogs, social platforms, YouTube, smartphones. The measurement industry pivoted from counting column inches to counting clicks, shares, retweets, likes, and mentions.

At first, it felt like progress. Metrics were available instantly. Dashboards refreshed in real-time. Executives could see Share of Voice plotted on trendlines. The volume of data was intoxicating.

But with digital visibility came a dangerous assumption: if your brand is being talked about, you must be winning. Visibility ≠ value, but volume metrics don't tell the difference.

When "Going Viral" Became a Risk

The digital era created a new goal: Go viral. The assumption was that massive reach and engagement meant campaign success. But volume-based measurement couldn't differentiate between good attention and bad attention.

Starbucks #RaceTogether (2015). Designed to spark national dialogue about race, the campaign encouraged baristas to write "Race Together" on cups and engage customers in conversations about racial inequality.

It immediately went viral—not as intended. Critics called the campaign tone-deaf and exploitative. Social media exploded with backlash. The dashboards showed skyrocketing Share of Voice, millions in reach, and record social engagement. From a volume standpoint, the campaign was a "success." From a brand equity standpoint, it was a disaster. Trust scores declined. The campaign was pulled within days.

United Airlines Passenger Removal (2017). Video of a passenger being forcibly dragged off an overbooked flight went viral globally. The dashboards showed record reach, highest-ever engagement, and dominant Share of Voice. What actually happened: stock dropped 4% ($1 billion in market value), the CEO faced Congressional hearings, brand perception was damaged for years, and competitors gained market share. Maximum visibility during a crisis isn't a KPI—it's a catastrophe metric.

Bud Light Influencer Boycott (2023). A collaboration with transgender influencer Dylan Mulvaney triggered a nationwide boycott. Dashboards showed record visibility, unprecedented reach, and dominant Share of Voice in the beverage category. What actually happened: parent company AB InBev lost $5+ billion in market value within days, sales declined for months, and competitive brands gained significant market share. Being talked about constantly doesn't mean being valued. Sometimes it means being boycotted.

Share of Voice vs. Share of Trust

Many communications teams still rely heavily on Share of Voice—measuring how often a brand is mentioned relative to competitors. The logic: If we're mentioned more than competitors, we're winning. The problem: SOV says nothing about whether those mentions build trust, reinforce leadership, or position the brand favorably.

A brand can dominate Share of Voice during a crisis and see trust collapse. A brand can have low Share of Voice but high Share of Trust—and win.

Why Generation 1 Metrics Still Dominate

Despite their limitations, Generation 1 metrics remain the most widely used in PR and communications. They're easy to count and report, provide "proof" that PR activity happened, allow comparison to competitors, and align with digital platform analytics.

But they fail where it matters: They can't differentiate good attention from bad, can't connect coverage to business outcomes, can't predict reputation impact, and can't guide strategic decisions. They create false confidence.

According to Meltwater's Data-Driven Communications research (2025), teams relying primarily on output metrics score an average of 24 points out of 100 on measurement maturity—firmly in the "Consumer" level (Level 1). These teams can report what happened, but they can't answer "so what?" or "what should we do?"

The lesson from 100+ years of output metrics: Volume is not insight. Reach is not impact. Activity is not value.

The industry needed to evolve beyond counting to actually measuring perception and trust. That's where Generation 2 emerged.

Generation 2: Survey-Based Reputation Models (2000s-present)

When the Industry Learned to Measure Perception—But Not Fast Enough

As organizations realized that volume metrics were insufficient, the industry turned to a fundamentally different approach: asking stakeholders directly what they think. If output metrics couldn't tell us whether coverage built trust or shaped perception, maybe surveys could.

The Rise of Survey-Based Reputation Research

In the late 1990s and early 2000s, several companies pioneered systematic reputation measurement. RepTrak (from the Reputation Institute) focused on reputation across multiple stakeholder groups. Harris Poll developed the Reputation Quotient for long-running corporate reputation tracking. Edelman launched the Trust Barometer for annual global trust research across institutions and brands. Other entrants included Brand Keys' Customer Loyalty Engagement Index (focused on emotional engagement), Fortune's Most Admired Companies (based on executive surveys), and CoreBrand (focused on brand power among business decision-makers).

Each brought a slightly different methodology, but all shared a common approach: Survey representative samples of stakeholders to measure perception.

How Survey-Based Reputation Models Work

While methodologies vary, most survey-based reputation solutions follow a similar four-part structure.

Sample Selection. Providers survey 1,000-2,000 respondents per market to achieve statistical representativeness. They target the general public, customers, employees, or specific stakeholder segments depending on the research objectives. Most field surveys annually or quarterly, though some offer continuous tracking options at premium pricing.

Multi-Dimensional Measurement. Different providers measure different dimensions, but most include variations of core reputation drivers. RepTrak's model measures seven dimensions: Products & Services; Innovation; Workplace; Governance; Citizenship; Leadership; and Performance. Harris Poll takes a slightly different approach with six dimensions: Products & Services; Financial Performance; Vision & Leadership; Workplace Environment; Social Responsibility; and Emotional Appeal. The Edelman Trust Barometer focuses more narrowly on four trust attributes: Competency; Integrity; Dependability; and Purpose.

Despite the variations, you'll notice significant overlap. Products and services matter in every model. Leadership appears in various forms. Workplace and social responsibility show up consistently. The models agree more than they differ—which suggests these dimensions genuinely capture what shapes reputation.

Reputation/Trust Scoring. Providers aggregate survey responses into an overall reputation or trust score, typically on a 0-100 scale. They benchmark your organization against competitors and industry averages, then track changes over time to identify trends. The single score becomes a powerful executive communication tool—easy to report, easy to compare, easy to track year over year.

Reporting. Results are delivered through annual or quarterly reports that include competitive rankings, dimensional breakdowns, and stakeholder segment analysis. The better providers offer diagnostic insights explaining *why* scores moved, though the depth of analysis varies significantly across vendors.

What Survey-Based Models Got Right

Before we examine their limitations, let's acknowledge their genuine contributions to the field.

Survey-based models proved that perception is measurable—reputation is no longer just a "soft" metric that can't be quantified. They created standardized benchmarks, allowing companies to compare reputation scores across industries and over time. They got executives to care, because a single reputation score like "67/100" is powerful and easy to communicate. They validated that multiple dimensions matter—reputation isn't one thing but is shaped by products, leadership, workplace, citizenship, and more. They shifted focus from outputs to outcomes, moving the conversation from "Did we get coverage?" to "How are we perceived?" And they provided stakeholder segmentation, revealing that different groups—customers, employees, investors—perceive brands differently.

These were important advances. Survey-based reputation research moved the industry forward significantly.

The problem isn't that survey models are wrong. It's that they're insufficient for the speed, specificity, and strategic demands of modern measurement professionals.

Why Survey-Based Models Fall Short for Modern Measurement

Let's examine six critical limitations that prevent survey-based reputation models from serving today's measurement professionals effectively.

1. Too Slow for Real-Time Decision-Making

Survey-based reputation models typically operate on quarterly or annual cycles—far too slow for today's media environment. The typical timeline runs 8-12 weeks: survey fielding in weeks 1-4; data analysis and validation in weeks 5-8; and report preparation and delivery in weeks 8-12. By the time you receive results, the data is 90+ days old.

Consider this scenario: A competitor launches a major product partnership on Monday. During weeks 1-4, media coverage happens, narratives form, perception shifts, and your competitor dominates the "innovation" conversation. By week 8, your next quarterly reputation survey fields. By week 12, results arrive showing your Innovation score dropped 4 points while your competitor's rose 6 points.

Your CEO asks: "Why are we losing competitive positioning on innovation?" You can't answer effectively because the perception shift happened 12 weeks ago, the media narratives that caused it are long past, you have no insight into which specific events drove the change, and you can't recommend corrective action because the moment has passed.

Signal-based intelligence would have flagged the competitive threat in Week 1, identified the narrative gap immediately, recommended counter-narrative strategy by Friday, and measured impact within 2-4 weeks.

When reputation reshapes in hours, 90-day measurement cycles aren't strategic insight—they're autopsy reports.

2. Too Broad for Actionable Strategy

Most survey-based models measure 6-7 dimensions. While comprehensive, this creates an actionability problem.

Your quarterly results arrive: Innovation down 3 points, Leadership up 2 points, Workplace flat, Citizenship down 1 point, Products & Services up 1 point, Performance down 2 points, Governance flat. Now what do you do?

The survey tells you perception changed across multiple dimensions—but it can't tell you which specific events, articles, or narratives caused each change. It can't explain whether Innovation dropped because of a product delay, a competitor move, or negative coverage. It can't clarify whether Leadership rose because of CEO visibility or strategic announcements. And it can't prescribe what actions to take to improve the dimensions that declined.

Survey data is diagnostic, not prescriptive. It tells you the patient has symptoms. It doesn't tell you the diagnosis or treatment.

Measurement professionals need to connect perception shifts to specific narratives, media moments, and competitive dynamics. Survey models can't do that because they're disconnected from the real-time media environment that shapes perception.

3. Not Communications-Native

Survey dimensions were designed for annual stakeholder research—not for real-time media intelligence and communications strategy.

Try this exercise: Map a media article to survey dimensions. Consider this headline: "Company X launches AI-powered platform, reducing customer onboarding time by 60%. CEO says it represents 'the future of enterprise software.' Early customers report strong ROI."

Which dimensions does this affect? Products & Services (it's about a product)? Innovation (AI is innovative)? Leadership (CEO is quoted)? Performance (customer ROI suggests performance)? All of the above? How do you weight each?

And critically: Does it matter that this appeared in TechCrunch versus a low-tier blog? Does it matter that the CEO was quoted? Does it matter that two customers were named as proof points? Does it matter that competitors weren't mentioned? Does it matter that the article appeared above-the-fold?

Survey dimensions don't map cleanly to earned media analysis. They were designed for different purposes. Signal-based frameworks, by contrast, are built specifically for media intelligence—tracking prominence, source authority, competitive framing, and thematic signals.

4. Sample Size Limitations for Persona Insights

Survey-based models typically survey 1,000-2,000 respondents per market. That's statistically valid for broad population estimates. But it's not granular enough for the persona-specific questions executives actually ask.

What do healthcare CIOs specifically think about our cybersecurity innovation? How do regulatory insiders in financial services perceive our compliance reputation? What narrative are venture capital investors forming about our growth trajectory? How do enterprise buyers in manufacturing view our sustainability commitment?

Survey samples aren't large enough or targeted enough for niche persona analysis.

Signal-based measurement analyzes thousands of media mentions, social posts, analyst statements, and stakeholder discourse—providing granularity to decode perception by specific persona (CIOs, CFOs, CTOs); industry sector (healthcare, finance, manufacturing); geography

(North America, EMEA, APAC); source type (tier-1 media, trade publications, analysts, influencers); and narrative theme (innovation, trust, pricing, reliability).

When executives ask persona-specific questions, survey models can't answer. Signal-based intelligence can.

5. Expensive and Immovable

Survey-based reputation programs typically cost $50,000-$150,000+ annually per market. For global companies operating in multiple markets, costs can exceed $1 million per year.

Once you commit to a survey-based program, you're locked into their methodology, their timeline, and their question set. There's limited ability to customize or pivot.

Consider this scenario: Your CEO suddenly cares about AI innovation perception after a major competitor announcement. With a survey-based program, you can't add "AI innovation" as a tracked dimension mid-cycle. You have to wait for the next survey wave—3-12 months. You might be able to append questions if budget allows and timing works. Then you'll wait another three months for results.

Your measurement framework should adapt to your business priorities—not force your priorities to fit a rigid survey structure.

Signal-based intelligence, by contrast, can pivot immediately. Need to track AI innovation perception starting tomorrow? Adjust your monitoring queries, update your signal definitions, and start tracking. No waiting. No budget approval. No structural constraints.

6. Disconnected from Day-to-Day Media Strategy

Perhaps the most critical limitation for measurement professionals: Survey-based reputation models don't inform daily, weekly, or monthly communications decisions.

You're crafting a media pitch today. You're responding to a competitor announcement this week. You're advising your CCO on messaging strategy this month. Survey-based reputation data won't help you with any of those decisions.

It tells you how perception stood 90 days ago—not what's happening now. It can't tell you which narratives are forming this week. It can't identify which media outlets drive the most reputation impact. It can't help you frame your message against competitors. It can't flag emerging crisis risk.

Survey models are diagnostic tools for understanding historical perception. They aren't strategic tools for shaping future perception.

That's the fundamental gap: Survey models measure outcomes. They don't decode the signals that create those outcomes.

The Integration Strategy: Best of Both Worlds

Here's the important nuance: You don't have to choose between survey-based models and signal-based intelligence. The smartest measurement professionals use both—but for different purposes.

Use survey-based reputation models for annual benchmarking against competitors and industry; board-level reporting (executives and directors recognize brand names like RepTrak and Edelman); long-term trend validation over years; stakeholder perception confirmation that validates what your signal data suggests; and executive compensation metrics where companies tie bonuses to reputation scores.

Use signal-based reputation intelligence for active decision support with weekly and monthly strategic guidance; campaign effectiveness measurement; competitive narrative tracking; crisis early warning systems that detect weak signals before they explode; stakeholder-based insights on how specific external personas perceive you; and media strategy guidance on which outlets matter most and which narratives to pursue.

Think of it like financial reporting. Survey-based models are your annual report—comprehensive, backward-looking, standardized, and board-facing. Signal-based intelligence is your weekly P&L—active, forward-looking, actionable, and operations-facing.

You need both. But if you only have one, you need the weekly P&L—not just the annual report. An annual report tells you whether the company was profitable last year. A weekly P&L tells you whether you're profitable now—and what to do about it.

PRO TIP

THE INTEGRATION STRATEGY

Use survey-based models (RepTrak, Edelman) for annual bench-marking and board reporting—executives recognize these brands. Use signal-based intelligence for weekly/monthly decisions, competitive tracking, and early warning.

Think of survey models as your annual physical exam, and signal intelligence as your fitness tracker. You need both, but the tracker guides daily decisions.

Case Study: When Low Volume Creates High Equity—The EcoGear Example

EcoGear is a composite case study representing patterns observed across outdoor apparel brands implementing circular economy initiatives. While the company name is fictitious, the dynamics described reflect published research on sustainability communications and brand perception.

While survey-based models focus on broad population perception, they often miss what matters most: signal quality over quantity.

EcoGear's Circular Economy Expansion

In late 2023, an outdoor apparel company—let's call it EcoGear—quietly expanded its circular economy program, allowing customers to repair, resell, and recycle outdoor gear. There was no flashy launch campaign. No celebrity partnerships. No paid media blitz.

The media coverage was modest: limited earned media mentions in the launch quarter, modest social media buzz, no viral moments. By traditional metrics, it wouldn't register as "newsworthy."

Yet research on circular economy brand perception suggests this approach often outperforms high-volume campaigns over time. A 2025 systematic literature review published in the *Journal of Cleaner Production* found that "authentic, sustainable branding enhances long-term brand value, while misleading sustainability claims weaken consumer trust." The same research noted that circular economy practices, when genuinely implemented, create stronger brand differentiation than traditional "green" marketing campaigns.

Why the Disproportionate Impact?

While volume was low, signal quality was extraordinary.

High-authority sources picked up the story: industry publications framing the initiative as "infrastructure for a post-consumer economy;" business innovation coverage emphasizing systemic change; coverage in climate-focused podcasts and sustainability newsletters; and mentions by influential sustainability thought leaders on social media.

Narrative density was strong. Coverage consistently emphasized values in action rather than just talk, framed the initiative as systemic change rather than a one-off program, and positioned the brand as category leader with competitors playing catch-up.

Community amplification was authentic. Buy-it-for-life communities championed the program, outdoor enthusiast forums discussed it extensively, and micro-influencers shared repair stories organically.

Research from the journal *Circular Economy and Sustainability* (2023) confirms this pattern: "Loyal customers significantly contribute to building a positive brand image by reinforcing the perceptions of trust and reliability. This relationship is particularly relevant in the circular economy, where customers prioritize brands that align with their values of sustainability and responsible consumption."

What Would Different Measurement Systems Have Shown?

Traditional volume metrics would have shown low mention count, low reach compared to competitor product launches, and concluded the campaign underperformed.

A survey-based reputation model wouldn't detect the shift for 6-12 months. When finally measured, it would show improvement but wouldn't explain why—creating an attribution challenge.

Signal-based intelligence would have detected the high-authority source concentration immediately; flagged narrative quality indicators around values, systemic change, and leadership positioning; tracked community amplification patterns; identified Innovation and Trust signal strengthening; and connected the media narrative to reputation driver movement.

The Lesson: Volume is vanity. Signal quality is strategy.

Generation 3: Signal-Based Reputation Intelligence (2020s+)

Track Signals, Decode Meaning, Drive Action

This is where the field is heading—and where you need to operate.

Signal-based reputation intelligence represents a fundamental shift in how measurement professionals work. It combines real-time data from media, social, analyst discourse, and stakeholder statements with AI-powered scale to analyze thousands of signals continuously. It layers in human strategic judgment to interpret context, nuance, and competitive dynamics. It uses communications-native dimensions designed for earned media rather than surveys, delivers persona-based insights tailored to different decision-makers, and provides predictive capability to spot weak signals before they become crises.

Instead of asking 1,000 people what they think once a quarter, you analyze thousands of real-world signals continuously.

Organizing Signals Around Business Priorities

Instead of tracking seven abstract survey dimensions—or defaulting to generic metrics—Generation 3 measurement organizes signals around your business priorities. The specific pillars you track should map directly to what your organization actually cares about.

At one global financial services company, we built measurement around five pillars validated by the Chief Communications Officer: Platform/Partner (cross-border capabilities, network reach); Digital Leader (technology, customer channels); Responsible Corporate Citizen (ESG, community impact); Employer of Choice (workplace, talent); and Performance (financial results, analyst sentiment). These weren't generic categories—they were extracted from the company's strategic plan and executive communications.

At an automotive manufacturer, the priorities looked completely different: Product (innovation, quality, technology); Corporate (leadership voice, strategic direction); Performance (sales, market position); Workplace (labor relations, employee experience); and Society (sustainability, community impact). Their EV leadership strategy meant "Product" carried heavy weight in their scoring model.

The important insight: There's no universal framework. RepTrak uses seven drivers. Some organizations need ESG-specific signals. Others prioritize regulatory and policy dimensions. The pillars must emerge from understanding who needs intelligence and what decisions they're making—which is exactly what Persona-Based Insights (Chapter 4) helps you discover.

Why not just pick standard pillars and use them everywhere? Two decades of building measurement systems revealed a consistent pattern: Organizations that try to apply generic frameworks end up with metrics that don't resonate with leadership. Executives tune out reports that don't connect to their actual priorities. The measurement team drowns in data that doesn't drive decisions.

The strategic sweet spot is three to five pillars—enough to capture complexity but few enough to drive action. The signals must map directly to executive questions, be communications-native (designed for earned media intelligence), and be persona-adaptable (different stakeholders care about different signals).

For this book, I'll illustrate the methodology using four strategic signals that work across many contexts:

> **Innovation:** Are we seen as shaping the future or following it?
>
> **Trust:** Do stakeholders believe in our intent, competence, and consistency?
>
> **Perception:** How are we positioned versus competitors in stakeholders' minds?
>
> **Reputation:** What enduring narrative are we building over time?

These four emerged from years of field-testing and correlate well with RepTrak's research. But they're illustrative—not prescriptive. Your organization may need different pillars entirely. The MRS methodology you'll learn in Chapter 5 works regardless of which pillars you choose.

Your CEO doesn't need a seven-dimension report. They need answers to the questions that matter to them. At the financial services company, those questions were: Are we seen as digital leaders? Are we a responsible corporate citizen? Is our performance story landing with analysts? At the automotive company: Are we winning the EV narrative? How's our workplace reputation post-union negotiations?

These questions drive billion-dollar decisions.

Why Generation 3 Outperforms Generation 2

Let's compare the same scenario across both approaches.

Scenario: Your competitor announces a major partnership with a leading technology company Monday morning.

Generation 2 (Survey-Based Model) Response

During weeks 1-4, media coverage happens. The narrative forms: "Competitor X partners with Tech Giant, positioning as AI innovation leader." Perception shifts. Social discourse amplifies. Industry analysts upgrade competitor positioning.

By week 8, your next quarterly reputation survey fields. By week 12, results arrive showing your Innovation score dropped 4 points while your competitor's rose 6 points.

Your analysis: "We lost Innovation perception versus competitor." Executive question: "What should we have done differently?" Your answer: "We'll track it more closely next quarter."

Outcome: Missed opportunity. Narrative has solidified. Too late for counter-positioning.

Generation 3 (Signal-Based Intelligence) Response

Monday 10:00 AM: Competitor announcement breaks. Monday 2:00 PM: Your monitoring platform flags coverage surge. Monday 4:00 PM: You deliver a SIGNAL brief to your CCO.

The brief opens with the **Signal**—what changed: Competitor X launched a partnership narrative positioning them as "AI innovation leader for mid-market," with coverage concentrated in tier-1 business and tech media.

Next, the **Implication**—why it matters: They're claiming the innovation position you need for your Q2 product launch. If the narrative sticks, you'll be positioned as "catching up" versus "leading." Your Innovation signal could drop 8-12 points over the next 30 days based on historical precedent.

Then, the **Gap**—what's missing: You have no counter-narrative in market. Your last innovation story ran six weeks ago. Competitive coverage ratio over the past 90 days shows them mentioned 3:1 versus you on "innovation" themes. You're invisible in this conversation.

The **Narrative**—the emerging story: They're framing as "AI innovation for mid-market." You're being positioned by default as "enterprise legacy player." This is the narrative dynamic that cost IBM market share versus Amazon Web Services in 2015-2017.

The **Action**—your recommendation: Launch a counter-narrative by Friday. Secure an exclusive customer case study in *Forbes*, *TechCrunch*, or *VentureBeat*. Lead with measurable ROI proof points showing your AI already delivers results, not vaporware. Position as "proven innovation versus unproven partnership." Get a CEO byline or interview for voice and authority. Amplify through your industry analyst channel.

The **Lift**—expected impact: an 8-point recovery in Innovation signal within 30 days; prevention of a 15-point competitive perception gap forming; protected Q2 product launch positioning; and maintained share of the "innovation" narrative. Investment: $15K for freelance writer, media relations, and analyst outreach. ROI: Prevent significant launch marketing waste if you have to reposition later, and protect your product launch investment.

Tuesday 9:00 AM: Your CCO presents the brief in the executive meeting. Tuesday 11:00 AM: Counter-narrative campaign approved. Friday: Customer success story published in target outlets. Week 2: You measure narrative penetration and adjust messaging. Week 4: Innovation perception gap neutralized. Your brand positioned as "proven AI leader."

The Difference

Survey model: 12 weeks to understand what happened—too late to act.

Signal intelligence: Six hours to decode the threat and recommend action.

This is why signal-based intelligence is Generation 3. It operates at the speed of modern media—not the speed of annual surveys.

The Barcelona Principles: Progress, but not Transformation

No discussion of measurement evolution is complete without examining the Barcelona Principles—the PR industry's most influential framework for modern measurement.

The 2010 Watershed Moment

By the late 2000s, the communications industry had reached a crisis point. AVE was widely used despite being fundamentally flawed. Digital metrics were producing massive data volume with minimal insight. Executives were growing frustrated with measurement that couldn't answer basic questions. There were no industry-wide standards for what "good measurement" looked like, and different agencies and teams used different methodologies, making comparison impossible.

In 2010, the International Association for Measurement and Evaluation of Communication (AMEC) convened global PR leaders, measurement experts, and communications professionals in Barcelona. Their mission: create a unified framework for credible, consistent, strategic communications measurement that the entire industry could adopt.

The result: the Barcelona Principles—seven guidelines that fundamentally redefined how communications should be measured.

The Evolution: Barcelona 1.0 → 2.0 → 3.0 → 4.0

The principles have evolved to keep pace with industry changes.

Barcelona 1.0 (2010) established the initial framework with a primary focus on killing AVE and emphasizing outcomes over outputs. It established the foundation for modern measurement.

Barcelona 2.0 (2015) updated the principles for social media and digital transformation, added emphasis on organizational performance and stakeholder impact, and recognized that communications measurement must tie to business results.

Barcelona 3.0 (2020) further refined the framework for integrated communications, emphasized organizational outcomes and societal impact, and acknowledged the need for transparency and ethical measurement.

Barcelona 4.0 (2025), launched at the AMEC Global Summit in Vienna, places stronger emphasis on AI usage, data integrity, and methodological transparency. It aligns more closely with AMEC's Integrated Evaluation Framework (IEF) and uses sharper language reflecting a technology-driven, stakeholder-centric world.

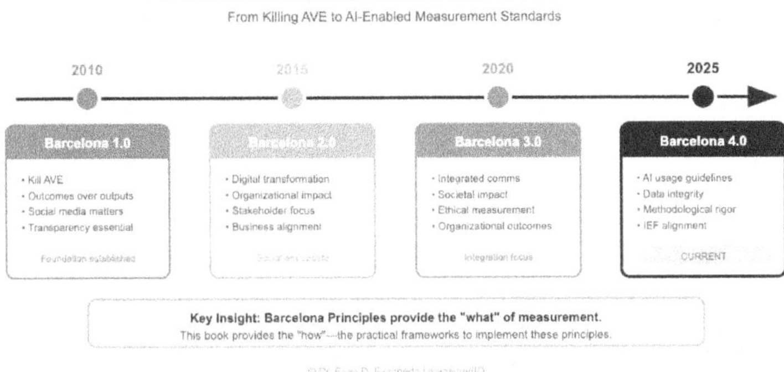

Figure 2.2: The Barcelona Principles Evolution—From Killing AVE
to AI-Enabled Measurement Standards

The Seven Principles (Barcelona 4.0, 2025)

Principle 1: Setting clear, measurable objectives is a critical prerequisite for effective communication planning, measurement, and evaluation. You can't measure success without defining what success looks like. Goals must be specific, measurable, and tied to business objectives—not just communications activity. The updated principle emphasizes that objectives are dynamic guideposts for iterative communication, not static endpoints.

Principle 2: Defining and understanding all stakeholder audiences are essential steps to plan, build relationships, and create lasting impact. Don't just measure what happened to your organization. Understand and measure impact on all stakeholder audiences—customers, employees, communities, investors—and broader society. The updated principle deepens emphasis on stakeholder engagement across polarized, fragmented audiences.

Principle 3: Comprehensive communication measurement and evaluation should be applied to all relevant channels used to understand and influence audience stakeholders. You can't measure just media, or just social, or just events. Modern communications spans multiple channels including emerging platforms like Discord, AI search outputs, and newsletters. Measurement must be similarly integrated across all relevant online and offline channels.

Principle 4: Effective measurement and evaluation of communication require qualitative and quantitative analysis. Numbers alone don't tell the story. Qualitative insights—why people think what they think—are essential for understanding perception. The updated principle strengthens the mandate for mixed methods and human insight alongside AI tools. Dashboards tell us what happened; qualitative insight tells us why.

Principle 5: Invalid measures such as advertising value equivalents (AVEs) should not be used. Instead measure and evaluate the contribution of communication by its outcome and impact. This principle explicitly rejects AVEs and provides actionable alternatives. Don't just say what NOT to do—measure and evaluate outcomes and impact instead. Business leaders demand credible, strategy-linked metrics.

Principle 6: Measurement and evaluation of communication should demonstrate value and inform future strategy and tactics. Measurement isn't just about accountability—it's about improving strategy, performance, and trust. Show how communications contributes to organizational value and use insights to inform future decisions.

Principle 7: Ethics, governance, and transparency with data, methodologies, and technology builds trust and drives learning. New in 4.0, this principle places stronger emphasis on AI usage, data integrity, and methodological transparency. Measurement isn't credible without ethical rigor. This principle ensures practices are future-proof and stakeholder-safe, with particular focus on responsible AI use and transparent methodology.

What the Barcelona Principles Achieved

These principles represented genuine progress. They killed AVE—the industry's explicit rejection of a fundamentally flawed metric. They emphasized outcomes over outputs, shifting focus from activity to impact. They required goal-setting, ending measurement for measurement's sake. They promoted a holistic view, measuring across all channels rather than in silos. They demanded transparency about methodology and limitations. And they insisted on business alignment, connecting communications to organizational goals.

Major PR agencies, corporations, and measurement vendors publicly committed to following the Barcelona Principles. Trade associations promoted them. Universities incorporated them into curricula.

The Barcelona Principles moved the industry forward significantly.

KEY CONCEPT

BARCELONA PRINCIPLES: NECESSARY BUT NOT SUFFICIENT

The Barcelona Principles (now 4.0) advanced the field significantly. But they don't provide consistent benchmarks, don't address predictive analytics, don't include competitive positioning frameworks, and don't guide speed and cadence.

The principles tell you WHAT to measure. This book tells you HOW to measure it at the speed modern business demands.

Where the Barcelona Principles Fall Short

But while foundational, the Barcelona Principles aren't sufficient for today's measurement professionals. They have critical gaps:

No Consistent Benchmarks. The principles encourage goal-setting but offer no standard for what "good" looks like. What's a strong reputation score—70? 80? How much should trust improve quarter-over-quarter—two points or five? What's competitive parity in Innovation perception? How do you know if you're winning or losing? Without benchmarks, teams can't contextualize their performance.

No Integration with AI or Predictive Analytics. The media ecosystem moves faster than the principles anticipated. They haven't evolved to address active signal detection capabilities, AI-powered pattern recognition, predictive risk assessment algorithms, or automated narrative clustering and thematic analysis.

No Framework for Competitive Positioning. Brands want to know not just "how are we performing?" but "how are we performing relative to competitors?" The principles don't address competitive intelligence gathering, relative positioning analysis, share of narrative (not just Share of Voice), or strategic differentiation measurement.

No Emphasis on Brand Equity as Strategic Asset. The principles focus on communications measurement but don't connect measurement to brand equity frameworks used by CFOs, CMOs, and boards. Modern measurement professionals need to speak the language of brand equity valuation, intangible asset measurement, reputation risk quantification, and trust as business drivers.

No Guidance on Speed and Cadence. The principles don't address the timing question. How often should you measure? What requires daily monitoring versus quarterly tracking? How do you balance real-time alerts with strategic analysis? When is speed more important than comprehensiveness?

Put simply: The Barcelona Principles are a great foundation. But they're not sufficient for Generation 3 measurement professionals who need to detect signals that align to business priorities; benchmark against competitors; provide insight based on persona need; predict reputation risks before they materialize; prove business impact in executive language; and operate at the speed of modern media.

The principles tell you *what* to measure (outcomes, not just outputs). They don't tell you *how* to measure it at the speed and specificity modern business demands.

The Path Forward: Integrating Three Generations

So where does this leave you?

You've now seen the complete evolution of measurement.

Generation 1: Output Metrics (1900s-2010s) evolved from press clippings to AVE to digital volume metrics. It counted activity, not impact. It's still widely used but increasingly insufficient. Status: necessary for reporting activity, insufficient for proving value.

Generation 2: Survey-Based Models (2000s-present) includes Rep-Trak, Harris Poll, Edelman, and others. It measured actual perception and created benchmarks, but it's too slow for modern strategy and disconnected from daily decisions. Status: valuable for annual benchmarking, insufficient for strategic guidance.

Generation 3: Signal-Based Intelligence (2020s+) encompasses reputation signal detection, persona-based insights, and predictive capability. It's designed for the speed and specificity of modern communications. Status: the evolution you need to make.

You've seen why traditional tools miss $100 million crises. You've seen why even sophisticated survey models can't keep pace with reputation shifts that happen in hours. You've seen how the Barcelona Principles—now in their fourth iteration, released June 2025—advanced the field, but even with updates for AI and ethics, they don't go far enough for real-time strategic needs.

The Integration Strategy

The smartest measurement professionals don't abandon old approaches entirely. They strategically integrate.

Annual Layer (Generation 2). Use survey-based reputation models for annual benchmarking. Present to board and C-suite—they recognize the brand names. Track long-term trends and year-over-year reputation trajectory. Validate perception shifts detected through other methods.

Strategic Layer (Generation 3). Use signal-based intelligence for daily, weekly, and monthly decisions. Track the Four Signals: Innovation, Trust, Perception, and Reputation. Detect competitive threats early. Guide media strategy and campaign planning. Provide crisis early warning. Deliver persona-based insights.

Tactical Layer (Generation 1). Track output metrics for activity reporting. Use for campaign logistics and coverage documentation. Report to internal teams and agencies. But never confuse outputs with outcomes.

Think of it this way: Generation 1 is your activity log—what you did, what you got. Generation 2 is your annual physical exam—a comprehensive snapshot at a moment in time. Generation 3 is your fitness tracker—continuous monitoring, real-time insights, predictive alerts.

You need all three. But if you only have one, get the fitness tracker—not just the annual exam or activity log.

What This Framework Replaces

Before we build forward, let's be explicit about what you're leaving behind.

Signal-based intelligence isn't another layer on your reporting stack. It replaces practices that no longer serve you.

It replaces monthly decks that summarize activity without prescribing action. If a report doesn't recommend a decision, it doesn't belong in an executive conversation.

It replaces dashboards built for monitoring platforms, not decision-makers. Executives think in risks and tradeoffs, not charts. That's why SIGNAL briefs exist.

It replaces lagging explanations that arrive after perception has already shifted. Telling someone why something went wrong three weeks later isn't insight—it's documentation.

It replaces sentiment averages that flatten nuance. A single negative mention from a high-authority source often matters more than hundreds of positive posts. This framework recognizes that asymmetry.

And it replaces the false comfort of "alignment." Alignment without activation is theater. Real alignment exists when intelligence changes what leaders decide to do.

This isn't an enhancement to traditional measurement. It's a different operating model.

What's Next: Building the System

You now understand why output metrics (Generation 1) can't differentiate good attention from bad—and why volume never equaled value. You understand why survey-based models (Generation 2) were important progress but are too slow and broad for strategic communications. You understand why signal-based intelligence (Generation 3) represents the evolution modern measurement professionals need. You know how to integrate all three approaches strategically. And you understand why the Barcelona Principles advanced the field but don't go far enough.

You understand WHY measurement must evolve.

But understanding the problem isn't enough. You need the solution—the actual system.

That's what Chapter 3 delivers.

In the next chapter, we'll open the hood on signal-based intelligence. You'll learn what distinguishes true signals from noise and why different organizations track different reputation dimensions based on their unique priorities. You'll see illustrative pillars—Trust, Innovation, Perception, and Reputation—while understanding that your pillars will emerge from the discovery work in Chapter 4. You'll explore the Three Intelligence Layers and how they transform data into strategic recommendations. And you'll understand how the Maturity Model, expanded with Meltwater's Data-Driven Communications Research Lab, shows where you are and how to advance.

You'll see exactly how Generation 3 measurement works—and why the methodology must be grounded in stakeholder priorities before it can deliver value.

Ready to see the system?

Let's go.

References

AB InBev. (2023). Q3 2023 Earnings Report. Leuven, Belgium: Anheuser-Busch InBev.

AMEC (International Association for Measurement and Evaluation of Communication). (2010). Barcelona Principles 1.0. London, UK: AMEC.

AMEC. (2015). Barcelona Principles 2.0. London, UK: AMEC.

AMEC. (2020). Barcelona Principles 3.0. London, UK: AMEC.

AMEC. (2025). Barcelona Principles 4.0. London, UK: AMEC. https://amecorg.com/resources/barcelona-principles-4-0/

Ansoff, H. I. (1975). Managing Strategic Surprise by Response to Weak Signals. *California Management Review*, 18(2), 21-33.

Coombs, W. T. (2007). Protecting Organization Reputations During a Crisis: The Development and Application of Situational Crisis Communication Theory. *Corporate Reputation Review,* 10(3), 163-176.

Edelman. (2025). Edelman Trust Barometer 2025. New York, NY: Edelman.

Harris Poll. (2024). The Harris Poll Reputation Quotient. New York, NY: The Harris Poll.

Jeon, S., & Baeck, S. (2020). The Impact of Food Safety Events on the Value of Food-Related Firms: An Event Study Approach. *Journal of Hospitality & Tourism Research,* 44(8), 1218-1239.

Li, C., & Zhang, W. (2020). Food Safety Trust, Risk Perception, and Consumers' Response to Company Trust Repair Actions in Food Recall Crises. *International Journal of Environmental Research and Public Health,* 17(4), 1187.

Meltwater. (2025). Data-Driven Communications assessment findings (internal research, used with permission).

Paraskevas, A. (2006). Signal Detection as the First Line of Defense in Tourism Crisis Management. *International Journal of Hospitality Management,* 25(4), 587-602.

Reputation Institute. (2024). RepTrak Methodology Overview. Boston, MA: Reputation Institute.

Santos, A., et al. (2025). Enhancing Brand Value Through Circular Economy Service Quality: The Mediating Roles of Customer Satisfaction, Brand Image, and Customer Loyalty. *Sustainability,* 17(3), 1332.

ScienceDirect. (2025). Redefining Marketing Strategies Through Sustainability: Influencing Consumer Behavior in the Circular Economy. *Journal of Cleaner Production.*

The New York Times. (2023, May 28). Bud Light's Sales Slump Continues as Boycott Enters Second Month.

United Airlines. (2017). Q2 2017 Earnings Call Transcript. Chicago, IL: United Airlines.

WARC. (2024). *Eco-Innovation Strategies that Drive Long-Term Brand Value*. London, UK: WARC.

Xiang, R., Wang, M., Lin, L., & Wu, D. (2021). A Research on the Crisis Spillover Effect of Food Safety Incidents on Competitive Firms. *Frontiers in Public Health*, 9, 766385.

Note on Sources

The QuickServe Food Safety Crisis is a composite case study representing patterns observed across multiple documented food safety incidents at global restaurant chains. The company name is fictitious, but the damage profiles, timelines, and recovery costs reflect documented industry patterns and academic research on crisis management impacts. Specific figures (75-150 infections, $100 million recovery investment) represent typical ranges observed across comparable incidents, not a single company's experience.

The three-generation framework (Output Metrics, Survey-Based Models, Signal-Based Intelligence) is an original taxonomy developed by the author to contextualize the evolution of communications measurement.

The Barcelona Principles discussion draws on publicly available documentation from AMEC (Association for Measurement and Evaluation of Communication).

CHAPTER 3

DECODING SIGNALS

How Media Coverage Becomes Strategic Intelligence

Your dashboard shows 6,247 mentions this week. Sentiment: 68% positive. Reach: 8.2 million.

Your CEO leans back in her chair and asks: "So what should we do?"

You don't have an answer.

This is the measurement trap — and if you're stuck in it, you're not alone. Most communications teams still default to reach and impressions as their primary success metrics, yet those same professionals will tell you those numbers rarely move executive decisions. The data bears this out: Meltwater's Data-Driven Communications assessments of 500+ communications professionals found that only 8% had reached the Visionary level — where measurement actually drives strategy. The other 92% are still reporting outputs and hoping someone notices.

The gap between data and decisions persists because most measurement systems were built for reporting, not intelligence. They count what happened after it happened. They describe activity, not insight. They answer "what was said" but not "what's changing" or "what should we do."

This chapter introduces signal-based intelligence—the conceptual foundation that transforms media coverage from noise into strategic intelligence.

You've already seen why this matters. Chapter 1 showed you the activation gap: measurement professionals drowning in data but starving for impact. The Monday Morning Test revealed that strategic advisors deliver intelligence, not just metrics. Chapter 2 traced the evolution of measurement across three generations. Generation 1 (output metrics) and Generation 2 (survey-based models) couldn't provide early warning or actionable timing. Generation 3—signal-based intelligence—emerged as the solution.

Now we need to understand what signal-based intelligence actually is.

This chapter answers five critical questions:

1. What is a reputation signal (and how is it different from a metric or mention)?

2. How do you define the reputation pillars that matter to your business?

3. How do signals become strategic intelligence?

4. What capability do you need to build to detect and interpret signals?

5. How do signals connect to action and business outcomes?

By the end of this chapter, you'll understand the conceptual framework that underlies all modern reputation intelligence—including the Persona-Based Insights framework in Chapter 4, the Media Reputation Score methodology we'll detail in Chapter 5, and how to activate within your organization in Chapters 6-9.

Here's the shift we're making:

From: "What was said about us?"

To: "What's changing in our reputation—and what should we do about it?"

Let's start with the most fundamental question: What is a signal?

Section 1: What Is a Reputation Signal?

A signal is a pattern of change that indicates future reputation movement—not just a snapshot of current state.

Signals are fundamentally different from the metrics most measurement professionals track. A metric tells you what happened: "We had 6,247 mentions this week." A mention is a single data point: "*The Wall Street Journal* covered our earnings." A signal reveals what's changing: "Trust language is declining 40% week-over-week in regulatory sources—pattern matches pre-crisis indicators from similar cases."

The difference matters because metrics describe the past, signals predict the future.

Traditional measurement captures snapshots. Signal-based intelligence detects trajectories. And in a world where reputation can reshape in 24 hours (remember YesMadam from Chapter 1?), trajectory matters more than position.

KEY CONCEPT

SIGNAL VS. METRIC VS. MENTION

A mention is a single data point: "The WSJ covered our earnings." A metric tells you what happened: "We had 6,247 mentions this week." A signal reveals what's changing: "Trust language declining 40% in regulatory sources—pattern matches pre-crisis indicators."

Metrics describe the past. Signals predict the future.

The Anatomy of a Reputation Signal

Not every change in your data is a signal. Most of it is noise—random fluctuations that don't indicate meaningful shifts in reputation.

So what makes something a signal versus just data? A true reputation signal has six components:

Volume: How Much Is Being Said. Volume alone is meaningless. YesMadam generated 162 million impressions in 24 hours—and it destroyed the brand. High volume can signal crisis as easily as success.

But volume becomes meaningful when compared to baseline. If your normal volume is 200 mentions per week and you suddenly hit 2,000, that's a signal. If your normal volume is 5,000 mentions per week and you drop to 500, that's also a signal. Volume matters as change, not as absolute number.

Velocity: How Fast It's Spreading. Acceleration matters more than absolute numbers. A story that goes from 10 mentions to 100 mentions in 6 hours is more significant than a story that generates 500 mentions slowly over 3 weeks.

Velocity reveals two critical dynamics: amplification (is this spreading virally or organically?) and urgency (how much time do we have to respond?).

Source Authority: Who Is Saying It. A mention in *The Wall Street Journal* carries more weight than a random blog post. A regulatory inquiry carries more weight than a customer complaint. A CEO resignation covered by *Bloomberg* matters more than the same resignation covered by a trade publication.

Source authority weighting is critical to signal intelligence—not because some sources are "better" than others, but because different sources indicate different types of reputation impact. Tier 1 media like the WSJ,

NYT, and *Bloomberg* signals mainstream visibility and C-suite attention. Regulatory sources like the Food and Drug Administration, Securities and Exchange Commission, and Federal Trade Commission signal compliance risk and governance concerns. Expert commentary from analysts and academics signals credibility assessment and long-term trends. Social platforms signal grassroots sentiment and viral potential. Trade publications signal industry positioning and competitive context.

Thematic Consistency: Is It a Pattern or Noise? A single mention is a data point. Repeated themes across disconnected sources are a signal.

Pattern recognition separates signal from noise. If one article mentions "trust issues," that's data. If five articles from different outlets mention "trust erosion" within 48 hours, that's a pattern. If those mentions cluster around similar themes—transparency, accountability, credibility—that's a signal.

Thematic clustering reveals narrative shifts—changes in how your brand is being framed, positioned, or understood. This is where human analysts add irreplaceable value. AI can identify keywords. Humans recognize when disconnected mentions are telling the same story.

Geographic and Temporal Clustering: Where and When. Signals often appear in specific regions or time windows before spreading nationally. Regional patterns can predict national crises. Local media often detects weak signals before tier 1 outlets.

Time-of-day patterns reveal urgency (crisis stories break morning, trend through day). Historical patterns show cyclical versus structural changes. Where and when something is said matters as much as what is said.

Sentiment Trajectory: Not Just Positive or Negative, But Direction. Traditional sentiment analysis gives you a snapshot: 68% positive, 20% neutral, 12% negative.

Signal-based intelligence tracks trajectory. Is trust eroding or building? Is innovation perception rising or falling? Is the sentiment stable or volatile?

Direction matters more than position. A brand with 60% positive sentiment but rising trajectory is in better shape than a brand with 80% positive sentiment but declining trajectory.

The "So What" Test: When Data Becomes Signal

Not all signals are actionable. The question isn't "Is this changing?" but "Does this change matter?"

Every signal must pass the "So What" test—three questions that separate data from intelligence:

First: What's changing? Be specific. "Mentions are up" isn't enough. "Trust language declining 40% in tier 1 media while innovation mentions rising 60% in tech outlets" is a signal.

Second: Why does it matter? Connect to business outcomes. "This matters because trust erosion precedes customer churn, and we're in renewal season with enterprise clients."

Third: What should we do? Provide an actionable recommendation. "Launch transparency campaign targeting enterprise decision-makers with proof points on reliability and governance."

If you can't answer all three questions, it's data—not intelligence.

QUICK CHECK

THE "SO WHAT" TEST

Every signal must answer three questions: 1. What's changing? (Be specific) 2. Why does it matter? (Connect to business outcomes) 3. What should we do? (Actionable recommendation) If you can't answer all three, it's data—not intelligence.

Section 2: Defining Your Reputation Pillars

Not all reputation dimensions are equal. Some predict investor confidence. Others drive customer loyalty. Some protect you in crisis. Others position you for growth.

Understanding which signals matter—and when—is the difference between reactive reporting and strategic intelligence.

The pillars I'm about to detail aren't meant to be adopted wholesale. They emerged from years of field-testing across dozens of organizations and industries, validated against RepTrak's seven-pillar model, cross-referenced with academic research on reputation drivers, and refined through real-world implementation. They represent one proven configuration—but not the only one.

Remember the financial services company from earlier? Their pillars were Platform/Partner; Digital Leader; Responsible Corporate Citizen; Employer of Choice; and Performance. The automotive manufacturer used Product; Corporate; Performance; Workplace; and Society. Neither used the four signals I'll describe below—because their business priorities demanded different frameworks.

Here's the critical insight: effective measurement requires organizing media signals around reputation drivers that matter to your business. The scoring methodology (which you'll learn in Chapter 5) is universal. The pillars are not.

That said, you need somewhere to start. The four signals below—Trust, Innovation, Perception, and Reputation—provide a solid foundation that works across many industries. Use them as your starting framework, then customize based on what you discover through Persona-Based Insights (Chapter 4). Many organizations find that two or three of these signals map directly to their priorities, while one or two need to be replaced with something more specific to their business.

Illustrative Pillars: Trust, Innovation, Perception, Reputation

KEY CONCEPT

YOUR PILLARS WILL BE DIFFERENT

The four signals presented here—Trust, Innovation, Perception, Reputation—are a starting framework. Your organization's actual pillars will emerge from the PBI work in Chapter 4. Many organizations use 3-5 pillars customized to their strategic priorities. The financial services company used Platform/Partner; Digital Leader; Responsible Corporate Citizen; Employer of Choice; and Performance. The automotive manufacturer used Product; Corporate; Performance; Workplace; and Society.

The methodology is consistent; the pillars are yours to define.

These four strategic signals cover: Trust (credibility, reliability, transparency, safety); Innovation (forward-thinking, leadership, differentiation); Perception (overall favorability and brand positioning); and Reputation (long-term narrative and stakeholder equity).

Let me show you how each one works—and more importantly, how I learned which signals matter most in different contexts.

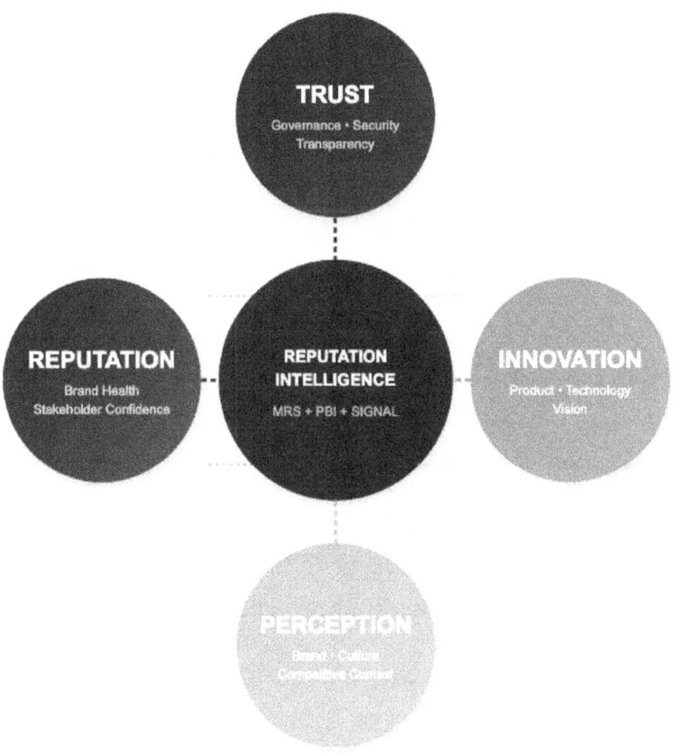

Figure 3.1: The Four Signals Framework—Trust, Innovation, Perception, and Reputation (customize based on your organization's priorities discovered through PBI in chapter 4)

Signal 1: TRUST

What It Measures

Trust is the foundation of all stakeholder relationships. It reflects whether people believe your brand is credible (you tell the truth); reliable (you deliver on promises); transparent (you operate openly); safe (you protect stakeholders from harm); and ethical (you do the right thing).

Trust isn't measured by what you say about yourself. It's measured by what credible third parties say about you—and whether their assessments suggest you can be trusted to act in stakeholders' interests.

Why It Matters

Trust is the single most predictive signal of long-term brand health.

Trust predicts crisis resilience. Brands with high trust recover faster from negative events. Trust creates "benefit of the doubt" during controversies. Low trust amplifies negative news—every mistake confirms the pattern.

Trust drives customer retention and loyalty. It correlates directly with repeat purchase and advocacy. In B2B contexts, trust determines contract renewals and expansion. Trust is the moat that protects market share during competitive attacks.

Trust influences investor confidence during volatility. Governance issues (low trust) trigger stock sell-offs. ESG investors weight trust heavily in valuation models. Trust signals predict regulatory scrutiny and legal risk.

Trust determines your "permission to operate." Regulators, policymakers, and community groups grant or withhold social license based on trust. Low trust invites intervention, investigation, and restriction. High trust creates operating freedom and partnership opportunities.

Trust is the hardest signal to build and the easiest to destroy. It accumulates slowly through consistent behavior over time. It can be lost overnight through a single breach of credibility, safety, or ethics.

How Trust Manifests in Media Coverage

Positive trust indicators include regulatory compliance and governance coverage with positive tone; safety and security associations ("most trusted," "reliable," "safe choice"); transparency and accountability framing ("open," "honest," "forthcoming"); ethical behavior recognition through awards, rankings, and endorsements; and expert credibility assessments where analysts and academics validate claims.

Negative trust indicators include regulatory investigations, violations, and sanctions; safety incidents, recalls, and liability issues; transparency failures such as delayed disclosure or hidden information; ethical lapses including conflicts of interest and misrepresentation; and source authority escalation where consumer complaints lead to regulatory action.

The source matters enormously. Trust signals from regulatory bodies, independent experts, and tier 1 investigative journalism carry 5-10x the weight of consumer reviews or promotional coverage.

Example: The Vacation Rental Trust Gap

Let me share an example from recent competitive analysis work. Two major vacation rental platforms—let's call them PlatformA and PlatformB—were competing for perception leadership in Q2 2025. Traditional metrics showed PlatformA dominating: 2:1 advantage in total media volume, higher innovation framing, stronger brand awareness.

But signal-based analysis revealed a different story. PlatformB's Trust signal scored significantly higher than PlatformA.

Why? Family-focused travel media consistently framed PlatformB as "safer choice for families." Consumer reports highlighted PlatformB's host verification and property standards. Travel advisors recommended PlatformB for "reliable, predictable experiences." Regulatory coverage showed fewer safety incidents and disputes.

PlatformB was associated with "host reliability," "safety," "consistency," and "family-friendly." PlatformA was associated with "unique experiences" and "innovation," but also "safety concerns" and "host issues." Trust language appeared 40% more frequently in PlatformB coverage.

And here's the critical insight: PlatformB's trust sentiment was steadily rising (6.5 to 8.0 over 8 weeks) while PlatformA's trust sentiment was declining (7.5 to 6.0 over the same period).

The strategic implications were clear: For PlatformB, the trust advantage positioned them as the "stable, reliable choice," particularly strong with repeat customers and families. Less exciting than the competitor, but more trusted. Their strategy: lean into trust positioning, especially for long-term rentals and family travel.

For PlatformA, innovation leadership was clear, but trust vulnerability was emerging. High visibility without trust foundation equals risk. Their strategy: Address trust signals proactively before they become crisis.

PlatformB didn't "win" the category—PlatformA maintained market leadership. But PlatformB carved out a defensible position based on trust differentiation. Different stakeholders value different signals.

Remember: these pillars—Trust, Innovation, Perception, Reputation—were the right framework for this particular analysis. Your pillars may look different. The automotive manufacturer I mentioned earlier would have analyzed this same competitive landscape through Product, Corporate, Performance, Workplace, and Society. The methodology is universal; the pillars are not.

This is the power of signal-based intelligence: It reveals strategic positioning that volume metrics miss.

Signal 2: INNOVATION

What It Measures

Innovation reflects whether your brand is perceived as forward-thinking (focused on the future, not the past); a market leader (setting direction, not following); differentiated (unique positioning versus competitors); relevant (aligned with emerging trends and stakeholder needs); and cutting-edge (associated with progress, advancement, disruption).

Innovation isn't measured by R&D spend or patent counts. It's measured by whether media coverage and stakeholder discourse position your brand as an innovation leader—regardless of actual innovation activity.

Perception of innovation drives business outcomes, even when it decouples from innovation reality.

Why It Matters

Innovation signals have outsized impact on three critical areas.

First, competitive positioning and market share: Innovation leaders attract "early adopter" customers who pay premium prices. Innovation perception predicts market share shifts 6-12 months out. "Fast follower" brands struggle to command pricing power. Innovation territory is won or lost through narrative, not just product.

Second, investor confidence and valuation: Growth investors weight innovation heavily in valuation models. Innovation signals predict future earnings potential. "Innovative" brands trade at higher multiples than "legacy" brands. Innovation narrative drives M&A interest and partnership opportunities.

Third, talent acquisition and retention: Top talent wants to work for "innovative" companies. Innovation perception correlates with Glassdoor scores and recruiting success. "Legacy" or "behind the curve" perception triggers talent flight. Innovation signals make you an employer of choice.

Innovation is the growth signal. It positions you for the future and attracts stakeholders who value progress over stability.

When Innovation Became the Primary Driver

Here's a story from my time at a global financial services company that fundamentally shaped how I think about signal prioritization.

When I joined the communications team, we were using RepTrak's seven-pillar framework to measure reputation: Products and Services; Innovation; Workplace; Governance; Citizenship; Leadership; and Performance. It was a solid, academically validated approach.

But as we implemented what would become the Persona-Based Insights framework (which you'll learn in Chapter 4), something unexpected emerged: Our investor and business media audiences weren't equally interested in all seven pillars. When we mapped stakeholder priorities to reputation drivers, one signal kept rising to the top: Digital Leadership.

The executive who cared most about this was the head of investor relations. "Analysts keep asking whether we're a legacy player or a digital innovator," he told me. "That's the narrative that moves our stock price. I don't need to know about all seven RepTrak pillars. I need to know if we're winning the digital transformation story."

At the time, the company was in the middle of a massive digital transformation—evolving from a traditional financial services business to a cross-border payments platform. Fintech competitors were emerging rapidly. The narrative battle wasn't about whether we were a "good corporate citizen" or had strong "workplace culture"—though both mattered. The narrative battle was about whether we could innovate.

So we made a strategic decision. Rather than spreading our measurement equally across seven pillars, we leaned heavily into the Digital Leadership signal. We built the Media Reputation Score methodology specifically to track how our innovation narrative was performing against competitors. His priorities shaped our pillars. Not the other way around.

The results were revealing. We could see exactly which stories moved the Innovation needle. We could benchmark against competitors. We could identify which publications and which types of coverage drove perception shifts. And critically, we could provide the C-suite with intelligence that actually answered their questions: "Are we winning the digital leadership narrative?"

This experience taught me that while you can start with established pillar frameworks, you must discover which signals actually matter most to your specific business context. The illustrative pillars I present in this chapter—Trust, Innovation, Perception, and Reputation—are a proven foundation. But within that foundation, you'll likely find that one or two signals dominate your strategic priorities at any given time.

For that financial services company, Digital Leadership (mapping to Innovation) was the signal that mattered most. For a pharmaceutical company facing regulatory scrutiny, Trust might dominate. For a consumer brand in a competitive market, Perception might be the priority. For an automotive company navigating EV transition, Product might carry the heaviest weight.

The methodology stays the same. The signal weighting changes based on what you discover through PBI.

Example: The Beverage Category Innovation Battle

Let me share another example: In Q1 2025, two major beverage companies—let's call them BeverageA and BeverageB—were engaged in their perennial battle for category leadership. Volume metrics showed the usual pattern: BeverageA with higher overall coverage.

To demonstrate how pillar selection shapes analysis, consider a beverage CMO focused on younger demographics. Through PBI conversations, Innovation emerges as the critical pillar—this executive cares most about "future of category" positioning. So the competitive analysis is built around Innovation as the primary lens, with Trust, Perception, and Reputation as supporting dimensions.

Signal-based analysis revealed BeverageB gaining innovation territory.

BeverageB positioned its EV infrastructure investment as "future-focused supply chain." Coverage framed BeverageB as "leading on sustainability and logistics innovation." Business media highlighted how BeverageB was "reinventing distribution for the climate era."

Tech and business outlets like *Bloomberg*, WSJ, and *TechCrunch* gave BeverageB extensive innovation coverage. Sustainability and logistics publications positioned BeverageB as industry leader. Comparative coverage framed it as "BeverageB innovates while BeverageA maintains tradition."

BeverageB was associated with "EV infrastructure," "supply chain innovation," "sustainability leadership," and "forward-thinking." BeverageA was associated with "iconic brand," "tradition," "classic," and "legacy"—positive framing, but not innovative.

The strategic implications were clear. BeverageB's innovation signal gains provided competitive differentiation. They were positioned for partnership opportunities with sustainability-focused retailers, attractive to ESG-conscious investors and younger consumers. Their strategy: amplify innovation narrative and own "future of beverage" positioning.

For BeverageA, strong brand equity was evident but an innovation gap was emerging. There was risk of "legacy brand" perception with younger demographics. Their strategy: launch innovation initiatives AND ensure media coverage frames them as leadership, not catch-up.

BeverageB didn't overtake BeverageA in total market share. But BeverageB captured valuable innovation territory that positions them for long-term growth with sustainability-conscious stakeholders.

The Innovation Insight: You don't need to out-innovate competitors on product. You need to out-narrate them on innovation perception. Media coverage drives perception. Perception drives business outcomes.

And here's the critical point: Innovation was the right pillar to prioritize for this situation. A different brand—say, one whose executive sponsor cared most about regulatory relationships—might have analyzed the same two companies through a Trust lens and reached entirely different strategic conclusions. The methodology is consistent. The pillar selection comes from PBI.

Signal 3: PERCEPTION

What It Measures

Perception reflects overall favorability and brand affinity: likability (do people feel positively toward the brand?); affinity (do stakeholders have emotional connection?); favorability (is the brand viewed in a positive light?); consideration (would stakeholders choose this brand?); and advocacy (would stakeholders recommend this brand?).

Perception is the "baseline brand health" signal—the general sentiment that surrounds your brand across all coverage and discourse.

Why It Matters

Perception drives three critical stakeholder behaviors:

First, purchase consideration and intent. Positive perception predicts product consideration in B2C contexts. Perception correlates with "likelihood to recommend" in B2B sales. Low perception creates friction at every stage of the customer journey.

Second, word-of-mouth and organic advocacy. High perception brands benefit from positive organic conversation. Perception drives social sharing and recommendation behavior. Low perception limits viral potential and advocacy.

Third, crisis resilience and reputation buffer. Strong perception creates "benefit of the doubt" during negative events. Perception acts as a reputation reservoir during temporary setbacks. Brands with high perception recover faster from PR issues.

Perception is your brand equity reservoir. It's the goodwill you've built that buffers you against bad news and amplifies good news.

Leading versus Lagging Indicator

Perception is often a lagging indicator—but it can lead behavioral change.

The relationship is complex. Trust and Innovation drive Perception: if Trust is high and Innovation is high, Perception rises. But Perception can remain high even as Trust and Innovation decline due to lag effect. Once Perception shifts, it predicts behavioral change in purchase, advocacy, and loyalty.

The timing typically works like this: Innovation signals rise, then 3-6 months later Perception improves. Trust signals decline, then 2-4 months later Perception weakens. Perception declines, then 1-3 months later purchase behavior changes.

This means strong Perception without underlying Trust or Innovation is vulnerable. It's a trailing indicator of past success, not a predictor of future strength.

The Perception Paradox

Returning to our vacation rental example, PlatformA maintained higher overall Perception scores than PlatformB—despite PlatformB's Trust advantage.

Why? PlatformA had a 2:1 advantage in total earned media volume, more diverse coverage types spanning travel, business, lifestyle, and tech, higher celebrity and influencer association, and more "unique experience" and aspirational framing.

Innovation coverage created a positive halo effect. "Future of travel" narratives prominently featured PlatformA. Product launches generated favorable coverage. Years of market leadership created a perception reservoir. Even as Trust declined, overall Perception remained strong. Brand affinity and emotional connection buffered negative signals.

High Perception + Low Trust = Short-term strength, long-term vulnerability.

For PlatformA, the perception advantage sustains market leadership today. But Trust erosion threatens Perception sustainability. Without a Trust foundation, Perception will eventually follow Trust down. Their strategy: Address Trust signals before the Perception reservoir depletes.

For PlatformB, lower Perception despite higher Trust means the Trust foundation is strong but less visible. Their strategy: Build Perception through visibility and emotional connection while maintaining Trust advantage.

The Lesson: Perception tells you where you are today. Trust and Innovation tell you where you're going tomorrow.

Signal 4: REPUTATION

What It Measures

Reputation reflects the enduring narrative and long-term stakeholder equity your organization has built over time. It encompasses overall credibility and standing in the market; stakeholder confidence in your organization's trajectory; competitive positioning relative to peers; strategic narrative territory you own versus competitors; and resilience—your ability to weather setbacks and maintain momentum.

Reputation isn't the same as Perception. Perception captures how people feel about you today. Reputation captures what they believe about you over time—the accumulated story of who you are, built through consistent behavior across Trust, Innovation, and Perception dimensions.

To be clear: Trust, Innovation, Perception, and Reputation are four distinct signals—not three signals feeding into a fourth.

Why It Matters

Reputation is the most predictive signal of long-term business performance.

Reputation predicts financial outcomes. It correlates with stock price, valuation multiples, and investor confidence. High-reputation brands command pricing power and market share. Reputation crises trigger measurable financial impact through stock drops and sales decline.

Reputation determines stakeholder decisions. Investors decide where to allocate capital. Customers decide which brands to trust with loyalty. Employees decide where to build careers. Partners decide which companies to align with. Regulators decide which companies to scrutinize or support.

Reputation is your strategic moat. High reputation creates competitive advantage. Low reputation makes every business activity harder. Reputation compounds over time—momentum matters.

Reputation is the outcome of Trust + Innovation + Perception working together. It's not a simple average—it's a weighted composite based on context.

The Relationship Between Signals

Trust, Innovation, Perception, and Reputation are four distinct signals that together create a complete picture of brand health.

Different contexts demand different signal priorities.

During Crisis: Trust dominates. Crisis tests credibility—stakeholders want to know if they can rely on you. Boeing's collapse wasn't about

Innovation or Perception—it was Trust failure. When evaluating crisis response, weight Trust highest.

During Growth and Competition: Innovation leads. Competitive battles reward Innovation positioning. EV automakers' brand strength has been driven primarily by Innovation signal despite Trust challenges. When fighting for market position, weight Innovation highest.

In Mature Markets: Perception and Reputation matter most. Established categories reward consistency, favorability, and long-term narrative. Legacy CPG brands sustain market position through Perception and Reputation even when Innovation lags. When defending market leadership, weight these signals highest.

For B2B and Enterprise: Trust and Reputation dominate. Business buyers prioritize reliability, credibility, and track record. Enterprise technology companies build on Trust foundation plus Reputation for delivery. When selling to business customers, weight Trust and Reputation highest.

The key insight: all four signals matter, but their relative importance shifts based on your business context—which is exactly why PBI (Chapter 4) must come before MRS (Chapter 5). You need to discover which signals matter most to your organization before you build your scoring model.

Section 3: From Signals to Intelligence Layers

Detecting signals is step one. Interpreting what they mean—and recommending what to do—is where measurement professionals become strategic advisors.

This is the activation layer from Chapter 1.

Remember the Monday Morning Test? The difference between the $95K data provider and the $180K strategic advisor wasn't access to better data. Both had the same monitoring platforms. Both could see the same mentions.

The difference was what they did with the signals.

The data provider reported: "Here's what was said."

The strategic advisor delivered: "Here's what it means, why it matters, and what we should do."

The gap between those two responses is the intelligence layer.

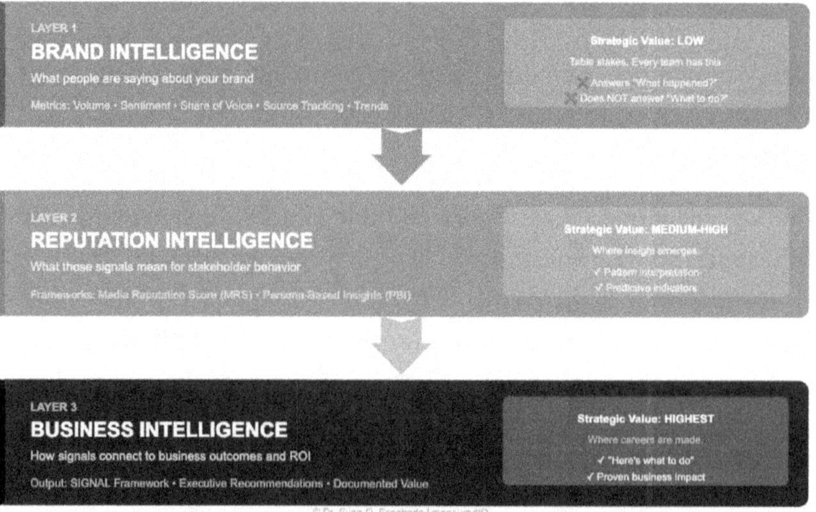

Figure 3.2: The Three Intelligence Layers—Brand Intelligence, Reputation Intelligence, and Business Intelligence

Signal-based reputation intelligence operates across three layers. Most measurement professionals stop at Layer 1. The career opportunity—and the business value—is in Layers 2 and 3.

Layer 1: BRAND Intelligence

Definition: What people are saying about your brand

Brand Intelligence is the foundation layer—the raw detection and classification of signals. It encompasses volume of mentions across sources, thematic analysis of what topics are being discussed, sentiment distribution across positive, neutral, and negative, source tracking of who is saying what, competitive mention tracking for share of voice, and basic trending and historical comparison.

This is what traditional media monitoring provides.

Value Delivered: Brand Intelligence provides awareness of what's being said. It offers historical tracking ("Here's our mention volume over time"); trend detection ("Mentions spiked 300% this week"); topic identification ("Top themes are product launch, pricing, customer service"); and competitive context ("We have 45% share of voice vs. competitor's 30%").

Limitation: Descriptive, Not Diagnostic. Brand Intelligence answers "what happened" but not "what it means" or "what we should do."

Strategic Value: LOW. This is table stakes. Every communications team has access to this level of intelligence. It's necessary but not sufficient.

This is where most teams get stuck—and where careers plateau.

Layer 2: REPUTATION Intelligence

Definition: What those signals mean for stakeholder behavior and reputation outcomes

Reputation Intelligence adds interpretation and strategic context. It includes pattern recognition across disconnected signals; pillar-based analysis against the reputation dimensions that matter to your business;

source authority weighting and credibility assessment; thematic narrative mapping of what stories are being told; competitive benchmarking and positioning analysis; early warning indicators and trend prediction; and stakeholder impact assessment.

This is where signal detection becomes reputation intelligence.

Note: Technology enables this layer, but human expertise is irreplaceable. AI can identify patterns. Humans understand what they mean in YOUR business context.

Value Delivered: Reputation Intelligence provides understanding of why signals matter. It delivers pattern interpretation ("Trust language declining 40% in regulatory sources—this matches pre-crisis patterns from similar cases"); strategic context ("Innovation gap widening vs. competitor—we're losing 'future of category' positioning"); competitive positioning ("Competitor capturing Trust territory we owned 6 months ago"); predictive indicators ("Based on signal velocity and source authority escalation, expect mainstream crisis coverage in 2-3 weeks"); and stakeholder impact ("Enterprise customers weight Trust heavily in renewals—this signal threatens Q3 retention targets").

Strategic Value: MEDIUM-HIGH. This is where insight emerges. You're no longer just reporting data—you're providing intelligence that shapes decisions.

Two frameworks operationalize Reputation Intelligence:

Persona-Based Insights (PBI), covered in Chapter 4, aligns intelligence to stakeholder priorities; maps signals to business decision triggers; ensures the right intelligence reaches the right personas at the right time; and connects reputation intelligence to business actions.

Media Reputation Score (MRS), detailed in Chapter 5, quantifies the reputation impact of each signal; connects media coverage to reputation drivers; enables benchmarking and prediction; and provides scoring methodology for Trust, Innovation, Perception, and Reputation.

Together, PBI + MRS transform signals into reputation intelligence.

Layer 3: BUSINESS Intelligence

Definition: What actions to take and expected business outcomes

Business Intelligence adds strategic recommendations and activation. It encompasses specific, actionable recommendations with rationale; ROI projections and impact quantification; risk mitigation strategies and prevention plans; opportunity capture roadmaps; activation playbooks (Signal to Narrative to Action); proof chains connecting leading indicators to lagging outcomes; and cross-functional coordination and alignment.

This is where reputation intelligence becomes business intelligence.

Note: This layer requires strategic judgment, business acumen, and executive communication skills—capabilities that separate strategic advisors from tactical analysts.

Value Delivered: Business Intelligence provides actionable recommendations executives can implement. It offers strategic recommendations ("Here's what we should do, why, and what we'll gain"); ROI justification ("Here's the cost of action vs. cost of inaction"); risk mitigation ("Here's how we prevent the worst-case scenario"); opportunity capture ("Here's how we leverage this signal for competitive advantage"); activation roadmaps ("Here's the specific plan, owners, and timeline"); and proof metrics ("Here's how we'll measure success and prove impact").

Dino Delic, who has assessed hundreds of communications teams through Meltwater's DDC program, puts it simply: "The teams that break through to Level 3 and 4 maturity share one characteristic—they stopped asking 'what happened?' and started asking 'what does this mean for our business?' That shift in question changes everything."

Strategic Value: HIGH. This is C-suite decision intelligence. You're not reporting data or providing analysis—you're shaping strategic decisions that drive business outcomes.

This is career-defining capability: $180K-$300K+ compensation, VP-level trajectory.

PRO TIP

MOVE FROM LAYER 1 TO LAYER 3

Layer 1 (Brand Intelligence): What was said. You can probably do this already. Layer 2 (Reputation Intelligence): What it means. Start here by adding interpretation. Layer 3 (Business Intelligence): What to do. The goal—strategic recommendations with ROI. Progress deliberately.

Master each layer before advancing. Most teams get stuck at Layer 1. The career opportunity is in Layers 2 and 3.

Section 4: Building the Capability

Most measurement professionals blame their tools for their inability to provide strategic intelligence. "If only we had better monitoring… If only our dashboards were more sophisticated…"

This is false. The limitation is process and capability, not technology.

You can deliver Layer 3 intelligence with Google Alerts and a spreadsheet if you have a clear understanding of what signals matter, a disciplined "So What" test for every signal, strategic judgment to connect signals to business outcomes, executive communication skills to deliver recommendations, and a proof methodology to validate impact.

Tools amplify these capabilities. They don't replace them.

The Five Skills That Make You Indispensable

Skill 1: Contextual Interpretation. This is understanding whether a signal matters in your specific industry, competitive, and business context.

AI flags: "Mentions of 'pricing' increased 200% this week."

Human interprets: "This is normal—we just announced pricing, of course there's coverage. Not a signal." Or alternatively: "This is abnormal—pricing mentions are up but we didn't announce anything. A competitor must have leaked our pricing, creating market uncertainty. This is a strategic threat."

Skill 2: Strategic Judgment. This is deciding whether to monitor, investigate, act, or escalate based on risk, opportunity, and organizational capacity.

AI flags: "Negative sentiment spike in regional coverage."

Human decides: "Our threshold for regional signals is a 3-week sustained pattern. This is day 2. Monitor but don't activate." Or alternatively: "This is Tier 1 media picking up a regional story. Escalate immediately—national coverage likely within 48 hours."

Skill 3: Pattern Recognition Across Disconnected Sources. This is seeing connections between signals that don't obviously relate but tell the same story.

Consider four signals that appear unrelated: a LinkedIn post from an employee about "unsustainable workload," a Glassdoor review mentioning "burnout culture," a trade publication article about "high turnover in tech sector," and an investor call question about "talent retention strategy."

AI sees four unrelated mentions across different sources. A human recognizes an early warning pattern of a workplace culture issue that threatens talent retention and investor confidence.

Skill 4: Executive Translation. This is communicating signal intelligence in language executives understand and act on.

Analyst output: "Trust signal declining 15 points, driven by regulatory source authority escalation and thematic clustering around governance language with negative sentiment trajectory…"

Executive translation: "We're seeing early warning signs of a potential regulatory investigation. Based on historical patterns, we have 2-3 weeks to address this proactively before it becomes a public crisis. Recommendation: Engage counsel and prepare transparency strategy."

Skill 5: Competitive Intelligence Framing. This is positioning every signal in competitive context—understanding what it means for your position relative to competitors.

Signal: "Innovation mentions up 40% this quarter."

Without competitive context: "Great! We're getting innovation coverage."

With competitive context: "We're up 40% but our competitor is up 120%. We're losing innovation territory. The gap is widening. Action needed."

Section 5: The Evolution—Where This Is Headed

Everything I've described so far—the four signals, the three intelligence layers, the Media Reputation Score methodology—represents what we might call the first generation of signal-based reputation intelligence.

It works. I've seen it transform communications functions from report generators into strategic advisors. I've seen it detect crises before they explode. I've seen it capture competitive territory that traditional measurement missed.

But there's a limitation built into the approach: We're measuring signals through a single lens—qualitative media data.

The Single-Lens Limitation

Media Reputation Score, as we'll detail in Chapter 5, analyzes earned media coverage. It captures what's being said about your brand, by whom, with what tone, at what velocity, in which channels.

This is enormously valuable. Media coverage shapes stakeholder perception. It's public, observable, and measurable. It provides early warning of reputation shifts before they show up in surveys.

But media signals are only half the picture.

Media signals can tell you what narratives are being amplified, which stories are gaining traction, how your coverage compares to competitors, whether tone and themes are shifting, and which sources are driving conversation.

Media signals can't tell you what stakeholders actually believe, whether media narratives are landing with audiences, whether there's a gap between what's being said and what people think, or whether your goodwill is being captured or wasted.

The Dual-Lens Evolution: Brand Equity Score

This is where the evolution is headed.

Brand Equity Score represents the next generation of reputation intelligence. Instead of measuring through a single lens (media signals), it measures through two lenses simultaneously.

The Qualitative Lens captures earned media and social conversation—reach-weighted, credibility-tiered, deduplicated, and filtered for bots and sarcasm. This is what Media Reputation Score does.

The Quantitative Lens captures consumer sentiment through nationally representative survey data—weighted by age, gender, region, and income. Core metrics like awareness, favorability, trust, advocacy, and community impact are mapped to reputation pillars.

The Composite merges both lenses. Signals are normalized by pillar and merged into a single score for head-to-head comparison.

The Breakthrough: PSGI—The Public Signal Gap Index

Here's where it gets interesting.

When you measure through both lenses, you can see something that neither lens reveals alone: the gap between what people believe and what narratives are being told.

We call this PSGI—the Public Signal Gap Index.

PSGI measures the misalignment between public sentiment (Quant) and narrative framing (Qual). It answers a critical strategic question: Is the story matching the reality?

A larger positive gap means under-leveraged goodwill. Public sentiment is stronger than narratives suggest. You have untapped equity that isn't being activated through media and communications. The public likes you more than coverage would suggest.

A near-zero gap means alignment. Public sentiment matches narrative framing. What's being said reflects what people believe.

A negative gap means over-indexed narrative. You're talking more than sentiment supports. Coverage is stronger than public feeling warrants. There's risk of perceived inauthenticity.

The PSGI Action Matrix

PSGI creates four strategic quadrants.

Aligned: Low gap in both media and social. Your narratives reflect reality. Strategy: maintain and optimize.

Reframe Earned: High media gap, low social gap. Traditional media isn't capturing your story, but social sentiment is strong. Strategy: press-first approach—get earned media to reflect what audiences already believe.

Mobilize Community: Low media gap, high social gap. Media coverage is accurate, but social and community conversation isn't amplifying it. Strategy: social-first approach—activate communities and creators.

Do Both: High gap in both media and social. Significant untapped goodwill that isn't reflected in either media or community coverage. Strategy: accelerate storytelling across press and social to convert latent goodwill into outcomes.

Why This Matters

In the Q2 2025 competitive analyses I mentioned earlier, both major beverage brands landed in the "Do Both" quadrant—meaning each had significant untapped goodwill that wasn't reflected in media or community coverage. This gap represents strategic opportunity: brands that accelerate storytelling across press and social can convert that latent goodwill into market advantage.

The dual-lens approach transforms reputation intelligence from "What are they saying about us?" to "Is what they're saying aligned with what people believe—and are we capturing or wasting the gap?"

This is the future of reputation intelligence. We're not there yet—Brand Equity Score requires both media data and survey data, which means more infrastructure, more cost, and more complexity. But for organizations that can make the investment, the strategic insight is transformational.

For now, Media Reputation Score provides the foundation. It's actionable, affordable, and immediately implementable. Master it first. Then evolve.

What You Can Do Starting Tomorrow

First, assess your current signal capability. Which DDC Maturity Level are you operating at—Level 1, 2, 3, or 4 from Chapter 1? Which Intelligence Layer do you operate at—Layer 1, 2, or 3? What skills do you need to develop among contextual interpretation, strategic judgment, pattern recognition, executive translation, and competitive framing?

Second, start building baselines. Collect 30-90 days of data across your core sources. Establish normal ranges for volume, sentiment, source mix, share of voice, and themes. Create a simple tracking spreadsheet—you don't need fancy tools yet.

Third, practice the "So What" test. For every signal you identify, answer three questions: What's changing? Why does it matter? What should we do? If you can't answer all three, it's data—not intelligence. Build this discipline daily.

Fourth, move from Layer 1 to Layer 2 to Layer 3. Layer 1 is what was said—you can probably do this already. Layer 2 is what it means—start here by adding interpretation and context. Layer 3 is what to do—this is the goal, delivering strategic recommendations with ROI. Progress deliberately. Master each layer before advancing.

Fifth, identify your primary signal. Based on your business context, competitive situation, and stakeholder priorities—discovered through PBI (Chapter 4)—determine which reputation dimension matters most right now. Organizations in growth mode often prioritize innovation or product leadership. Organizations recovering from crisis typically focus on trust or governance. Organizations defending market position may emphasize competitive perception or financial performance. Your pillars will be specific to your context—the examples throughout this book are illustrative, not prescriptive. The methodology stays the same. The pillar weighting changes based on what your internal stakeholder priorities.

Bridge to Chapter 4

You now understand what signals are and why they matter. You know the six components that distinguish true signals from noise. You've seen how different organizations define different reputation pillars based on their unique business priorities.

But here's the question you should be asking: How do I know which pillars matter for my organization?

You could guess. You could adopt the four signals I've outlined and hope they fit. But the organizations that get the most value from reputation intelligence don't guess—they discover. They systematically uncover who needs intelligence, what decisions those people make, and what reputation dimensions actually drive those decisions.

That's what Persona-Based Insights provides.

In Chapter 4, you'll learn how to identify the stakeholders who consume your intelligence, map their decision-making patterns, and extract the business priorities that should drive your measurement framework. This isn't optional groundwork—it's the foundation that makes everything else work. You can't build an effective Media Reputation Score (Chapter 5) without first understanding what you're measuring and why.

Persona-Based Insights is how you transform generic measurement into intelligence that matters—to the specific people who need it, for the specific decisions they're making.

Let's build it.

References

Meltwater. (2025). Data-Driven Communications assessment findings (internal research, used with permission).

Journal of Cleaner Production. (2025). Systematic literature review on authentic sustainable branding and long-term brand value.

Circular Economy and Sustainability. (2023). Research on customer loyalty, brand image, and trust in circular economy contexts.

Note on Sources

The signal-based measurement approach and the Three Intelligence Layers are original methodology developed by the author, informed by the Meltwater Data-Driven Communications curriculum and validated through implementation across multiple organizations. The four illustrative pillars (Trust, Innovation, Perception, Reputation) represent one proven configuration; as emphasized throughout this chapter, organizations should define pillars based on their unique business priorities discovered through Persona-Based Insights (Chapter 4).

Statistics regarding maturity level distribution (including the 8% Visionary finding) are drawn from Meltwater's DDC assessments of 500+ communications professionals. The Dino Delic quotes are used with permission.

Any illustrative examples in this chapter represent composite scenarios based on patterns observed across multiple implementations rather than specific client engagements.

CHAPTER 4

PERSONA-BASED INSIGHTS

Aligning Intelligence to the People Who Need It

For years, I operated like most communications measurement professionals. My team tracked dozens of metrics across multiple markets. We produced comprehensive monthly reports with beautiful charts showing media volume, sentiment trends, share of voice, and competitive benchmarks. We delivered them to the CCO, who would flip through before our monthly check-in.

And almost nobody else read them.

The reports that took us two weeks to produce every month sat in inboxes. They gathered digital dust. They influenced almost nothing. We were data providers, throwing reports over the fence, hoping someone would find something useful.

I knew something was broken. I just didn't know what.

The breaking point came during a quarterly business review at a global financial services company. I was presenting the communications scorecard to the executive team when one of the regional presidents—let's call him Marcus—interrupted me mid-slide.

"I appreciate all this work," he said, gesturing at my share-of-voice chart. "But I have a very specific problem. We're losing the digital transformation narrative in key markets. Our competitors are being seen as innovation leaders while we're perceived as legacy. I need to know: Are we making progress on that story? Are we losing ground? What should I do differently?"

I looked at my slides. I had global sentiment. I had worldwide share of voice. I had competitive benchmarks against five companies. But I had nothing—absolutely nothing—that answered Marcus's question about digital transformation perception in his specific markets.

"I'd have to pull a custom report," I said.

Marcus nodded politely. But I saw it in his eyes: Why am I in this meeting?

That night, I couldn't sleep. I kept thinking about the disconnect. I had data. Marcus had a decision to make. And somehow, all my measurement sophistication couldn't bridge the gap.

What was I missing?

Marcus wasn't being difficult. He was being honest. And he taught me the most important lesson of my career: you cannot build effective measurement until you understand who you're serving and what they actually need.

Throughout this book, you'll follow Sophia as she learns this same lesson with Henrik—the Regional President at TechFinance whose journey from skeptical executive to active intelligence partner illustrates how persona-based insights transform the measurement relationship. Their story is a composite drawn from experiences like the one I just described, and from the methodology I developed in response.

That's what this chapter is about. Before you calculate a single MRS score, before you build a dashboard, before you create your first SIGNAL brief—you need to do the discovery work. You need to find your Marcus, your Henrik, understand their world, and document the priorities that will shape everything that follows.

The Problem: One Report Serves No One

My situation wasn't unusual. It was universal.

Across organizations, communications measurement teams face the same frustrating pattern: They produce impressive dashboards filled with data, and executives don't engage. Reports get filed, not used. The measurement team becomes a cost center that produces dashboards, not a strategic function that drives decisions.

The traditional model looks like this: The comms measurement professional's main stakeholder is the CCO. You produce a monthly report, send it up the ladder, and hope it gets reviewed. Maybe the CCO shares a few charts in the next leadership meeting. Maybe someone asks a follow-up question. But there's no systematic connection between your intelligence and the decisions being made across the organization.

This creates a credibility problem. Executives see you as a data provider—someone who reports what happened—rather than an advisor who helps them figure out what to do. You struggle to gain trust beyond your immediate team because your work doesn't connect to what other leaders actually care about.

The root cause isn't bad data. It's misalignment.

Here's what typically happens: The measurement team measures what's measurable—they track reach, impressions, sentiment, share of voice, the metrics their tools can capture. Then they report what they measured, producing monthly dashboards that show trends across all metrics, all regions, all competitors, with comprehensive coverage of everything. Finally, they hope someone finds it useful. The report goes to the CCO, who shares it with whomever might be interested. Maybe someone will spot something actionable.

This approach treats measurement as a broadcast function: Create content, distribute widely, hope for engagement.

But decision-makers don't need broadcasts. They need answers to specific questions at specific moments. And those questions vary dramatically by role.

The CFO doesn't need sentiment trends across all markets. She needs Trust signal analysis focused on investor confidence, delivered two weeks before the earnings call, formatted as "what to tell analysts."

The Chief Product Officer doesn't need year-over-year volume comparisons. He needs Innovation benchmarking versus three specific competitors, delivered before the monthly product roadmap meeting, formatted as "perception gaps to close."

A Regional President doesn't need global share of voice. He needs digital transformation narrative tracking in his specific markets, delivered when he's making strategic decisions, formatted as "are we winning or losing this story?"

The CHRO doesn't need competitive analysis. She needs Workplace culture signals correlated with employee sentiment trends, delivered in real-time when issues emerge, formatted as "retention risks to address."

One comprehensive report cannot serve all these needs. When you build measurement around what you can track rather than what stakeholders need to know, you end up with data that impresses no one and influences nothing.

Your New Mantra: Don't Start with Data. Start with a Persona

Here's the fundamental problem with traditional communications measurement: When you start with data, you're trying to retrofit metrics to fit stakeholders.

You pull share of voice numbers, sentiment trends, reach figures, and competitive benchmarks. Then you package them into a report and hope different stakeholders find something relevant. You're essentially saying: "Here's what we can measure. Hopefully some of it matters to you."

This is backwards.

Share of voice doesn't answer the CFO's question about investor confidence. Sentiment trends don't tell the regional president whether he's winning the digital transformation narrative. Reach figures don't help the CHRO understand retention risk. You're giving everyone the same data and expecting them to extract their own value.

The result? They don't. The report gets filed. The data sits unused. And you wonder why no one sees you as a strategic partner.

When you start with a persona, you build measurement around decisions. You ask: What does this specific person need to know? What decisions are they making? What questions keep them up at night? Then you design intelligence that answers those questions directly.

This is the mindset shift that changes everything. Starting with data sounds like "Here's our share of voice this month." Starting with a persona sounds like "Here's whether you're winning the narrative that matters to your region." Starting with data sounds like "Sentiment improved 3%." Starting with a persona sounds like "Trust signals with investors are stable ahead of earnings." Starting with data sounds like "We got 47 tier-1 placements." Starting with a persona sounds like "Your key message landed in 8 of the 12 outlets your customers read." Starting with data sounds like "Competitor X had more mentions." Starting with a persona sounds like "Competitor X is gaining ground on the innovation story—here's what to do."

Same underlying data. Completely different framing. One approach produces reports that get filed. The other produces intelligence that drives decisions.

"Don't start with data. Start with a persona."

This isn't just a slogan—it's a discipline. It means resisting the temptation to lead with what your tools can measure. It means having conversations before building dashboards. It means understanding the human being who will use your intelligence before you decide what intelligence to produce.

This mantra should guide every decision you make in communications measurement. Before configuring a dashboard, ask: Who is this for? What decision will it inform? Before building a report, ask: What question is this answering? For whom? Before tracking a metric, ask: Which stakeholder needs this? Why? Before presenting to leadership, ask: What do they need to know to act?

When you internalize this mantra, you stop being a data provider and start being a decision partner. That's the transformation PBI enables.

KEY CONCEPT

THE MANTRA

Don't start with data. Start with a persona. When you start with data, you retrofit metrics to fit stakeholders. When you start with a persona, you build measurement around decisions.

This mantra should guide every choice you make in communications measurement.

The Breakthrough: Borrowing from Agile

A few weeks after that painful quarterly review, I had coffee with a friend who ran product development at a software company. I was venting about my frustration—all this data, and nobody using it—when he said something that stopped me cold.

"You're building features nobody asked for."

He explained the Agile methodology his team used. Before they built anything, they wrote user stories: "As a [user], I need [feature], so that I can [outcome]." This forced them to understand who they were building for, what that person needed, and why it mattered to them.

"You're building measurement like old-school software," he said. "You decide what to build based on what's technically possible, then you ship it and hope someone likes it. No wonder nobody's using your reports. You've never asked them what they actually need."

That conversation crystallized the mantra: Don't start with data. Start with a persona. So obvious. So simple.

I had been doing exactly what he described. I started with what my tools could measure—volume, reach, sentiment, share of voice—and then tried to make it relevant to stakeholders. I was retrofitting data to fit people, instead of designing intelligence around people.

The next week, I scheduled thirty minutes with Marcus—not to present anything, but to listen. Instead of starting with my data, I started with him. I asked one simple question: "What decisions do you make where reputation intelligence could help?"

Marcus leaned forward. For twenty minutes, he talked about his world.

He explained that digital transformation perception was his biggest strategic challenge. Competitors were winning the "innovation leader" narrative while his company was still perceived as a legacy player. He described the decisions this created: Should he invest more in executive visibility at tech conferences? Should he accelerate product announcements in key markets? Should he adjust messaging to emphasize digital capabilities?

"What I need to know," Marcus said, "is whether we're making progress on the digital innovation story. Not globally—specifically in the markets where I compete. I need to know if we're gaining ground or losing it, and I need to know fast enough to adjust."

Then I tried something new. I borrowed my friend's Agile format:

"So if I'm hearing you correctly: As the Regional President, you need innovation narrative tracking in your priority markets versus your key competitors, so that you can adjust digital positioning strategy and demonstrate progress to the board."

Marcus's response was immediate: "Yes. Exactly. That's exactly what I need. Can you actually do that?"

I wasn't sure. But I had just learned something crucial: I finally knew what to build.

PRO TIP

THE AGILE PERSONA STATEMENT

"As a [PERSONA], I need [SIGNAL], so that I can [OUTCOME]." Example: "As the Regional President, I need innovation narrative tracking in my priority markets versus my key competitors, so that I can adjust digital positioning strategy and demonstrate progress to the board."

If you can't complete this sentence, you don't yet understand your stakeholder.

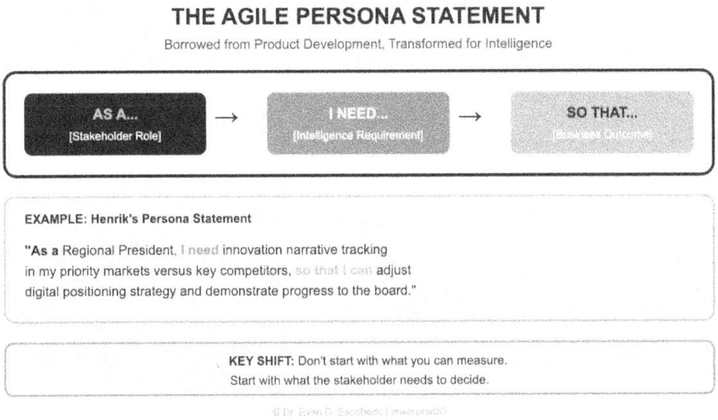

Figure 4.1: The Agile Persona Statement—Borrowed from
Product Development, Transformed for Intelligence

From Concept to System: The Four Tools That Changed Everything

That conversation with Marcus gave me a single persona statement. But I quickly realized that one statement wasn't enough. If I was going to deliver what Marcus needed, I had to get specific about four things.

First, which markets actually mattered to him? He didn't care about global coverage—he cared about specific regions where he was competing for business.

Second, which media outlets influenced his stakeholders? Not all coverage was equal. Some publications shaped perception with his customers and partners; others didn't matter at all.

Third, which competitors did he need to beat? He wasn't competing against everyone in the industry—just three or four companies fighting for the same narrative space.

Fourth, what business priorities was he trying to advance? His intelligence needs connected to specific strategic objectives, not abstract reputation metrics.

This realization led me to develop four simple tools that transformed PBI from an interesting concept into an operational system. These tools became the foundation for everything that followed—including the Media Reputation Score framework described in Chapter 5.

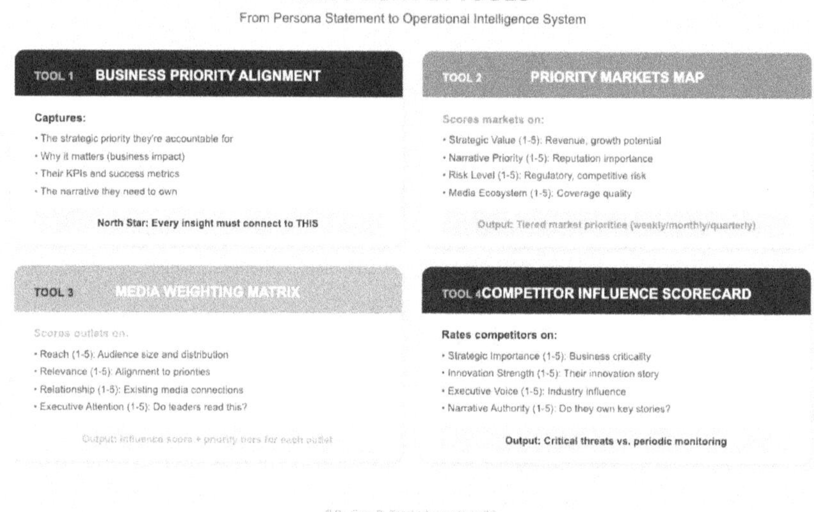

Figure 4.2: The Four PBI Tools—From Persona Statement to Operational Intelligence System

Tool 1: Business Priority Alignment

Before anything else, I needed to understand what Marcus was actually trying to achieve. Not "improve reputation"—that's too vague. What specific business outcome was he accountable for?

Through our conversations, we documented the essentials. The priority was establishing digital transformation leadership in his region. It mattered because market share, customer retention, and talent acquisition all depended on being seen as an innovator rather than a legacy player. His KPIs included digital product adoption rates, customer perception scores, and competitive win rates. The one narrative he needed to own:

"Leading the industry's digital transformation." Three specific competitors threatened this priority by positioning aggressively on innovation.

This Business Priority Alignment became the North Star for everything else. Every piece of intelligence I delivered had to connect back to this priority. If it didn't help Marcus advance digital transformation leadership, it didn't matter.

Tool 2: Priority Markets Map

Marcus operated across multiple markets, but they weren't equally important. Some drove most of his revenue. Some carried higher risk. Some had stronger media ecosystems.

I built a simple scoring matrix to prioritize markets based on four factors: Strategic Value (revenue importance and growth potential); Narrative Priority (how important reputation is in this market); Risk Level (regulatory, competitive, or reputational risk); and Media Ecosystem (quality of local coverage and relationships). Each factor was scored 1-5.

The result was a ranked list of markets with clear tiers: critical markets requiring weekly monitoring, important markets requiring monthly tracking, and others requiring only quarterly check-ins. This focused our resources where they mattered most.

Tool 3: Media Weighting Matrix

Not all media outlets carried equal influence. *The Wall Street Journal* mattered to Marcus's board, but not to the customers making purchasing decisions. Local business publications in key markets mattered to customers, but his CEO never saw them. Tech analyst reports mattered to investors, but not to regulators.

I built a weighting matrix that scored outlets across four dimensions: Reach (audience size and distribution); Relevance (alignment to Marcus's business priorities); Relationship (quality of existing media relationships); and Executive Attention (do key stakeholders actually read this?). Each dimension was scored 1-5.

The matrix auto-calculated an influence score for each outlet and ranked them into priority tiers. This told us exactly which coverage to prioritize in our analysis and which outlets to cultivate relationships with.

Tool 4: Competitor Influence Scorecard

Marcus didn't compete against everyone in the industry—just a handful of companies fighting for the same narrative space. But those competitors weren't equally threatening.

I built a scorecard that rated competitors across five dimensions: Strategic Importance (how critical is this competitor to your business?); Product/Innovation Strength (how strong is their innovation story?); Executive Voice (do their leaders shape industry conversation?); Market Overlap (how much do you compete in the same space?); and Narrative Authority (do they own key market narratives?). Each dimension was scored 1-5.

The scorecard calculated a weighted influence score and flagged which competitors were "critical threats" requiring intensive monitoring, versus those requiring only periodic tracking.

QUICK CHECK

HAVE YOU FOUND YOUR MARCUS?

Before proceeding to Chapter 5, you should have: • Identified your executive sponsor (your Marcus) • Completed the Agile persona statement for them • Built your Media Weighting Matrix based on their input • Documented their business priorities and decision triggers. If you skip this work, the MRS methodology in Chapter 5 will measure the wrong things.

The Transformation: From Data Provider to Trusted Advisor

With these four tools in place, everything changed.

Within three months, I had completed the same process with five stakeholders across the organization—not just Marcus, but the CFO, the Chief Product Officer, the CHRO, and the Chief Marketing Officer. Each conversation followed the same pattern: Understand their world, capture their persona statement using the Agile format, then build out their Priority Markets, Media Weighting, and Competitor Scorecard based on their specific needs.

The results were dramatic.

For Marcus, I delivered a monthly "Digital Transformation Narrative Brief"—a two-page document showing his innovation positioning versus three competitors across five priority markets. When it showed a competitor gaining ground on "AI innovation" messaging, Marcus accelerated a product announcement. When it showed his company winning on "customer experience transformation," he doubled down on that narrative.

For the CFO, I delivered Trust signal tracking focused on governance and investor confidence metrics, timed to her quarterly earnings preparation cycle.

For the CPO, I delivered Innovation perception benchmarking versus product competitors, delivered before monthly roadmap meetings.

For the CHRO, I delivered Workplace culture signal monitoring correlated with employee sentiment trends.

Each stakeholder received intelligence designed specifically for them, delivered when they needed it, answering questions that mattered to their decisions.

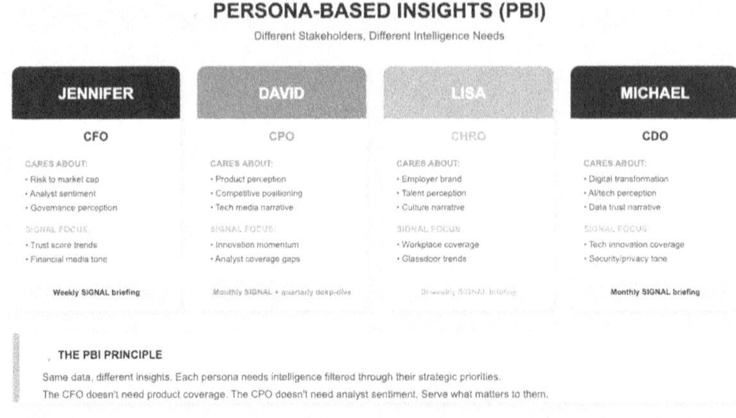

Figure 4.3: Persona-Based Insights—Different Stakeholders, Different Intelligence Needs

Within six months, my relationship with the organization had completely changed. I was no longer the person who produced the monthly report nobody read. I was the person stakeholders called when they needed to understand what was happening in their narrative landscape.

Marcus put it best: "You're not telling me what happened anymore. You're helping me see what's coming and decide what to do about it."

This was the transformation: from data provider to trusted advisor. And it happened because I stopped starting with data and began starting with people.

Why This Builds Trust

Here's what I learned that transformed my career: Persona-Based Insights isn't just a measurement methodology. It's a trust-building exercise.

When you sit down with a regional president, a product leader, or a C-suite executive and ask "What do you need to know to make better decisions?"—something shifts. You're not positioning yourself as a reporter of what happened. You're positioning yourself as a partner in what happens next.

The act of asking demonstrates something powerful: You care about their success.

Most measurement professionals never have this conversation. They assume they know what stakeholders need, or they assume stakeholders don't know what they need, or they're simply too busy producing reports to ask.

But when you take the time to understand a stakeholder's world—their priorities, their pressures, their competitive anxieties, their decision windows—you're doing something rare. You're treating them as a client whose success matters, not an audience for your dashboard.

Taking them through the PBI process—the Agile persona statement, the Priority Markets exercise, the Media Weighting matrix, the Competitor Scorecard—shows them that you're serious about understanding their world. When you show them that first dashboard aligned completely with their priorities, you're no longer seen as a data provider. You're seen as an advisor.

This is how you build trust across the organization. Not by producing better reports—by demonstrating that you care about what each stakeholder is trying to achieve and that you've built something specifically to help them succeed.

How These Tools Became the Foundation for MRS

Something unexpected happened as I rolled out PBI across the organization: the tools I'd built to understand stakeholder needs became the foundation for a completely new approach to measurement.

Let me tell you how it evolved.

When I first arrived at this global fintech company, they were using Rep-Trak—the standard seven-pillar reputation framework that many organizations use. The pillars were solid: Products & Services; Innovation; Workplace; Governance; Citizenship; Leadership; and Performance. But there was a disconnect. These generic reputation dimensions didn't map to what our Corporate Affairs and Communications (CACO) team was actually trying to achieve.

So we modified the framework. We created five CACO-aligned pillars that reflected our specific priorities: Digital Leader (our innovation and technology positioning); Platform/Partner (our ecosystem and partnership narrative); Responsible Corporate Citizen (our ESG and community impact); Employer of Choice (our workplace and talent story); and Performance (our financial results and business momentum).

This was progress. We were measuring reputation dimensions that mattered to our communications strategy. But something was still missing.

The breakthrough came during a PBI conversation with the Senior Vice President for Middle East and Africa. I walked him through the standard discovery: "What are your priorities? Which sources matter? Who are your competitors in this region?"

His answer surprised me.

"Look, I care about all five pillars," he said. "But if you're asking what keeps me up at night—it's Digital Leadership. We're being perceived as a legacy money transfer company. Our competitors are positioning as innovative fintechs. If we don't win the digital narrative in my region, we lose the market. Digital Leadership isn't just one of five priorities. It's THE priority."

That conversation changed everything.

Suddenly I understood: Business priority alignment wasn't just about understanding which pillars to track. It was about understanding which priority was number one—and for different stakeholders in different regions, the answer was different.

The SVP for Middle East and Africa cared most about Digital Leadership because that's where his competitive battle was being fought. The CFO cared most about Performance because that's what analysts and investors watched. The CHRO cared most about Employer of Choice because talent acquisition was her mandate.

Same five pillars. Completely different weighting based on business context.

This insight led directly to the Media Reputation Score framework described in Chapter 5.

- Business Priority Alignment became Reputation Drivers—instead of treating all reputation dimensions equally, MRS lets you weight drivers based on stakeholder priorities, so Digital Leadership might be 40% of the score for one stakeholder and 15% for another.
- Priority Markets Map became Geographic Weighting—an article in a priority market receives higher weight than coverage in a peripheral market, so the SVP for Middle East and Africa got intelligence weighted toward his region rather than diluted by global averages.
- Media Weighting Matrix became Source Authority—we identified target publications that mattered for each pillar in each region, making a mention in a tier-1 business publication about Digital Leadership worth more than ten mentions in tier-3 blogs.
- Competitor Scorecard became Competitive Benchmarking—we tracked the specific competitors threatening each priority in each market, recognizing that the SVP's competitive set in Middle East and Africa was different from the competitive set in North America.

The methodology evolved into something sophisticated: eight scoring factors applied to every article (Target Source, Key Message Penetration, Prominence, Salience, Sentiment, and Voice), weighted by stakeholder priorities and benchmarked against competitors.

But here's what made it work: We started with the stakeholder, not the methodology.

The scoring algorithm didn't come first. The PBI conversations came first. We understood what each stakeholder needed to know, and then we built measurement capable of answering their questions.

This is why PBI is essential groundwork before implementing MRS. You can't build an effective Media Reputation Score (Chapter 5) without first understanding what your stakeholders need and which reputation dimensions drive their decisions. The pillars you identify through this chapter become the foundation of your scoring model.

PBI is the discovery layer. MRS is the measurement layer. Together, they create intelligence that actually drives decisions.

How to Use the Tools: A Practical Guide

The four PBI tools are available as free interactive applications at measuredio.com/book/tools. Here is how to put them to work.

Tool 1: Persona-Based Insights™ Builder (Start Here)

This is your foundation. Before touching the other tools, complete this application with your executive sponsor's priorities in mind — ideally right after your first discovery conversation with Henrik.

Open the PBI Builder and work through the four guided steps. Step 1 captures the Business Priority: the ONE strategic goal your organization cannot miss, the narrative you need to own, and what's at stake if it stalls. Step 2 builds the Persona Canvas: Henrik's title and mandate, the KPIs he reports to leadership, his decision cadence and upcoming windows, the sources he actually reads, what keeps him up at night, and what proof he needs to act. Step 3 defines the Signal: your three to five reputation pillars, what evidence would show the priority advancing, and what early warning signals would tell you trouble is coming before Henrik sees it. Step 4 assembles the Agile Persona Statement — the formula that makes everything actionable.

Use these key prompts during your discovery conversation: "If you could own a single story in the market, what would it be?" "What proof would convince your CEO or board of progress?" "Which competitors currently shape this narrative?"

The output is a print-ready PBI Statement that becomes the North Star for all measurement work that follows. Every piece of intelligence you deliver must connect back to this document.

Tool 2: Priority Markets Map

Use this when your organization operates across multiple regions or markets — because not every market deserves the same intelligence resources.

Open the Priority Markets Map and list every market or region where you need to track reputation. Score each market on four dimensions using a one-to-five scale: Strategic Value (revenue importance and growth potential), Narrative Priority (how much reputation shapes outcomes in this market), Risk Level (regulatory, competitive, or crisis exposure), and Media Ecosystem (quality of local coverage and relationships). The tool auto-calculates a weighted Priority Index and assigns markets to tiers.

The output is a clear resource allocation: Critical markets (Tier 1) receive weekly monitoring and dedicated coverage. Important markets (Tier 2) receive bi-weekly monitoring and shared coverage. Monitor markets (Tier 3) receive monthly check-ins and exception-based alerts.

Tool 3: Media Weighting Matrix

Use this to establish which outlets carry real influence for your specific stakeholder — because Henrik's reading list is not the same as the CFO's, and both are different from industry defaults.

Open the Media Weighting Matrix and list the outlets you currently track or want to track. Score each outlet on four dimensions: Reach (audience size and distribution), Relevance (alignment to your stakeholder's business priorities), Relationship (quality of your existing connections at this outlet), and Executive Attention (does Henrik actually read it?). The tool auto-calculates an average score and assigns a tier with the corresponding MRS weight multiplier.

The output is a ranked outlet list that feeds directly into your Source Authority scores in Chapter 5. Tier 1 outlets (score 4.0 and above) carry three times the weight in MRS calculations — coverage here is gold. Tier 2 outlets (2.5 to 3.9) carry two times the weight. Tier 3 (below 2.5) carries standard weight — track for trends but don't overweight. Build one matrix per persona. Henrik's matrix and the CFO's will look different, and that difference is the point.

Tool 4: Competitor Influence Scorecard

Use this to focus competitive intelligence on the rivals who actually threaten your narrative — not every company in your sector.

Open the Competitor Influence Scorecard and list your key competitors — typically five to ten companies fighting for the same narrative space. Score each on five dimensions: Strategic Importance (how critical to your business strategy), Innovation Strength (how compelling is their innovation story), Executive Voice (do their leaders actively shape industry conversation), Market Overlap (how directly do you compete for the same customers), and Narrative Authority (do they own key narratives in your space). The tool auto-calculates a weighted Influence Index and assigns a monitoring tier.

The output is a ranked competitor list with clear monitoring intensity: Close Watch competitors receive weekly monitoring and regular competitive briefs. Monitor competitors receive bi-weekly tracking. Awareness competitors receive monthly check-ins.

This connects directly to MRS: the Competitor Influence Scorecard determines which rivals to include in your MRS benchmarking in Chapter 5, and which competitive gaps are worth tracking over time. Knowing that Competitor A is gaining on your Innovation pillar while you're declining is the kind of intelligence that gets Henrik's attention — and that comparison starts here.

Putting It All Together: The PBI Workflow

Here is the recommended sequence for implementing PBI.

Weeks 1-2: Business Priority Alignment. Complete the template with your executive sponsor. Document their priority, why it matters, their KPIs, the narrative they need to own, and the competitors threatening that priority. This becomes your North Star.

Weeks 3-4: Priority Markets and Media Weighting. Score and rank your markets using the Priority Markets Map. Score and rank your media outlets using the Media Weighting Matrix. Align both to your Business Priority—if a market or outlet doesn't connect to your stakeholder's priority, question whether it belongs in your monitoring scope.

Weeks 5-6: Competitor Scorecard and Validation. Score and rank competitors using the Competitor Influence Scorecard. Then validate your work: schedule a 30-minute review with your executive sponsor to confirm that the tools reflect their priorities accurately. Adjust based on feedback.

Weeks 7-8: Configure and Launch. Configure your monitoring platform based on tool outputs—prioritize Critical markets, Tier 1 outlets, and Critical/High threat competitors. Build your first stakeholder-specific dashboard or brief. Launch, gather feedback, and iterate.

Ongoing: Quarterly Review. Revisit Business Priority Alignment—has the priority shifted? Update tool scores based on market changes, new competitors, or media landscape shifts. Expand to additional stakeholders as you build credibility.

The tools are designed to work together. Your Business Priority determines which signals matter. Your Priority Markets Map determines where to focus. Your Media Weighting Matrix determines which coverage to prioritize. Your Competitor Scorecard determines who to benchmark against. Together, they create the architecture for persona-based intelligence that connects directly to MRS measurement (Chapter 5).

The PBI Conversation Guide

The quality of your Persona Canvas depends on the quality of your stakeholder conversations. Here is a practical guide for conducting effective PBI interviews.

Before the Meeting. Review the stakeholder's role, responsibilities, and recent priorities. Understand their position in the Business Priority Alignment. Prepare to listen more than talk—aim for 80/20.

Opening (2 minutes). "I'm working to ensure that our reputation intelligence directly supports your decisions. I'd like to understand your priorities, the questions you need answered, and how you prefer to receive information. This will help me design intelligence specifically for you."

Understanding Their World (10 minutes). Ask: "What are your top 2-3 priorities for the next 6-12 months?" "What decisions do you make where reputation intelligence could help?" "What does success look like in your role? How is it measured?"

Identifying Intelligence Needs (10 minutes). Ask: "When you think about reputation or media coverage, what do you need to know?" "Which competitors matter most in your context?" "What intelligence have you wished you had? Can you give me a specific example?" "If you could ask me one question about our reputation every week, what would it be?"

Understanding Timing (5 minutes). Ask: "Walk me through your decision calendar—when are your key meetings and planning moments?" "When would intelligence need to arrive to influence those decisions?" "What events would trigger a need for immediate intelligence?"

Delivery Preferences (5 minutes). Ask: "How do you prefer to consume information—dashboard, report, brief, conversation?" "What level of detail is useful? Headlines or deep analysis?" "Best time or channel to reach you?"

Closing (3 minutes). Summarize what you heard. Confirm the "As a… I need… so that…" statement. Commit to follow-up: "Based on this, I will design an intelligence approach for you. Can we review it together in two weeks?"

After the Meeting. Complete the Persona Canvas within 24 hours while the conversation is fresh. Draft their "As a… I need… so that…" statement. Identify 2-3 quick wins you can deliver to demonstrate value early.

COMMON MISTAKE

DON'T SKIP THE DISCOVERY

The most common implementation failure: jumping straight to measurement without doing PBI work. You end up with elegant dashboards tracking pillars nobody cares about. Marcus taught me this directly: "Where's Platform/Partner? Where's Digital Leader? These aren't our priorities." He was right. I'd skipped the discovery work. We started over.

Key Takeaways

Persona-Based Insights transforms communications measurement from a broadcast function to a decision support system.

The Mantra: Don't start with data. Start with a persona. This single mindset shift is the foundation of everything else. When you start with data, you retrofit metrics to fit stakeholders. When you start with a persona, you build measurement around decisions. This is the difference between producing reports and driving action.

The core principles are straightforward.

- First, start with a persona, not with data—don't ask "What can we measure?" but rather "What does this person need to know to make better decisions?"

- Second, use the Agile formula: "As a [PERSONA], I need [SIGNAL], so that I can [OUTCOME]." This forces clarity about whom you are serving, what they need, and why it matters. If you cannot complete this sentence, you do not yet understand your stakeholder.

- Third, build the four tools that operationalize PBI—Business Priority Alignment, Priority Markets Map, Media Weighting Matrix, and Competitor Scorecard transform the persona-first concept into an actionable system.

- Fourth, anchor everything in Business Priority Alignment. Your North Star is what the organization must achieve. Every persona's intelligence should connect to these priorities. Different stakeholders may weight the same dimensions differently based on their context.

- Fifth, build trust through conversations. The act of asking stakeholders what they need demonstrates that you care about their success. Taking them through PBI—the discovery conversations, the tools, the persona-specific dashboards—shows you are serious about helping them win.

- Sixth, recognize that PBI is the discovery layer for MRS. You cannot build an effective Media Reputation Score without first understanding what your stakeholders need to know. PBI reveals how to weight reputation drivers, which sources matter, which competitors to track, and which markets to prioritize.

Marcus taught me this lesson definitively. Early in our work together, I brought him a beautifully designed dashboard tracking Trust, Innovation, Perception, and Reputation—the four pillars I'd used successfully at other organizations. He looked at it for thirty seconds and said, "Where's Platform/Partner? Where's Digital Leader? These aren't our priorities."

He was right. I'd skipped the discovery work. I'd assumed generic pillars would resonate. They didn't. We started over—this time beginning with his strategic plan, his board presentations, his actual priorities. The Media Reputation Score we eventually built was completely different from what I'd originally proposed. And it was infinitely more valuable because it measured what he actually cared about.

The transformation PBI enables is profound. You stop being the team that produces reports nobody reads. You become the function that helps the organization see around corners.

That is not just better measurement. That is strategic value.

What Is Next

You now have the frameworks to detect signals (Chapter 3) and align intelligence to stakeholders (Chapter 4). Now it's time to build the scoring methodology that quantifies reputation against the priorities you've just discovered.

Let's go.

References

Reputation Institute. (n.d.). RepTrak seven-pillar reputation measurement framework. Reputation Institute.

Beck, K., et al. (2001). *Manifesto for Agile Software Development.* agile-manifesto.org.

Note on Sources

The Persona-Based Insights (PBI) methodology and the four supporting tools (Documented Priorities, Priority Markets, Media Weighting Matrix, Competitor Scorecard) are original frameworks developed by the author based on professional experience implementing stakeholder-aligned intelligence systems.

The PBI approach draws conceptual inspiration from Agile methodology's emphasis on iterative development and stakeholder collaboration, adapted for communications measurement contexts.

Marcus's organizational case study, including the documented priorities and transformation outcomes, is a composite illustration based on the author's professional experience. Specific metrics and timelines have been adjusted to protect client confidentiality while preserving the operational principles demonstrated.

CHAPTER 5

MEDIA REPUTATION SCORE

From Priorities to Measurement

Developed in close collaboration with Michael Samuels, Meltwater.

If you've worked through Chapter 4, you now know something most measurement professionals never discover: exactly what your stakeholders care about and why.

Like Sophia, you've identified your Henrik—the executive sponsor whose questions drive your intelligence program. You've mapped their decision cadence, documented their business priorities, and built a Media Weighting Matrix that reflects which sources actually influence their thinking. You've moved from "what can we measure?" to "what do they need to know?"

Now comes the crucial next step: building a scoring methodology that quantifies reputation against those priorities.

The Question That Changed Everything

I was once in a C-level meeting when a CEO looked directly at me and asked: "Why do we even need Meltwater and media measurement? I get *The Wall Street Journal* and *The Financial Times* every morning."

The room went quiet. I could feel my colleagues shifting uncomfortably.

And here's the thing—he had a point.

We'd been sending him monthly reports full of impressive-sounding numbers. Mentions up 34%. Reach in the millions. Sentiment trending positive. Share of voice increasing against competitors. Beautiful charts. Comprehensive data.

But what did any of it actually tell him about the health of his company's reputation? What decisions could he make based on "reach in the millions"? When a crisis hit, could our metrics predict how stakeholders would respond?

The honest answer was no. We were measuring activity, not impact. We were counting mentions, not meaning.

That moment stuck with me. It forced me to confront an uncomfortable truth: traditional media measurement doesn't answer the questions executives actually care about. "How's our reputation doing?" can't be answered with "mentions are up."

What I didn't understand then—but do now—is that the problem wasn't just the metrics. It was the disconnect between what we measured and what that CEO actually cared about. We hadn't done the PBI work. We didn't know his priorities. We were measuring generically and hoping something would resonate.

Marcus taught me this lesson years later. When I first presented a reputation dashboard to him, he pushed back immediately: "These pillars don't match our strategic plan. Where's Platform/Partner? Where's Digital Leader? You're showing me Trust and Innovation, but that's not how our board talks about the business."

He was right. And that's when everything clicked. The scoring methodology I'm about to share with you is powerful—but only when applied to pillars that matter to your organization. That's why PBI comes first.

So I started building something different—a methodology that would score media coverage based on how much it actually mattered to reputation, not just how much of it existed.

The idea was simple in concept, complex in execution: Not all coverage is created equal. A passing mention in a random blog isn't the same as a feature story in *The Wall Street Journal*. A positive story about your quarterly earnings isn't the same as a positive story about your CEO's leadership. A crisis mention in a tier-1 outlet reaching institutional investors is fundamentally different from the same mention in a consumer lifestyle blog.

We wanted to know: Which coverage actually moves the needle?

That question led me down a rabbit hole of academic research, competitive analysis, and methodology development. I tested it across multiple organizations. I refined it through trial and error. I validated it against actual reputation outcomes.

What emerged was the Media Reputation Score—the foundation for everything in this book.

Why Traditional Metrics Fail

Before we build the solution, let's understand the problem.

The communications measurement industry has been stuck on the same metrics for decades: mentions, reach, impressions, sentiment, share of voice. These aren't useless—they provide useful context. But they don't answer the questions that matter to executives.

The fundamental issue: Volume doesn't equal impact.

I learned this viscerally during a crisis response. We generated massive coverage—thousands of mentions, millions in reach. By traditional metrics, it was a "successful" communications effort. But the coverage was predominantly negative, concentrated in tier-1 financial media, and directly attacked our trust positioning with investors. Our "high volume" was actually accelerating reputation damage.

Traditional metrics couldn't see this. They just showed big numbers going up.

Academic research confirms this blind spot. A 2023 study in the *Schmalenbach Journal of Business Research* found that corporate reputation actually amplifies the impact of media coverage on market value—both positive and negative. The researchers concluded that media favorability and visibility have a positive effect on corporate reputation, but the relationship isn't linear. Context matters enormously. Similarly, research by Kiousis et al. in the *Journal of Public Relations Research* found a partial but meaningful correlation between media coverage and corporate reputation, suggesting that while media coverage impacts reputation, other factors—such as customer experience and internal management—play equally significant roles.

The key insight: Media coverage influences reputation, but you need a methodology to understand how. That's what Media Reputation Score provides.

The Multi-Billion Dollar Measurement Gap

Let's put this in business terms.

The global media monitoring tools market reached $5.4 billion in 2024, according to Grand View Research, with major players like Meltwater (estimated at over $500 million in annual revenue) and Cision commanding significant market share. The online reputation management market adds another $6.9 billion, per Mordor Intelligence analysis. Meanwhile, organizations invest heavily in survey-based reputation research—RepTrak alone gathers more than one million company ratings annually across its global benchmarking database.

That's billions spent on reputation measurement—and most organizations still can't answer basic questions: Did that crisis actually move our reputation score? Which narratives are helping or hurting us? Are we winning or losing against competitors on trust? What's going to happen next?

The problem isn't the tools. RepTrak delivers excellent perception data. Meltwater delivers excellent media intelligence. The problem is the gap between them.

MRS bridges this gap. It's not a replacement for either system—it's the missing connection that makes both valuable.

The Core Insight: Not All Coverage Is Equal

Here's the foundational principle of MRS: Different coverage has different impact.

This seems obvious when stated directly, but most measurement systems ignore it completely. They treat every mention equally, or they weight only by reach (which creates its own problems—viral blog posts aren't necessarily more impactful than niche policy journals).

MRS scores coverage across multiple dimensions that determine actual reputation impact. The methodology is built on a simple truth: An article's influence on reputation depends on who said it, how they said it, where it appeared, and whether it advances or undermines your strategic narratives.

KEY CONCEPT

THE CORE INSIGHT

Not all coverage is created equal. A passing mention in a random blog isn't the same as a feature story in *The Wall Street Journal*. A positive story about quarterly earnings isn't the same as a positive story about CEO leadership.

MRS scores coverage based on how much it actually matters to reputation—not just how much of it exists.

The Multi-Dimensional Scoring Framework

While the specific weightings and calibrations are tailored to each organization's industry, competitive context, and stakeholder priorities, the MRS framework evaluates coverage across several key dimensions:

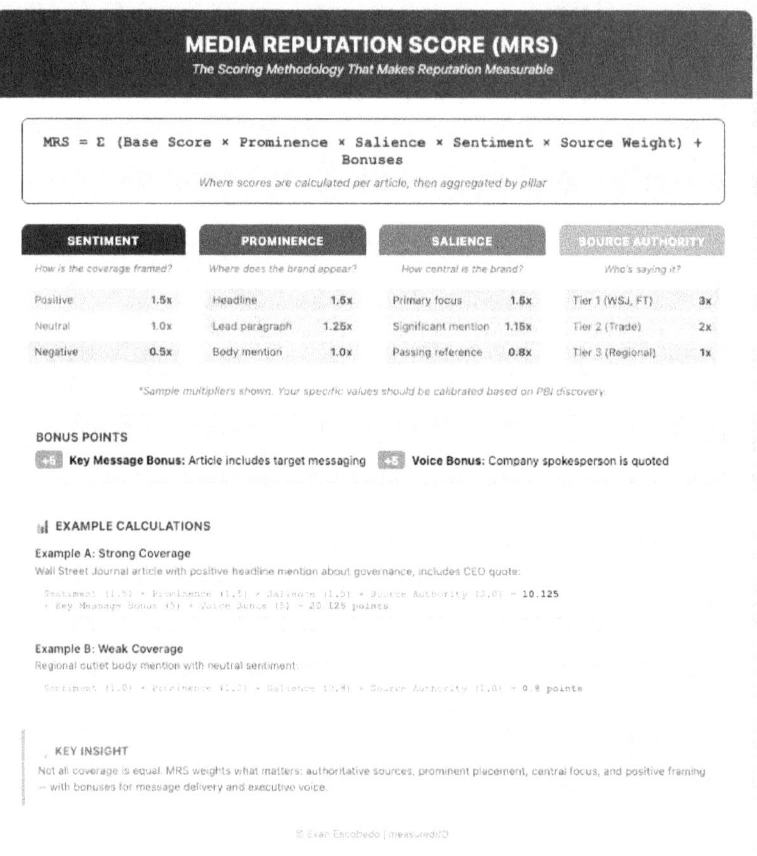

Figure 5.1: Media Reputation Score Methodology— Multi-Dimensional Scoring Framework

Sentiment Analysis

Not a simple positive/negative binary. Effective reputation scoring requires a nuanced scale that captures degrees of favorability—from strongly positive through neutral to strongly negative. Critically, different entities mentioned in the same article can receive different sentiment scores. A competitive comparison piece might praise one company while criticizing another. This multi-entity sentiment parsing is where human judgment becomes essential.

Source Authority

A mention in *The Wall Street Journal* carries different weight than a mention in a regional blog—not because one is "better," but because they reach different stakeholders with different credibility. The methodology uses tiered influence scoring that accounts for priority publications specifically important to your stakeholders; major national and international outlets with broad credibility; specialized trade and industry media; and general coverage sources.

The research supports this approach. Deephouse's foundational work on media reputation, published in *Journal of Management*, established that media reputation functions as a strategic resource that depends heavily on source credibility—journalists are viewed as independent intermediaries whose assessments carry more weight than company-generated content.

Prominence

There's a meaningful difference between being the focus of a story and being mentioned in passing. Headline mentions carry different weight than lead paragraph placement, which differs from body mentions or passing references. Determining true prominence requires reading comprehension, not just keyword location detection.

Salience

If an article mentions your brand alongside fifteen competitors, your salience is low. If you're the only company discussed, your salience is high. This dimension captures competitive positioning in coverage and affects both the score and strategic interpretation.

Voice

Who's speaking? Coverage where your executive demonstrates thought leadership carries different weight than coverage where a third party praises (or criticizes) your brand, which differs again from a straightforward company announcement. Voice affects credibility and impact.

Amplification

How is earned media content extended through social sharing and engagement? A story that generates significant social amplification has reach and resonance beyond its initial publication.

Key Message Alignment

This is where MRS fundamentally differs from traditional measurement. Does the coverage advance your strategic narratives—the messages that, if they appeared in coverage, would move business objectives forward? Coverage that advances priority narratives scores differently than coverage that merely mentions your brand without strategic alignment.

The Key Message Connection: Why This Changes Everything

Here's the problem with most media measurement: it counts coverage without asking whether that coverage advances your business objectives. You might get 500 mentions, but if none of them contain the narratives that matter to your strategy, what have you actually achieved?

Key Message Alignment solves this by connecting media measurement to business priorities.

The process works in four steps.

First, identify business priorities. You've already done this work in Chapter 4. Through Persona-Based Insights, you aligned with your executive stakeholders—your Henrik—to understand what dimensions of reputation matter most to them. Those documented priorities now become your MRS pillars.

For the financial services company I mentioned earlier, that meant scoring against Platform/Partner, Digital Leader, Responsible Corporate Citizen, Employer of Choice, and Performance. For the automotive manufacturer focused on EV leadership, it meant Product, Corporate, Performance, Workplace, and Society. Your pillars will reflect your organization's unique strategic priorities.

If you skipped Chapter 4, stop here. Go back and complete the PBI work. The most elegant scoring methodology in the world is worthless if it's measuring the wrong things. I've watched measurement programs fail not because the math was wrong, but because the pillars didn't connect to what leadership actually cared about. Henrik would send those reports straight to the trash folder.

Second, define priority narratives. Based on those business priorities, you define specific key messages—the narratives that, if they appeared in coverage, would advance strategic objectives. These aren't generic taglines. They're precise statements tied to business outcomes. For example, if the business priority is "Establish leadership in digital transformation," the corresponding key message might be "Company X is leading the industry's shift to real-time digital payments."

Third, measure alignment. MRS then tracks whether those specific key messages appear in scored coverage. Does the article contain one or more of your priority narratives?

Fourth, weight accordingly. Coverage with key message alignment scores higher because it's not just generating awareness—it's advancing business objectives. A tier-2 article with strong key message penetration may be more valuable than a tier-1 article that mentions your brand without advancing your narrative.

Why This Matters

Traditional measurement can't do this because it doesn't start with business priority alignment. It measures what happened in media without asking whether what happened actually mattered to the business.

When you're deliberate about first identifying and aligning to your company's business priorities, you can measure pull-through. You can answer: "Did our communications efforts translate into coverage that advances what leadership actually cares about?"

This is the difference between reporting "we got coverage" and reporting "we got coverage that moved our strategic narrative forward." The latter is what earns you a seat at the executive table.

PRO TIP

> ### KEY MESSAGE ALIGNMENT IS THE DIFFERENTIATOR
>
> This is where MRS fundamentally differs from traditional measurement. Does the coverage advance your strategic narratives? A tier-2 article with strong key message penetration may be more valuable than a tier-1 article that mentions your brand without advancing your narrative.
>
> Traditional measurement can't do this because it doesn't start with business priority alignment.

Mapping Coverage to Reputation Drivers

Scoring individual articles is step one. Connecting those scores to reputation dimensions is where MRS becomes strategic intelligence.

Every scored article is mapped to one or more reputation drivers. Different organizations use different frameworks—RepTrak's academically validated model uses seven dimensions (Products/Services;

Innovation; Workplace; Governance; Citizenship; Leadership; and Performance). Other organizations develop custom frameworks aligned to their strategic priorities.

As I've mentioned, when I implemented this methodology at a global financial services company, we used five pillars aligned with executive priorities: Digital Leadership (Innovation) covered forward-thinking, technology leadership, and fintech positioning; Responsible Corporate Citizen (Trust/ESG) encompassed ethics, sustainability, community impact, and regulatory compliance; Employer of Choice (Workplace) addressed culture, talent, employee experience, and diversity; Performance tracked financial results, business execution, and market position; and Platform/Partner captured ecosystem, partnerships, network scale, and cross-border capabilities.

The methodology is framework-agnostic—what matters is consistent application aligned to your organization's strategic priorities.

The Driver Mapping Process

The mapping combines automated and human intelligence. AI classification uses machine learning to categorize each article by likely driver based on keywords, topics, and themes. Human validation follows, with analysts reviewing high-impact stories to verify classification and catch nuance that AI misses. Multi-driver assignment recognizes that some stories touch multiple drivers—a story about your CEO announcing layoffs affects Leadership, Workplace, and Performance simultaneously.

This creates a driver-level view: How is your coverage performing on Innovation versus Trust versus Performance? Where are you strong? Where are you vulnerable?

Seeing MRS in Action: The Vacation Rental Analysis

Let me show you how this plays out with real competitive intelligence.

In Q2 2025, we analyzed over 40,000 earned media mentions across two major vacation rental platforms—let's call them HomeShare and VacationStay. Traditional metrics showed a predictable picture: HomeShare dominated on volume with roughly 2:1 advantage in total coverage. Case closed, right?

Not quite.

To demonstrate the methodology, we built this analysis around four pillars that would likely matter to a CMO in this space: Innovation (critical for investor relations and tech media positioning); Trust (essential for the family travel segment); Perception (overall brand health); and competitive positioning.

If this were an actual client engagement, these pillars would emerge from PBI conversations—not assumptions. But for this illustrative analysis, we selected dimensions that map to how vacation rental executives typically discuss their business. The methodology is real. The pillar selection shows how you'd apply it.

When we applied MRS methodology—scoring each mention for impact, mapping to these specific reputation drivers, and analyzing signal strength—a much more nuanced picture emerged.

The Pillar Breakdown

Innovation Signal. HomeShare scored significantly higher. Their coverage featured global partnerships, experiential campaigns, and "future of travel" narratives. Media framed them as industry trailblazers. VacationStay's innovation coverage was muted—operational partnerships and incremental updates that didn't capture narrative momentum. The strategic insight: HomeShare owns the innovation narrative. VacationStay would need sustained, bold initiatives to capture innovation territory.

Trust Signal. Here's where it got interesting. VacationStay scored notably higher on Trust.

Why? HomeShare's high visibility came with heightened scrutiny. Regulatory challenges appeared in tier-1 coverage. Service consistency concerns surfaced in consumer-focused media. The sentiment balance told the story: HomeShare had significantly more negative mentions than positive. VacationStay's ratio was healthier.

VacationStay's trust narrative centered on host verification, property standards, and family-friendly positioning. Travel advisors consistently framed them as "the reliable choice." The strategic insight: HomeShare's innovation leadership comes with trust vulnerability. High visibility without a foundation of trust creates reputational fragility.

Perception. HomeShare maintained higher overall Perception despite the trust gap. Years of market leadership created a perception reservoir—broad awareness, cultural relevance, celebrity association.

But here's the warning sign: Perception is a lagging indicator. It trails Trust and Innovation. HomeShare's strong Perception today could mask Trust erosion that will eventually catch up. The strategic insight: High Perception + Low Trust = short-term strength, long-term vulnerability.

The Strategic Recommendations

Here's what would be important to the CMO—not a data dump, but answers to her actual questions.

For HomeShare, the immediate priority is addressing Trust signals before the Perception reservoir depletes. The action: Integrate proof points on safety, regulatory compliance, and service consistency into innovation storytelling.

For VacationStay, the immediate priority is amplifying the innovation narrative while maintaining the trust foundation. The action: move beyond operational partnerships to bold, experiential storytelling. The opportunity: Capture "trustworthy innovator" positioning that Home-Share left open.

This is what signal-based intelligence delivers: not just "who's winning" but "why they're winning" and "what should we do about it."

From "So What?" to "Now What?"

Early in my career, an executive gave me feedback that changed how I think about intelligence delivery. After reviewing a comprehensive MRS analysis, he said: "The rigor in the index score is solid. But it's challenging for me to understand what I need to do to reverse course. I'm consistently at the bottom across key pillars, but it's not clear why—or what the leaders are doing differently."

He wasn't criticizing the methodology. He was asking for the bridge between measurement and action.

This is where many MRS implementations fall short. They answer "So what?"—here's what the scores mean—but not "Now what?"—here's what you should do about it.

Every MRS deliverable should include three components:

The Diagnosis: Where do you stand, and why? Not just "your Trust score is 48" but "your Trust score is 48, which trails the category leader by 15 points. The gap is driven by regulatory coverage in Tier 1 financial media, where competitors are earning positive governance narratives while your coverage focuses on compliance issues."

The Competitive Gap: What are the leaders doing differently? Not just "Competitor A scores higher on Innovation" but "Competitor A's Innovation score is driven by consistent executive thought leadership in tech media—their CTO has been quoted in 34 Tier 1 articles this quarter versus your CTO's 6 appearances. They're owning the 'future of category' narrative through spokesperson visibility."

The Action Path: What specific moves should you make? Not just "improve Trust scores" but "Recommendation: Launch a transparency initiative targeting Tier 1 financial media, featuring your Chief Compliance Officer discussing proactive governance measures. Timeline: Q3. Success metric: 10+ earned placements with positive Trust framing. Expected impact: 8-12 point improvement in Trust pillar score by Q4."

The executives I've worked with—the Henriks—don't want dashboards. They want answers to three questions: Where are we? Why? What should we do?

If your MRS output doesn't answer all three, you're still a data provider. Answer all three, and you're a strategic advisor. As Michael Samuels of Meltwater, who helped shape the MRS methodology, put it: "A score without a framework is just a number. Insight begins with interpretation."

This is exactly what the SIGNAL framework in Chapter 6 is designed to deliver. MRS gives you the scores, the gaps, the competitive context. SIGNAL gives you the structure to translate that intelligence into executive-ready communication that drives action. The two work hand-in-hand: MRS generates the insight, SIGNAL delivers it.

The AI + Human Partnership

Let me address the AI question directly, because I know you're wondering: Can't AI just do all of this?

The short answer: No. Not yet. Maybe not ever, for the parts that matter most.

What AI Does Well. AI excels at scale, processing thousands of articles in minutes. It delivers consistency, applying the same classification rules every time. It handles pattern recognition, identifying statistical anomalies and trends. And it provides baseline scoring through initial sentiment classification, topic tagging, and driver mapping.

What AI Still Struggles With

Sarcasm and Irony. Consider this tweet: "Oh great, another 'innovative' product launch from TechCo that nobody asked for." AI reads "innovative product launch" and scores it as a positive Innovation signal. A human reads sarcasm—negative sentiment that actually undermines the Innovation claim.

Strategic Framing. Three articles about the same product launch might read: "Company catches up to competitors with long-awaited feature" (frames you as a laggard); "Company leads market with innovative approach" (frames you as a leader); and "Company announces new feature" (neutral factual). AI sees three Innovation mentions with varying sentiment. A human recognizes that Article 1 is actually negative for your Innovation positioning—it frames you as behind, not ahead.

Contextual Relevance. An article in a niche policy journal about regulatory compliance reaches 500 readers, but they're the regulators who will decide your operating license. A viral blog post about product unboxing reaches 500,000 readers, but they're not your target stakeholders. AI sees the blog has 1000x reach and scores it as more important. A human knows the policy journal reaches decision-makers and has higher strategic impact.

The Hybrid Model

The solution isn't "AI or human." It's "AI for scale, human for judgment."

MRS uses AI to process the volume—classifying thousands of articles, scoring sentiment, tagging topics. Humans validate what matters—reviewing tier-1 coverage, assessing strategic framing, interpreting competitive positioning.

This hybrid approach is more accurate than AI alone and more efficient than human-only analysis. It's also more defensible—you can explain your methodology to skeptical executives because humans verified the important judgments.

Chapter 7 goes deep on how to operationalize this hybrid model at scale.

The Predictive Capability

Here's where MRS becomes genuinely strategic: prediction.

Media signals appear in coverage before they show up in surveys. Trust erosion surfaces in regulatory coverage weeks before RepTrak scores decline. Innovation momentum appears in tech media before brand perception shifts.

This creates a forecasting window.

The Lag Relationship. Research and field testing suggest these approximate lag windows between media signal changes and reputation survey movement.

Short lag signals (1-2 weeks) include Innovation and Products signals, performance-related coverage, and breaking news impact.

Medium lag signals (3-6 weeks) include leadership narratives, workplace coverage, and general perception shifts.

Long lag signals (6-10+ weeks) include governance and trust signals, citizenship and ESG narratives, and regulatory and compliance coverage.

These windows vary by industry, market, and competitive context. Your calibration will develop through practice and validation against actual outcomes.

The Early Warning System

MRS creates an early warning capability across four escalation levels:

- **Monitor** when a signal is declining but within normal variance.
- **Investigate** when a signal is down significantly from baseline in 30 days.
- **Act** when a signal is down substantially or source authority is escalating.
- **Escalate** when a regulatory investigation is announced or tier-1 investigative coverage appears.

The 2015 E. coli crisis at a major restaurant chain provides a textbook example. Traditional monitoring would have shown normal volume until the story broke nationally. Signal-based intelligence would have detected trust language declining in food safety mentions, source authority escalating from consumer reports to local health departments to state regulators, and sentiment trajectory turning sharply negative in regional coverage—all before the national headlines hit.

The Implementation Reality

Now let's get practical about what this requires.

Building MRS Capability

Implementing MRS effectively requires five elements: data infrastructure through a media monitoring platform with full metadata (source, reach, sentiment, topics); an analytical framework with scoring methodology calibrated to your industry and stakeholders; human expertise through trained analysts who understand your business context and can validate AI classifications; executive alignment with stakeholders who understand what they're receiving and how to act on it; and continuous calibration through ongoing refinement based on correlation with actual reputation outcomes.

The Skill Gap

Here's the reality: Most communications teams aren't equipped to build MRS capability from scratch. The methodology requires strategic alignment with business priorities (not just communications objectives); technical capability to process and score large volumes of coverage; analytical expertise to interpret patterns and generate insights; and executive communication skills to translate intelligence into action.

This is why implementation typically requires expert guidance—whether through consulting engagement, training programs, or technology partnerships that embed the methodology.

What You Can Start Tomorrow

That said, you can begin applying MRS principles immediately.

First, stop reporting volume as success. When you send your next report, lead with impact, not mentions.

Second, tier your sources. Create a simple classification: Priority (outlets your executives read), Tier 1 (major national/international), Tier 2 (regional/specialized), Tier 3 (everything else). Weight your analysis accordingly.

Third, map to business priorities. Before your next campaign, ask: "What narrative would advance our business objectives?" Then measure whether that narrative appeared in coverage.

Fourth, add competitive context. Never report your scores in isolation. Always show where you stand relative to competitors.

Fifth, track trajectory, not snapshots. Every metric should show direction—up, down, or stable—not just current position.

These principles will immediately elevate your measurement practice, even before you implement full MRS methodology.

Building Your MRS Scorecard

Let me show you how to actually build this. I've held back some of the specific calibrations that took years to refine—that's the IP that makes this methodology valuable. But I can give you enough to start building your own scorecard tomorrow.

Step 1: Define Your Pillars (From PBI)

Before you score a single article, you need to know what you're scoring against. This comes directly from your PBI work in Chapter 4.

Pull out your Henrik's documented priorities. What are the 3-5 reputation dimensions that matter most to your organization?

For the financial services company, our pillars were:

- Platform/Partner (cross-border capabilities, network reach, B2B relationships)
- Digital Leader (technology, innovation, customer channels, fintech positioning)
- Responsible Corporate Citizen (ESG, ethics, community impact, compliance)
- Employer of Choice (workplace culture, talent, DEI, employee experience)
- Performance (financial results, analyst sentiment, stock performance)

For the automotive manufacturer, the pillars were:

- Product (innovation, quality, technology, EV leadership)
- Corporate (leadership voice, strategic direction, vision)
- Performance (sales, market position, financial health)
- Workplace (labor relations, employee experience, safety)

- Society (sustainability, community impact, regulatory relationships)

Your pillars will be different. That's the point. Write them down. Define what each one means with specific keywords and themes. This becomes your tagging guide.

Step 2: Build Your Scoring Dimensions

Every article gets scored across multiple dimensions. Here's a framework you can adapt:

Source Authority (0-100 scale)

This reflects how much weight the outlet carries with your stakeholders.

Tier	Score	Description
Priority Outlets	100	Publications Henrik specifically identified in PBI—the ones he actually reads
Tier 1 National/ Global	75	WSJ, NYT, Bloomberg, Financial Times, major broadcast
Tier 1 Trade/ Industry	65	Leading publications in your specific industry
Tier 2 Regional/ Specialized	50	Regional business journals, specialized trades
Tier 3 General	25	General news, smaller outlets, blogs

Your Media Weighting Matrix from Chapter 4 feeds directly into this. Henrik told you which outlets matter—now you weight them accordingly.

Prominence (Multiplier: 1.0 - 1.5)

How prominently does your brand appear in the article?

Placement	Multiplier	Description
Headline Focus	1.5	Brand in headline, article is primarily about you
Lead/Opening	1.3	Brand in first paragraph, significant focus
Body - Significant	1.2	Multiple paragraphs, substantive discussion
Body - Mentioned	1.1	Clear mention but not the focus
Passing Reference	1.0	Brief mention, no substantive discussion

Salience (Multiplier: 1.0 - 1.5)

How uniquely are you featured versus competitors?

Context	Multiplier	Description
Sole Focus	1.5	Only your brand discussed
Primary Focus	1.3	You're the main subject, competitors mentioned briefly
Shared Focus	1.1	You and 1-2 competitors discussed equally
Competitive Roundup	1.0	Multiple competitors, you're one of many
Competitor Focus	0.8	Article primarily about competitor, you're mentioned

Sentiment (Multiplier: 0.5 - 1.5)

What's the tone toward your brand specifically?

Sentiment	Multiplier	Description
Very Positive	1.5	Strongly favorable, praise, endorsement
Positive	1.25	Generally favorable, constructive
Neutral	1.0	Factual, balanced, no clear sentiment
Negative	0.75	Critical, unfavorable, concerns raised
Very Negative	0.5	Strongly negative, damaging, crisis-level

Key Message Alignment (Bonus: +10-30 points)

Does the article contain your priority narratives?

Alignment	Bonus	Description
Strong Alignment	+30	Contains 2+ key messages with positive framing
Moderate Alignment	+20	Contains 1 key message with positive framing
Weak Alignment	+10	Touches on key message themes indirectly
No Alignment	+0	No key message presence
Counter-Message	-20	Directly contradicts or undermines key messages

Voice (Bonus: +5-25 points)

Who's speaking and how does that affect credibility?

Voice Type	Bonus	Description
Third-Party Expert Endorsement	+25	Analyst, academic, or industry expert praises your brand
Executive Thought Leadership	+20	Your executive quoted demonstrating expertise
Customer/Partner Testimonial	+15	Stakeholder speaks positively about experience
Company Spokesperson	+10	Your official statement included
No Company Voice	+0	No quotes or statements from your side
Negative Third-Party	-15	Expert or analyst criticizes your brand

Step 3: The Scoring Formula

Here's a simplified formula you can start with:

Article Score = (Source Authority × Prominence × Salience × Sentiment) + Key Message Bonus + Voice Bonus

Example calculation:

An article appears in *The Wall Street Journal* (Source Authority: 75) with your brand in the headline (Prominence: 1.5), as the sole focus (Salience: 1.5), with positive sentiment (Sentiment: 1.25). It contains one key message (Bonus: +20) and includes an executive quote (Voice: +10).

Article Score = (75 × 1.5 × 1.5 × 1.25) + 20 + 10 Article Score = (210.94) + 30 Article Score = 240.94

To normalize to a 0-100 scale, you'll need to establish your scoring range based on your data. In practice, we normalize by dividing raw scores by a calibration factor derived from your highest-scoring articles.

Normalized Score = (Raw Score / Calibration Factor) × 100

If your calibration factor is 3.0 (meaning your best possible article scores around 300 raw points), then:

Normalized Score = (240.94 / 3.0) × 100 = 80.3

This article scores 80 out of 100—an excellent piece of coverage.

QUICK CHECK

THE MRS FORMULA

Article Score = (Source Authority × Prominence × Salience × Sentiment) + KM Bonus + Voice Bonus.

Pillar Score = Average of article scores mapped to that pillar.

Overall MRS = Weighted average of pillar scores (weights from PBI).

The weights come from your stakeholder. Henrik's priorities determine the formula—not industry defaults.

Step 4: Your Spreadsheet Structure

A practical starting point: Most media monitoring platforms— Meltwater, Cision, Muck Rack, Signal-AI, and others—allow you to export mentions from your saved searches. These exports typically include date, headline, outlet, URL, reach, and basic sentiment. Start with that export as your foundation, then add the MRS-specific columns for Source Authority tier, Prominence, Salience, Key

Messages, Voice, and your pillar assignment. You're not building from scratch—you're enriching what your platform already provides.

Your job is to add the MRS-specific columns that transform raw mentions into reputation intelligence. The platform gives you the foundation; you add the strategic layer.

Build a spreadsheet with these columns (★ = typically provided by platform export, ✎ = you add manually):

Then update the table to:

Column	Source	Description
Date	★ Platform	Publication date
Headline	★ Platform	Article title
URL	★ Platform	Link to article
Outlet	★ Platform	Publication name
Reach	★ Platform	Audience size (useful context, not used in scoring)
Outlet Tier	✎ Manual	Priority/T1/T2/T3 (from your Media Weighting Matrix)
Source Authority	✎ Manual	0-100 (based on Outlet Tier)
Pillar	✎ Manual	Which reputation pillar (from your PBI)
Sentiment	★/✎ Platform + Review	V.Neg/Neg/Neutral/Pos/V.Pos (platform provides baseline, analyst validates)
Sentiment Score	✎ Manual	0.5-1.5 multiplier
Prominence	✎ Manual	Headline/Lead/Body/Passing
Prominence Score	✎ Manual	1.0-1.5 multiplier
Salience	✎ Manual	Sole/Primary/Shared/Roundup
Salience Score	✎ Manual	0.8-1.5 multiplier
Key Message 1	✎ Manual	Yes/No
Key Message 2	✎ Manual	Yes/No
Key Message 3	✎ Manual	Yes/No

Column	Source	Description
KM Bonus	✎ Calculated	Points based on KM alignment
Voice Type	✎ Manual	Expert/Exec/Customer/Spox/None
Voice Bonus	✎ Calculated	Points
Raw Score	✎ Calculated	Formula-driven
Normalized Score	✎ Calculated	0-100 scale
Notes	✎ Manual	Analyst observations and strategic context

Pro tip: Create a template with the manual columns pre-formatted and validation dropdowns for Pillar, Sentiment, Prominence, Salience, and Voice Type. This speeds up tagging and ensures consistency across analysts.

Step 5: The Tagging Workflow

Here's how this works operationally:

Daily/Weekly Intake

1. Media monitoring platform delivers new articles matching your brand queries
2. AI does initial processing: outlet identification, basic sentiment, topic tagging
3. Articles are queued for human review based on tier (Priority and Tier 1 get immediate attention)

Human Analyst Review

1. Read the article (yes, actually read it—not just the headline)
2. Assign pillar: Which of your PBI-defined pillars does this article primarily address?
3. Score sentiment: What's the tone toward your brand specifically?
4. Score prominence: How central is your brand to the story?

5. Score salience: How uniquely are you featured versus competitors?

6. Check key messages: Do any of your priority narratives appear?

7. Identify voice: Who's speaking and how does that affect credibility?

8. Add notes: What's the strategic significance? Any context the scores don't capture?

Quality Control

1. Senior analyst reviews a sample of scored articles weekly

2. Calibration sessions monthly to ensure consistency across analysts

3. Quarterly review of scoring rubrics—are the weights still right?

Roll-Up and Reporting

1. Calculate article scores using formula

2. Aggregate by pillar: Average score of all articles mapped to each pillar

3. Aggregate overall: Weighted average of pillar scores (weights from PBI)

4. Compare to competitors: Same methodology applied to competitor coverage

5. Track over time: Monthly trend lines for each pillar and overall MRS

Step 6: From Article Scores to Pillar Scores to MRS

Pillar Score = Average of all article scores mapped to that pillar for the reporting period

Example: In Q3, you scored 45 articles mapped to "Digital Leader":

- 12 articles scored 70+
- 18 articles scored 50-69

- 10 articles scored 30-49
- 5 articles scored below 30
- Average: 54.2

Your Digital Leader pillar score for Q3 is 54.

Overall MRS = Weighted average of pillar scores

The weights come from your PBI work. If Henrik told you Digital Leader is twice as important as Employer of Choice, weight accordingly.

Example:

- Platform/Partner: Score 48, Weight 25%
- Digital Leader: Score 54, Weight 30%
- Resp. Corp. Citizen: Score 61, Weight 15%
- Employer of Choice: Score 45, Weight 10%
- Performance: Score 58, Weight 20%

Overall MRS = (48 × 0.25) + (54 × 0.30) + (61 × 0.15) + (45 × 0.10) + (58 × 0.20) Overall MRS = 12 + 16.2 + 9.15 + 4.5 + 11.6 Overall MRS = 53.45

Your overall Media Reputation Score for Q3 is 53.

Step 7: Competitive Benchmarking

Apply the same methodology to competitors. Every article you score for yourself, score for competitors too (when they appear in the same coverage).

This creates apples-to-apples comparison:

Company	Platform	Digital	Corp Citizen	Employer	Performance	Overall MRS
Your Brand	48	54	61	45	58	53
Competitor A	62	71	55	52	49	59
Competitor B	41	48	68	61	44	51

Now Henrik can see: "We're losing to Competitor A on Digital Leader—the pillar I told you matters most. What are they doing that we're not?"

That's actionable intelligence.

What This Requires

Let me be direct: Building MRS capability requires investment.

If you're a team of one: Start with Priority and Tier 1 outlets only. Score 50-100 articles per month manually. Use a spreadsheet. It's not scalable, but it's a proof of concept.

If you're a team of 2-3: Add Tier 2 outlets. Score 200-500 articles per month. Build a shared spreadsheet with validation rules. Establish calibration routines.

If you need enterprise scale: Full MRS implementation—including calibrated scoring algorithms, analyst training, dashboard visualization, and competitive benchmarking—typically requires expert guidance. Organizations can build this capability internally over 6-12 months, or accelerate through partnerships with specialized firms like measuredIO that have refined these methodologies across dozens of implementations.

The methodology I've shared here will get you started. The refinements—the specific calibrations, the edge case handling, the visualization layer—come from doing this work repeatedly across different industries and contexts.

The Career Opportunity

Let me be clear about what this capability means for your career.

Communications professionals who master signal-based reputation intelligence are rare. The supply is low because the capability is new and requires both technical skill and strategic judgment. The demand is high because executives increasingly expect quantified reputation intelligence.

This creates asymmetric opportunity.

If you operate at Layer 1 (traditional metrics only), you're competing with dashboards and AI tools. Your job security is questionable. Your compensation ceiling is limited.

If you operate at Layer 2 (signal-based intelligence), you're providing intelligence no one else in your organization can generate. You become the person who answers the questions executives actually care about. Your compensation and career trajectory reflect that value.

If you operate at Layer 3 (intelligence + strategic recommendations + proof of impact), you're a strategic advisor. You have executive access. Your judgment shapes major decisions. You're on the path to VP, CCO, or consultancy.

But here's what I didn't understand at first: the scoring methodology is universal, but the pillars must be specific to your business. At that financial services company, we built MRS around five pillars that came directly from the Chief Communications Officer's strategic priorities. Marcus helped me see that the same methodology, applied to HIS pillars, produced reports that he didn't value.

The difference isn't talent. It's methodology.

Common Mistakes and How to Avoid Them

After implementing MRS across multiple organizations, I've seen the same mistakes repeatedly.

Over-weighting volume. The instinct is to celebrate high mention counts. Resist it. Always lead with impact scores, not volume.

Ignoring source authority. Treating all coverage equally is the original sin of media measurement. Implement tier classification from day one.

Skipping human validation. AI classification is good enough for most content. It's not good enough for the content that matters most. Build a validation workflow for high-impact coverage.

Measuring without acting. The most sophisticated methodology is worthless if it doesn't drive decisions. Every output should include actionable recommendations with clear owners.

Single-point-in-time analysis. Reputation isn't a snapshot. It's a trajectory. Always present scores with trend lines.

Analyzing your brand in isolation. Your reputation exists relative to competitors. Include competitive context in every analysis.

COMMON MISTAKE

FROM "SO WHAT?" TO "NOW WHAT?"

Many MRS implementations answer "So what?" but not "Now what?" Every MRS deliverable should include:

- The Diagnosis: Where do you stand, and why?
- The Competitive Gap: What are leaders doing differently?
- The Action Path: What specific moves should you make?

If your output doesn't answer all three, you're still just a data provider.

What You've Learned

This chapter gave you the conceptual foundation for signal-based reputation intelligence. You now understand why traditional metrics fail to answer executive questions; the multi-dimensional approach that captures actual reputation impact; how Key Message Alignment connects media measurement to business priorities; and driver mapping that reveals where your reputation is strong or vulnerable. You've seen real competitive intelligence examples showing MRS in action, the AI + Human hybrid model that combines scale with judgment, the predictive capability that creates early warning, and the career opportunity for professionals who master this methodology.

Bridge to Chapter 6

You now have the framework to think about media coverage in terms of reputation impact.

You started with PBI (Chapter 4)—discovering your Henrik, documenting his priorities, building the Media Weighting Matrix that reflects what actually influences his thinking. Then you built MRS scoring against those priorities—not generic pillars, but the specific dimensions that matter to your organization.

Now you have intelligence. Real intelligence. Scores that mean something. Signals that predict outcomes. Competitive positioning that reveals opportunities and vulnerabilities.

But here's what I learned the hard way: Intelligence that doesn't reach decision-makers in a format they can act on is just expensive data.

Marcus didn't want a dashboard. He didn't want a 40-page report. He wanted answers to specific questions, delivered at the moment he needed them, in language that connected to decisions he was actually making.

That's what the SIGNAL framework delivers.

In Chapter 6, you'll learn how to translate MRS intelligence into executive-ready communication. You'll build briefs that land—not because they're comprehensive, but because they're actionable. You'll master the structure that turns "here's what happened" into "here's what it means and what we should do."

From methodology to communication.

Let's make it land.

References and Further Reading

Market Data

Grand View Research (2024). "*Media Monitoring Tools Market Size, Share & Trends Analysis Report by Type, by Application, by End Use, by Region, and Segment Forecasts, 2025-2030.*" https://www.grandviewresearch.com/industry-analysis/media-monitoring-tools-market-report

Growjo (2024). "Meltwater Company Profile." https://growjo.com/company/Meltwater. Note: Revenue figures are third-party estimates, not official company disclosures.

Mordor Intelligence (2025). "*Online Reputation Management Market Size, Industry Trends & Analysis 2030.*" https://www.mordorintelligence.com/industry-reports/online-reputation-management-market

RepTrak Company (2025). "2025 Global RepTrak® 100." https://www.reptrak.com/globalreptrak/

Foundational Reputation Research

Fombrun, C.J., Ponzi, L.J., & Gardberg, N.A. (2015). "Stakeholder Tracking and Analysis: The RepTrak® System for Measuring Corporate Reputation.» *Corporate Reputation Review*, 18(1), 3-24.

Deephouse, D.L. (2000). "Media Reputation as a Strategic Resource: An Integration of Mass Communication and Resource-Based Theories." *Journal of Management*, 26(6), 1091-1112.

Media Effects on Reputation

Kiousis, S., Popescu, C., & Mitrook, M. (2007). "Understanding Influence on Corporate Reputation." *Journal of Public Relations Research*, 19(2), 147-165.

Schmalenbach Journal of Business Research (2023). "How and Why Does Corporate Reputation Moderate Mass Media News' Impact On Market Value?"

Industry Standards

Barcelona Principles 3.0 for PR and Communications Measurement (AMEC, 2020).

Note on Sources

The Media Reputation Score (MRS) methodology, including the weighted scoring approach, is original methodology developed by the author based on work at a global financial services company and refined through subsequent implementations across multiple industries. The specific pillars you apply—whether the illustrative Trust, Innovation, Perception, and Reputation framework, or custom pillars discovered through PBI—are adaptable to your organization's priorities.

The Vacation Rental Analysis is illustrative to demonstrate the MRS methodology. While based on realistic competitive dynamics, these represent teaching examples rather than proprietary client analyses.

The AI + Human partnership framework draws on documented research regarding AI limitations in sentiment analysis and the author's practical experience implementing hybrid intelligence systems.

CHAPTER 6

EXECUTIVE STORYTELLING

A Framework Born from a High-Performing Culture

During my 13 years at Cisco, I learned something that transformed the way I communicate with executives.

Cisco had a framework called SCIPAB that was embedded in the culture. It stood for Situation; Complication; Implication; Position; Action; and Benefit. The framework provided a logical flow to quickly establish relevance, create urgency, and clearly outline next steps for any proposed solution.

Here's what made it powerful: Everyone used it.

It didn't matter what your actual role was—engineer, marketer, finance, operations—at Cisco, everyone was in sales. Everyone was positioning something. And no one walked into an executive meeting without a SCIPAB filled in. It created focus and discipline. It forced you to think through not just what you wanted to say, but why the executive should care and what they should do about it.

When I moved into communications measurement, I kept thinking about SCIPAB. I was producing dashboards full of data—media volume, sentiment trends, share of voice, competitive benchmarks—but executives weren't acting on them. The data was accurate. The timing was right. The stakeholders were aligned.

But something was missing.

Then it hit me: I was giving executives data, not decisions. I was describing situations without complications, presenting information without implications, showing numbers without actions. I had forgotten the discipline that made Cisco meetings so effective.

So I adapted SCIPAB for the communications measurement context. I modified it to fit the specific challenge of translating reputation data into executive action. The result was SIGNAL—a framework designed to transform measurement into intelligence that drives decisions.

SIGNAL isn't a replacement for SCIPAB; it's an evolution for a specific purpose. Where SCIPAB works brilliantly for sales positioning and general business communication, SIGNAL is optimized for reputation intelligence—for taking media signals, competitive data, and stakeholder insights and packaging them in a way that executives can act on immediately.

Let me show you why this matters.

The Last-Mile Problem

You've done everything right.

You detected the signals (Chapter 3). You identified your stakeholders and their priorities using Persona-Based Insights (Chapter 4). You built the Media Reputation Score to quantify reputation against those priorities (Chapter 5). You know what Henrik needs—digital transformation narrative tracking in his priority markets. You know what the CFO needs—trust signals timed to earnings cycles.

You're delivering the right intelligence to the right person at the right time.

And yet… executives still don't act on it.

Not because they don't care. Not because they don't trust the data. Not because they're too busy.

They don't act because the intelligence isn't translated into their decision-making language.

This is the last-mile problem. You've built the infrastructure, but the final delivery fails.

Why Aligned Intelligence Still Fails

Here's what typically happens even after implementing PBI.

What Henrik receives: "Digital transformation narrative share of voice increased from 28% to 35% in your priority markets. Innovation signal improved from 68 to 75. Competitor gap narrowed from -14 to -7 points versus your primary rival."

What Henrik needs: "You're winning the digital transformation story—but only in tech media. The publications your enterprise customers actually read haven't picked it up yet. You have a 6-week window to secure tier-1 business coverage before the industry analyst reports lock in perception for the year. Recommend: CEO interview in Financial Times by April 15. Decision needed by Friday."

The difference? The first is measurement. The second is intelligence. The first describes what happened. The second prescribes what to do and why it matters. The first requires Henrik to interpret. The second delivers the interpretation.

This is the intelligence-to-action translation gap.

Measurement ≠ Intelligence

Most reputation measurement—even when aligned to personas—stays descriptive.

Descriptive measurement sounds like: "Innovation narrative share of voice increased from 28% to 35%." Or: "Trust signal declined 7 points in two weeks." Or: "Competitor coverage volume up 23% week-over-week."

Interpretive intelligence sounds like: "Innovation momentum is building, but only reaching technical audiences—6-week window to capture business media before analyst reports." Or: "Trust erosion matches the pattern that preceded analyst downgrades in 4 similar cases—proactive response needed within 2 weeks." Or: "Competitor is attempting to own the AI narrative—recommend accelerating our announcement to Q2."

The gap is clear. Measurement tells you scores; intelligence tells you stories. Measurement reports data; intelligence recommends actions. Measurement describes what changed; intelligence explains why it matters and what to do.

Executives make decisions based on stories, not scores. Your job isn't to report data—it's to translate data into decisions.

The Solution: The SIGNAL Framework

The SIGNAL Framework is the translation layer between measurement and action.

It's a structured storytelling system that converts reputation data into executive-ready intelligence. Every piece of intelligence—whether it's a weekly brief, a crisis alert, or a strategic recommendation—flows through this framework.

SIGNAL stands for six components: **S** is Signal (what changed—the data point); **I** is Implication (why it matters—the business consequence); **G** is Gap (what's missing—the strategic vulnerability or opportunity); **N** is Narrative (the emerging story—the pattern or trend); **A** is Action (what to do—the specific recommendation); and **L** is Lift (expected impact—the business outcome if action is taken).

If you know SCIPAB, you'll see the DNA:

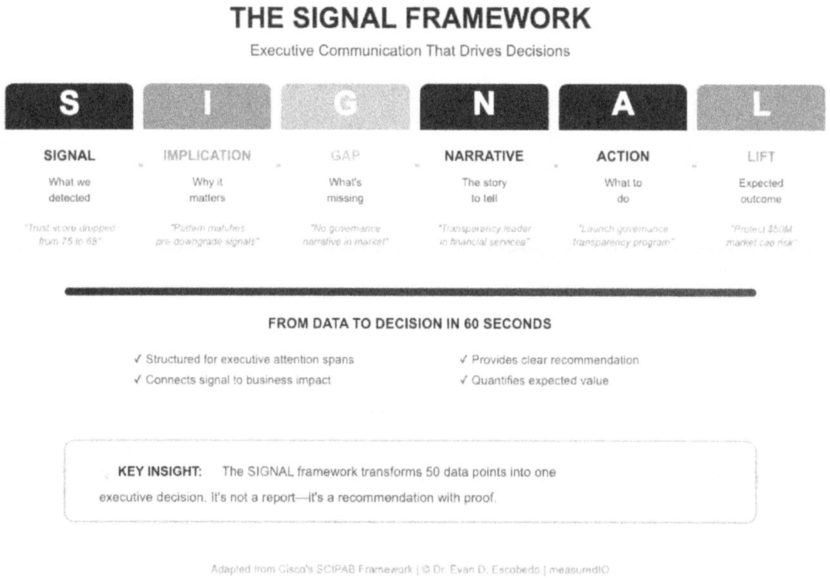

Figure 6.1: The SIGNAL Framework—Executive Communication That Drives Decisions

The key addition in SIGNAL is the explicit focus on Gap (what's missing or vulnerable) and Narrative (the emerging pattern)—both critical when translating reputation data into strategic intelligence. Executives need to understand not just what happened, but what should be happening and where the situation is heading.

This framework ensures consistency (every analyst uses the same structure), clarity (executives know exactly what's being communicated), actionability (every insight comes with a recommendation), and business relevance (every signal connects to outcomes).

Let's break down each component.

The Six Components of SIGNAL

S - SIGNAL (What Changed). The precise, measurable shift detected in your data. This is the factual foundation. Structure it as one sentence with a specific metric, directional movement, and time boundary. A good example: "Trust signal declined from 75 to 68 in the past 14 days, driven by Governance driver erosion (78 → 65)." A bad example: "Reputation is declining"—too vague, no metric, no timeframe. The rule: If you can't measure it, you can't SIGNAL it.

I - IMPLICATION (Why It Matters). The business consequence of the signal. What it means for strategy, risk, or opportunity. Structure it as one to two sentences with business context (not PR context) and stakeholder impact. A good example: "Trust erosion at this velocity historically precedes analyst downgrades within 6 weeks—putting Q2 earnings investor confidence at risk." A bad example: "This is concerning"—no business context, no stakeholder impact. The rule: If the executive reads your implication and says "So what?," you failed.

G - GAP (What's Missing). The absence, opportunity, or vulnerability revealed by the signal. What's not happening that should be. Structure it as one to two sentences, framed as an absence, pointing toward the action. A good example: "We have no proactive governance narrative to counter the erosion—our last governance communication was 6 months ago. Competitors published governance updates in the past 30 days." A bad example: "We need to do more"—too vague, no specific absence identified. The rule: Gap reveals WHERE to focus, not just THAT there's a problem.

N - NARRATIVE (The Emerging Story). The pattern or storyline forming. The strategic reframe that helps executives see the bigger picture. Structure it as one to two sentences that are forward-looking and connect to business priorities. A good example: "Governance trust is shifting from 'assumed' to 'proven'—the market now requires proactive transparency demonstrations, not reactive assurances." A bad example:

"Things are changing"—too generic, no storyline. The rule: If your narrative could apply to any company in any industry, it's not strategic enough.

A - ACTION (What to Do). The specific, executable recommendation. What to do, by when, with what resources. Structure it as one to three specific actions with owner assigned, timeline specified, and budget if relevant. A good example:"Launch proactive governance campaign within 2 weeks: CEO blog post by March 20, top 15 investor briefings March 25-April 5, board transparency announcement April 1. Owner: CFO + CCO. Budget: $500K." A bad example: "Improve governance communications"—no specificity, no timeline, no owner. The rule: If you can't assign an owner and a deadline, it's not an action.

L - LIFT (Expected Impact). The projected business outcome if the action is taken. The ROI justification. Structure it as one to two sentences, quantified when possible and time-bound. A good example: "Expected: Trust stabilization within 4 weeks, zero analyst downgrades (vs. 30% predicted probability), substantial market cap protection. Historical pattern: similar interventions delivered strong positive ROI." A bad example: "This will help"—no quantification, no timeline. The rule: If you can't quantify the lift, strengthen your recommendation.

KEY CONCEPT

THE SIGNAL FRAMEWORK

S — Signal: What changed (the data point) I — Implication: Why it matters (the business consequence) G — Gap: What's missing (the vulnerability or opportunity) N — Narrative: The emerging story (the pattern or trend) A — Action: What to do (specific recommendation) L — Lift: Expected impact (the business outcome) If you know SCIPAB, you'll see the DNA.

SIGNAL is optimized for reputation intelligence.

How SIGNAL Components Work Together

The six components create a complete decision-support narrative. SIGNAL establishes the fact (data credibility). IMPLICATION connects to business stakes (strategic relevance). GAP reveals the opportunity or vulnerability (insight). NARRATIVE reframes strategically (wisdom). ACTION prescribes what to do (decision support). LIFT quantifies expected value (ROI justification).

Together, they transform measurement into intelligence, data into story, observation into recommendation, and report into decision.

This is what executives need. This is what drives action.

SIGNAL in Action: Henrik and Sophia's Story Continues

Let's return to Henrik, the regional president we met in earlier chapters and Sophia, the measurement analyst supporting Henrik. Through PBI, Sophia learned that Henrik's top priority is digital transformation leadership—being perceived as an innovator rather than a legacy player in his markets.

Remember the mantra from Chapter 4: Start with a persona, not with data.

Sophia started with Henrik. She understood his world. She built intelligence around his decisions. Now she needs to deliver that intelligence in a way that drives action.

Three months into delivering persona-aligned intelligence, Henrik's weekly brief contains this SIGNAL:

SIGNAL BRIEF: Digital Transformation Narrative

Prepared for: Henrik, Regional President
Date: April 15
Context: Q2 industry analyst reports publish in 6 weeks

S - SIGNAL: "Digital transformation narrative share of voice in your priority markets increased from 28% to 36% over the past 90 days (+8 points). Innovation signal improved from 68 to 76 (+8 points). Competitive gap versus your primary rival narrowed from -14 to -6 points. Source breakdown: 81% of coverage in tier-2 tech publications, only 9% in tier-1 business media."

I - IMPLICATION: "You're winning the digital narrative in your region—but only in tech publications that your enterprise customers don't read. Tier-1 business media (*Financial Times*, Bloomberg, *The Economist*) still position your primary competitor as the innovation leader. This matters because enterprise buyers in your region cite tier-1 business coverage as the primary influence in vendor selection. The gap in tier-1 coverage: Competitor has 18 articles positioning them as 'digital leader,' you have three. Industry analyst reports publish in six weeks—these will lock perception for 12-18 months."

G - GAP: "Your digital transformation story has not penetrated the publications your enterprise customers actually read. Your competitor secured an FT exclusive on their digital platform last month and briefed Gartner analysts in February. You have no tier-1 business media momentum and no analyst briefings scheduled despite having superior product capabilities. The 6-week window before analyst reports is your opportunity—or your vulnerability."

N - NARRATIVE: "Digital leadership perception is consolidating now. Companies that establish tier-1 business media presence before analyst reports typically maintain 'leader' positioning for 18+ months. Companies that miss this window spend 12-18 months and significant resources trying to recover. You have built momentum in technical coverage—the foundation is solid. Now you need to translate that foundation into business coverage before the window closes. This is a timing problem, not a capability problem."

A - ACTION: "Secure tier-1 business media presence within six weeks. In Weeks 1-2, pitch an exclusive CEO interview to *Financial Times* on regional digital transformation strategy—your team has a relationship with the FT Brussels correspondent, so leverage it; target publication date is April 30, and the owner is Regional Comms Lead. In Weeks 3-4, brief the top 3 industry analysts (Gartner, Forrester, IDC) on the digital roadmap, ensuring they have your narrative before reports finalize, and provide data on digital adoption rates, customer success stories, and roadmap details; owner is Henrik plus Product Lead. In Weeks 5-6, announce the regional digital partnership (the fintech collaboration you've been negotiating) with coordinated Bloomberg/Reuters coverage, timing the announcement to land one week before analyst report deadlines; owner is Henrik plus Corporate Comms. Decision needed by Friday for Week 1 execution. Budget: $150K for media relations support, analyst briefing materials, and announcement coordination."

L - LIFT: "Expected impact: Tier-1 coverage increases from 3 articles to 10+ within 60 days. Analyst report positioning shifts to 'Leader' versus current trajectory of 'Strong Performer.' Business value: 'Leader' positioning correlates with 15% higher win rates in enterprise deals in your region, which based on your pipeline represents significant incremental revenue opportunity over 18 months. Probability of success: 78% based on 3 similar interventions in other regions that achieved 'leader' positioning with 6-week execution timelines. Downside if no action: Likely 'Strong Performer' categorization, 18-month recovery timeline, estimated $25M opportunity cost."

What Happened

Henrik reviewed the brief on his Tuesday morning flight. By the time he landed, he had approved the plan with one modification (moving the partnership announcement to Week 4 to align with a regional conference he was already attending), sent an email to his comms lead authorizing execution, and blocked time for analyst briefings in Weeks 3-4.

Response time: 2 hours (compared to the weeks it would have taken to interpret raw dashboards and develop his own action plan).

Outcome: FT interview published April 28. Three analyst briefings completed. Partnership announced May 6 at regional conference with Bloomberg coverage. Gartner report (June 1) positioned the company as "Leader" in regional digital transformation—first time in three years.

Henrik's feedback to Sophia: "This is the first time I've received intelligence I could actually act on. You didn't just tell me what was happening—you told me what to do about it and why it mattered. That's what I need."

A Second Example: The CFO and Trust Erosion

Different persona, different priority, same framework.

Jennifer, TechFinance's CFO — the same executive who had received that first Trust Erosion brief in the Preface — receives Trust signal analysis timed to earnings cycles. Through PBI, we know she cares about investor confidence, analyst perception, and anything that could affect market cap. Her decision windows align with the earnings calendar.

Here's what a SIGNAL brief looks like when there's a problem:

SIGNAL ALERT: Trust Erosion Detected

Prepared for: Jennifer, CFO
Priority: HIGH - Requires response within 48 hours
Date: March 10 Context: Q2 earnings call in 6 weeks; analyst briefings begin April 8

S - SIGNAL: "Trust signal declined from 75 to 68 in the past 14 days (-7 points, -9%). Primary driver: Governance sub-signal collapsed from 78 to 65 (-13 points, -17%). Velocity: -3.5 points per week—accelerating. Source shift: Coverage moved from consumer financial blogs (low authority) to tier-2 trade publications (high authority), with *American Banker, CFO,* and *Compliance Week* questioning board composition and audit committee independence following an industry peer's governance scandal."

I - IMPLICATION: "Trust erosion at this velocity matches the pattern that preceded analyst downgrades in four comparable fintech cases over the past three years. Case 1 (2023): Similar governance signal decline led to Morgan Stanley downgrade six weeks later with significant market cap decline. Case 2 (2023): Trust erosion pattern led to Goldman downgrade five weeks later with significant market cap decline. Case 3 (2022): Governance driver collapse led to two simultaneous downgrades with significant market cap decline. Case 4 (2021): Trust velocity at -3.2/week led to Barclays downgrade seven weeks later with significant market cap decline. Current trajectory suggests 30% probability of at least one downgrade by late April—directly impacting Q2 earnings narrative. Each downgrade carries significant market cap impact. Combined with earnings timing, potential exposure is substantial."

G - GAP: "No proactive governance narrative exists to counter the erosion. Last governance-related communication was September (six months ago)—a routine board composition update that received minimal coverage. In contrast, Competitor A published an enhanced governance framework in February; Competitor B announced an additional independent board member in January; and Competitor C released a transparency report with audit committee details in March. Institutional investors have no recent evidence of our governance leadership. Our silence in the context of industry governance concerns creates a vacuum that trade media is filling with skepticism. Analyst briefings are scheduled for April 8—they will ask governance questions. We currently have no answers prepared."

N - NARRATIVE: "Governance trust is shifting from 'assumed credibility' to 'demonstrated transparency' across the financial services sector. The market no longer accepts governance by implication—proactive demonstration is now required. This shift was triggered by recent industry scandals but has become a permanent expectation. Companies that demonstrate governance leadership proactively are being rewarded; companies that remain silent are being questioned. This creates both risk (if we stay silent, we confirm skeptics' concerns) and opportunity (if we lead proactively while competitors remain reactive, we establish governance leadership positioning). The 6-week window before analyst reports provides time to control the narrative rather than respond to questions."

A - ACTION: "Launch governance transparency initiative within two weeks. In Week 1 (March 18-22): Publish CEO governance blog post titled 'Our Commitment to Transparent Oversight'—draft by March 15, legal review March 16-17, publish March 19. Announce governance enhancements including an additional independent audit committee member (candidate identified) and enhanced audit committee charter with quarterly disclosure commitment. Issue press release March 20 with proactive distribution to *American Banker*, *CFO*, and *Compliance Week* (the outlets driving current narrative). In Weeks 2-3 (March 25-April 5): Conduct CFO-led investor calls with top 15 institutional investors—proactive briefing on governance enhancements before they ask. Prepare governance FAQ document for IR team to handle inbound inquiries. Create peer governance comparison positioning our governance versus sector peers (we compare favorably on 7 of 9 metrics—need to communicate this). In Week 4 (April 8-12): Integrate governance talking points into analyst briefings as part of standard earnings prep. Offer board member interviews to key trade publications. Monitor Trust signal for stabilization indicators. Owner: CFO (Jennifer) + CCO + General Counsel. Decision needed by Friday March 15 for Monday March 18 execution start. Budget: $800K, broken down as $300K for governance enhancements (board search, charter updates), $250K for communications (content, media relations, materials), $150K for investor outreach (roadshow logistics, materials), and $100K contingency."

L - LIFT: "Expected impact based on historical pattern analysis: Week 4 sees Trust decline arrested with stabilization at 67-68 (no further erosion). Week 6 sees Trust recovery begin, moving from 68 to 70. Week 8 sees Trust recovery to 72-73 (approaching baseline). Week 10 sees full recovery to 75+ with zero analyst downgrades. Probability assessment: With action, 87% probability of preventing downgrade based on four similar interventions. Without action, 30% probability of downgrade, rising to 45% if erosion continues. Financial impact: Protected value is substantial (single prevented downgrade). Potential upside is an additional $25M if governance leadership positioning attracts positive analyst commentary. Investment is $800K. ROI: 62:1 minimum, potential 94:1. Precedent: Four similar proactive governance interventions in our historical database averaged 87% success rate in preventing predicted downgrades, with average time to stabilization of 4 weeks, average time to full recovery of 8 weeks, and average ROI of 45:1."

What Happened

Jennifer reviewed the alert within an hour of receipt. She immediately forwarded it to General Counsel and CCO with the note "Let's discuss at 2pm today," called her IR lead to hold the investor outreach calendar for Weeks 2-3, and approved the budget at $1.2M (increased to add enhanced investor materials).

Response time: 4 hours from alert to approved plan.

Execution timeline: March 19 saw the CEO blog post published (received 12 positive trade media mentions). March 20 saw the governance enhancement announcement (*American Banker* led with "proactive transparency" framing). March 25-April 5 saw 14 of 15 institutional investor calls completed. April 8-12 saw analyst briefings completed—zero governance questions (proactive narrative had addressed concerns).

Outcome: Trust signal stabilized at 68 in Week 4, recovered to 73 by Week 8. Zero analyst downgrades. Q2 earnings call included unprompted positive analyst commentary on "governance leadership." Strong positive ROI.

Jennifer's feedback to Sophia: "You showed me a problem I didn't know I had, with enough time to fix it, and a plan that worked. That's worth more than any dashboard."

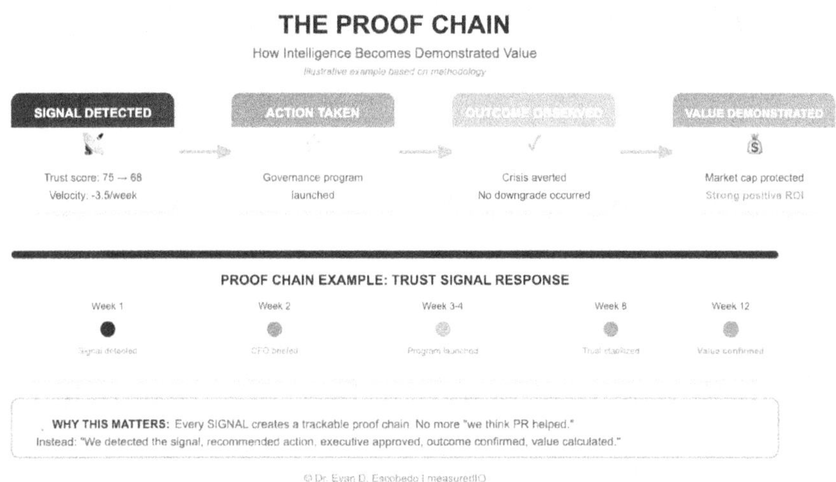

Figure 6.2: The Proof Chain—How Intelligence Becomes Demonstrated Value

The Activation Workflow: From Detection to Decision

SIGNAL stories don't appear magically. They require a systematic workflow that turns raw data into executive-ready intelligence. Here's the operational process.

Step 1: Signal Detection (Daily/Continuous). Monitor your MRS dashboards and alerts for threshold breaches (Trust drops below 70, Innovation gap widens beyond -10 points); velocity changes (any signal moving faster than 2 points per week); source authority shifts (coverage moving from low-authority to high-authority outlets); competitive movements (competitor scores changing significantly); and pattern matches (current data resembling historical patterns that preceded outcomes). Most days, nothing triggers. When something does, move immediately to Step 2.

Step 2: Pattern Matching (Within 2 Hours). When a signal is detected, check your historical database. Have we seen this pattern before? What happened next in similar cases? What interventions worked? What didn't? What was the timeline from signal to outcome? This historical context informs your Implication and Lift components. Without pattern matching, you're guessing. With it, you're predicting based on evidence.

Step 3: Stakeholder Mapping (Immediate). Ask yourself which persona this signal affects most directly, what decisions they make that this signal impacts, what their current context is (upcoming board meeting? earnings cycle? product launch?), and what their decision authority is (can they approve the likely action?).

Step 4: SIGNAL Draft (Within 24 Hours). Write the six components in order. Start with Signal—the data, precise, measured, time-bounded. Then Implication—what it means for THIS stakeholder's priorities. Then Gap—what's missing or vulnerable. Then Narrative—the strategic pattern or story. Then Action—specific recommendations with owners, timelines, budgets. Finally, Lift—expected outcomes with quantification.

Step 5: Review and Calibrate. Before sending, verify that the action matches the stakeholder's authority level, the timeline is realistic, the budget is defensible, and someone could execute without asking clarifying questions.

Step 6: Deliver in Context. Use the stakeholder's preferred channel and timing. Henrik wants mobile briefs for travel. Jennifer wants detailed analysis before Monday planning. Format matters.

Step 7: Track and Close Loop. After delivery, track whether they acted, what the outcome was, and whether your prediction was accurate. This builds your pattern library and credibility.

Four Narrative Patterns for Common Situations

Over time, you'll recognize recurring situations that call for SIGNAL responses. Rather than starting from scratch each time, experienced practitioners use narrative patterns—templates for common scenarios. Here are four patterns you'll use repeatedly.

Pattern 1: The Erosion Alert. Use this when a key signal is declining and approaching a threshold that historically predicts negative outcomes. The structure emphasizes Implication heavily—emphasize business stakes and historical pattern matching, showing what happened in similar cases. It also emphasizes Lift heavily—quantify the downside if no action is taken AND the upside of intervention. Action focuses on stabilization and prevention.

Example triggers include Trust dropping 7+ points in 14 days, Innovation gap widening 5+ points in 30 days, Governance driver collapsing while the industry faces scrutiny, or source authority shifting from friendly to skeptical outlets.

Template opening: "Trust erosion pattern detected—matches [N] cases that preceded [negative outcome] within [timeframe]..."

The Jennifer/CFO example a few pages back follows the Erosion Alert pattern.

Pattern 2: The Momentum Opportunity. Use this when positive movement creates a window to accelerate gains or capture positioning before the window closes. The structure emphasizes Gap heavily—what's missing to fully capitalize on the momentum? It also emphasizes Narrative heavily—frame the strategic window and why NOW matters. Action focuses on acceleration and capture.

Example triggers include share of voice increasing 20%+, competitive gap narrowing significantly, positive coverage surging following an announcement, or industry narrative shifting in your favor.

Template opening: "Innovation momentum building—narrow [N]-week window to capture [positioning] before [event that locks perception]..."

The Henrik example earlier follows the Momentum Opportunity pattern.

Pattern 3: The Competitive Threat. Use this when a competitor makes a move that threatens your positioning, narrative, or market perception. The structure emphasizes Implication heavily—what is the competitor trying to achieve, and how does it affect your positioning? It also emphasizes Gap heavily—where are you vulnerable, and what narrative space are they capturing? Action focuses on response (counter-positioning) or differentiation (own a different space).

Example triggers include a competitor announcement capturing narrative you need, competitor coverage surging in your priority media, competitor executive visibility in forums where you're absent, or competitor capturing "leader" positioning in analyst reports.

Template opening: "Competitive threat detected—[Competitor] is positioning to own [narrative] with [specific move]. This threatens [your positioning] because [business impact]..."

Key consideration: Not every competitor move requires response. The SIGNAL should assess whether the threat is material (affects your business priorities) or noise (competitor activity that doesn't impact your position).

Pattern 4: The Crisis Signal. Use this when negative coverage or signals spike suddenly, requiring immediate response rather than strategic planning. The structure emphasizes Signal heavily—precise scope of the problem, what exactly is happening, where, how fast is it spreading. It also emphasizes Action heavily—immediate response steps, often in hours rather than days. The compressed timeline throughout reflects the urgency.

Example triggers include negative coverage spiking 200%+; social amplification surging on a negative story; tier-1 media pickup of a damaging narrative; or crisis-level threshold breach.

Template opening: "[Issue] coverage spiked [X]% in past [hours/days], now reaching [tier-1 outlets]. Social amplification at [velocity]. Immediate response required..."

Key consideration: Crisis SIGNALs require pre-established escalation protocols. You don't have time during a crisis to figure out who approves what. Build the authority matrix in advance.

PRO TIP

FOUR PATTERNS FOR COMMON SITUATIONS

1. Erosion Alert: Signal declining toward negative threshold. Emphasize Implication and Lift. 2. Momentum Opportunity: Positive movement creates a window. Emphasize Gap and Narrative. 3. Competitive Threat: Competitor move threatens your position. Emphasize Implication and Gap. 4. Crisis Signal: Sudden negative spike. Emphasize Signal and Action.

Recognize the pattern, and you know which SIGNAL components to emphasize.

Applying the Patterns: Quick Reference

The Erosion Alert pattern triggers when a signal is declining toward a negative threshold. Key SIGNAL components are Implication (stakes) and Lift (downside/upside). Action focus is to stabilize and prevent.

The Momentum Opportunity pattern triggers when positive movement creates a window. Key SIGNAL components are Gap (what's missing) and Narrative (why now). Action focus is to accelerate and capture.

The Competitive Threat pattern triggers when a competitor move threatens your position. Key SIGNAL components are Implication (their intent) and Gap (vulnerability). Action focus is to respond and differentiate.

The Crisis Signal pattern triggers when there's a sudden negative spike. Key SIGNAL components are Signal (precise scope) and Action (immediate steps). Action focus is to contain and respond.

Most situations you encounter will fit one of these four patterns. When you recognize the pattern, you can draft faster because you know which SIGNAL components to emphasize and what type of action to recommend.

The SIGNAL Mindset

The framework is simple. The discipline is hard.

Most measurement professionals are trained to report data, not interpret it. They're uncomfortable making recommendations. They worry about being wrong. They defer to executives to draw conclusions.

This mindset must change.

You are not a reporter. You are an advisor.

Your job is to tell executives what the data means, not just what it shows. To recommend actions, not just present options. To quantify expected outcomes, not just describe possibilities. To own the interpretation, not just deliver the numbers.

This is uncomfortable at first. You're putting yourself on the line. If your recommendation is wrong, it's visible.

But here's the truth: Executives don't want hedged, tentative analysis. They want clear recommendations from people who understand the data better than they do. They can always modify your recommendation—but they can't create one from scratch while running a business.

The progression looks like this. Level 1 is Reporter: "Here's what happened in media this week." This is a data dump with no interpretation. Level 2 is Analyst: "Here's what happened and here's what it might mean." This includes interpretation but no recommendation. Level 3 is Advisor: "Here's what happened, what it means for your priorities, what you should do about it, and what outcome to expect." This is a complete SIGNAL.

Most measurement professionals operate at Level 1 or Level 2. SIGNAL pushes you to Level 3.

KEY CONCEPT

YOU ARE NOT A REPORTER. YOU ARE AN ADVISOR.

Your job is to: ◆ Tell executives what the data means, not just what it shows ◆ Recommend actions, not just present options ◆ Quantify expected outcomes, not just describe possibilities ◆ Own the interpretation, not just deliver numbers.

Executives don't want hedged, tentative analysis. They want clear recommendations from people who understand the data better than they do.

Common objections and how to overcome them:

"What if I'm wrong?" You will be sometimes. That's okay. Track your accuracy, learn from misses, and improve. Executives respect people who make clear predictions and own the outcomes—even when wrong—far more than people who hedge everything.

"I don't have enough data to be confident." Say so in the SIGNAL. "Based on limited historical data, estimated probability is 60-70% with moderate confidence." Quantified uncertainty is more useful than vague hedging.

"The executive might disagree with my recommendation." Good. Your job is to give them a clear recommendation to react to. They can modify it, reject it, or improve it. What they can't do is create strategic options from raw data while also running their business.

"What if they don't act on it?" That's their prerogative. Your job is to provide decision-grade intelligence. Their job is to decide. If they consistently don't act, that's feedback—either your recommendations aren't calibrated to their reality, or your credibility hasn't been established yet. Adjust accordingly.

When you deliver SIGNAL stories instead of measurement reports, you become indispensable. You're not the person who produces dashboards. You're the person who helps executives see around corners and make better decisions.

That's the transformation from data provider to strategic advisor.

COMMON MISTAKE

"WHAT IF I'M WRONG?"

You will be sometimes. That's okay. Track your accuracy, learn from misses, and improve. Executives respect people who make clear predictions and own the outcomes—even when wrong—far more than people who hedge everything. Quantified uncertainty ("60-70% confidence") is more useful than vague hedging.

Key Takeaways

The SIGNAL Framework transforms measurement into intelligence that drives decisions.

The Problem: Even aligned intelligence fails when it requires executives to interpret data themselves. They don't have time. They don't have context. That's your job.

The Solution: SIGNAL—a six-component framework that translates data into executive-ready decision support. Signal is what changed (the data). Implication is why it matters (the business stakes). Gap is what's missing (the vulnerability or opportunity). Narrative is the emerging story (the strategic pattern). Action is what to do (specific recommendations). Lift is expected impact (the business outcome).

The Mindset Shift: You are not a reporter delivering data. You are an advisor delivering recommendations. Own the interpretation. Recommend actions. Quantify expected outcomes.

The Result: Executives respond in hours instead of weeks. Intelligence drives decisions instead of sitting in inboxes. You become the person who helps the organization see around corners.

This is executive storytelling. This is how signals become actions. This is what makes measurement matter.

What's Next

You now have the complete system. Chapter 3 showed you how to detect signals—patterns of change that predict outcomes. Chapter 4 showed you how to align intelligence to stakeholders through PBI—discovering your Henrik and documenting the priorities that matter. Chapter 5 showed you how to quantify with MRS, building scores against those priorities. Chapter 6 showed you how to communicate with SIGNAL.

But methodology alone doesn't drive change—you need to operationalize it. Chapter 7 shows you how to combine AI scale with human judgment to make this system work at enterprise level. Then Chapters 8 and 9 provide the cultural foundation and implementation playbook to move from pilot to organizational transformation.

From framework to execution.

Note on Sources

The SIGNAL framework presented in this chapter is an original methodology developed by the author, adapted from the SCIPAB (Situation, Complication, Implication, Position, Action, Benefit) communication framework used at Cisco Systems during the author's 13-year tenure.

The Henrik and Jennifer case studies are composite illustrations based on the author's professional experience implementing persona-based intelligence systems.

AI + HUMAN INTELLIGENCE

The False Promise of Full Automation

In 2024, a major financial services company deployed an AI-powered reputation monitoring system with great fanfare. The promise: real-time sentiment analysis across millions of articles, instant crisis detection, automated executive briefings.

Six months later, they nearly missed a regulatory crisis.

An analyst at *American Banker* published a carefully worded piece questioning the company's compliance practices. The tone was professional, even neutral. The language was technical. The AI sentiment engine classified it as "informational" with a neutral score.

No alert was triggered. No executive was notified.

Three weeks later, the SEC announced an investigation. The stock dropped 12%. The CEO asked communications: "Why didn't anyone see this coming?"

The answer: The AI did see it. It just didn't understand it.

A human analyst reading that same *American Banker* article would have recognized the warning signs immediately: the sourcing (three unnamed "current employees"); the timing (just before quarterly earnings); the framing ("questions are emerging"—journalist code for "we've confirmed a problem"); and the context (similar language preceded four other regulatory actions in the sector).

The AI saw words. A human would have seen the pattern.

This is why AI alone will never be enough for strategic reputation intelligence.

But here's the other truth: Human analysis alone isn't enough either.

That same human analyst couldn't have manually reviewed the 47,000 financial services articles published that month. They would have missed the emerging *American Banker* narrative buried in article #3,847.

The answer isn't AI or human. It's AI and human.

KEY CONCEPT

> ### THE HYBRID MODEL
>
> AI alone will never be enough for strategic reputation intelligence. Human analysis alone isn't enough either. The answer isn't AI OR human—it's AI AND human. AI provides: Scale, speed, pattern detection, consistency. Humans provide: Context, judgment, relationships, strategic recommendations.
>
> Neither is sufficient alone. Both combined outperform either.

The Research Is Clear: AI Has Limits

The limitations of AI in high-context analysis aren't speculation—they're documented extensively in peer-reviewed research and industry benchmarks.

Vectara's Hallucination Leaderboard, a widely-cited industry benchmark that tests how often LLMs generate information not present in source documents, shows hallucination rates ranging from approximately 1% for the best-performing models to over 25% for others—even on straightforward summarization tasks. The methodology, published on GitHub and Hugging Face, has been referenced in academic papers including research published in npj Digital Medicine.

Gartner's 2025 AI Hype Cycle research notes that "organizations face governance challenges (e.g., hallucinations, bias and fairness)" and reports that "less than 30% of AI leaders report their CEOs are happy with AI investment return." Their June 2025 Data & Analytics predictions state that "poor semantics in GenAI lead to greater hallucinations," emphasizing the ongoing challenge.

A comprehensive 2022 survey in Artificial Intelligence Review documented that sentiment analysis faces persistent challenges with sarcasm, negation, domain adaptation, and "the evolving nuances of digital communication." The researchers emphasized that context, cultural references, and implied meaning remain difficult for algorithmic approaches.

Perhaps most relevant for reputation measurement: a 2024 peer-reviewed study in Scientific Reports found that sarcasm detection without contextual information achieved only 49% F1 score on Reddit data—essentially a coin flip. When context was added, accuracy improved to 75%. This demonstrates how dependent AI accuracy is on the kind of contextual understanding that human analysts provide naturally.

Where AI Fails in Reputation Analysis

Let me show you the specific failure modes we've observed across implementations.

Failure Mode 1: Surface-Level Positivity. AI sentiment models trained on consumer reviews are calibrated to detect "I love this product!" versus "This is terrible!" But professional journalism rarely uses such language.

Consider this *Financial Times* excerpt covering an ESG report: "The company's sustainability commitments are ambitious, though execution timelines remain unspecified and several environmental targets lack third-party verification."

AI classification: Mildly positive—flagged "ambitious" and "commitments."

Human analysis: Skeptical/negative—"though" signals skepticism, "unspecified" and "lack verification" are critical qualifiers. The FT rarely uses such language unless genuinely concerned.

Three months later, two ESG rating agencies downgraded that company. The signal was there. The AI just couldn't read professional skepticism.

Failure Mode 2: Missed Sarcasm and Cultural Context. Peer-reviewed research confirms that sarcasm remains a fundamental challenge for AI. As the research confirms, sarcasm detection without context performs barely better than chance. With context, accuracy improved to 75%, still leaving one in four sarcastic statements misclassified.

Consider a viral tweet during a product launch failure: "Oh great, just what we needed—another data leak 🙃 #privacy #innovation"

AI classification: Neutral—"great" and "needed" are positive words.

Human analysis: Highly negative viral sarcasm—"Oh great" is a sarcastic opener, the upside-down emoji indicates irony, and the hashtags are mocking.

That tweet was retweeted 47,000 times and became the dominant frame for the launch narrative. The AI missed it because it couldn't read cultural context.

Failure Mode 3: Context Collapse. AI analyzes each article in isolation. Humans recognize patterns across articles, time, and sources.

Consider three articles about a company over three weeks. Week 1, Tech-Crunch publishes "Company announces AI-powered tools"—AI scores it positive. Week 2, The Information publishes "Inside Company's struggle to compete on AI"—AI scores it negative. Week 3, Protocol publishes "Why Company is playing catch-up in AI"—AI scores it negative.

AI assessment: Average sentiment slightly negative.

Human pattern recognition: This is a narrative shift in progress. Three credible outlets, three weeks, consistent framing as "follower not leader." This isn't random negative sentiment—it's perception hardening. Strategic response required.

The AI missed the pattern because it processed three independent articles. A human saw the convergence.

Where AI Excels: Scale, Speed, and Pattern Detection

Despite its limitations, AI has unlocked capabilities that were impossible with human-only analysis. Let me be specific about what AI does exceptionally well.

Scale That Humans Can't Match. A human analyst can read and carefully analyze maybe 50-100 articles per day. AI can process 50,000+ with consistent methodology. For a large brand generating thousands of mentions monthly across global markets, there's simply no human-only alternative.

Consider the math: If your brand generates 5,000 relevant mentions per month, that's 250 per business day. At 10 minutes per article for thoughtful analysis, you'd need 40+ hours daily—two full-time analysts doing nothing but reading. And they'd still miss the cross-article patterns that only emerge from aggregate analysis.

AI makes comprehensive monitoring possible. The question isn't whether to use it—it's how to use it wisely.

Velocity Detection. AI excels at detecting rate of change—something humans struggle with when reading individual articles. When coverage volume spikes 121% week-over-week while sentiment drops 0.36 points, that's an anomaly worth investigating. AI flags it automatically.

This velocity detection is especially valuable for early warning. By the time a human notices "we seem to be getting more negative coverage lately," the narrative may have already hardened. AI catches acceleration patterns within days, providing intervention windows that human-only analysis would miss.

Cluster Formation and Theme Emergence. When 14 articles mentioning "board governance" appear in one week versus two the previous week, AI detects the cluster forming. Human analysts reading those articles individually—even if they could read all 14—might not recognize the connections or significance.

Platforms like Meltwater use topic modeling and entity clustering to identify emerging themes before they become obvious trends. This capability is invaluable for proactive reputation management: seeing a governance narrative forming in week 1, before it becomes a crisis in week 4.

Multilingual Coverage. Most companies operate globally but measure reputation primarily in English-language media. This creates massive blind spots.

AI processes 50+ languages simultaneously, detecting regional sentiment shifts that would require an army of multilingual analysts to track manually. When a regulatory story breaks in Brazilian Portuguese media four weeks before English-language pickup (a real pattern we've observed), AI-enabled multilingual monitoring provides early warning that human-only analysis would miss entirely.

Competitive Benchmarking at Scale. Tracking five competitors across four reputation dimensions (Trust, Innovation, Performance, Leadership) in six priority markets produces data volumes that require algorithmic processing. That's 120 competitive data points to track continuously—impossible for manual analysis, routine for AI.

Competitive benchmarking becomes strategic when it's comprehensive and consistent. AI makes both possible.

Summarization and Content Generation. Modern AI tools within platforms like Meltwater, Cision, and Brandwatch now offer summarization capabilities—condensing 50 articles on a topic into key themes and representative quotes. This doesn't replace human analysis, but it dramatically accelerates the review process.

Similarly, AI can generate first drafts of routine reports, freeing human analysts to focus on interpretation and strategic recommendations rather than data compilation.

COMMON MISTAKE

WHERE AI FAILS

Surface-Level Positivity: AI reads "ambitious commitments" as positive. A human recognizes the FT rarely uses such language unless genuinely concerned. Missed Sarcasm: AI sees "Oh great, just what we needed." A human reads devastating irony. Context Collapse: AI analyzes articles independently. Humans recognize when three articles from three outlets tell the same emerging story. Research confirms: Sarcasm detection without context performs barely better than chance.

The Hybrid Model: AI Detection + Human Interpretation

The solution isn't choosing between AI and human analysis. It's designing a system where each does what it does best.

AI's role is detection at scale: processing high volumes of coverage (thousands to tens of thousands monthly); flagging threshold breaches and velocity anomalies; identifying cluster formation and emerging themes; providing consistent scoring methodology across time and sources; and enabling multilingual and multi-market monitoring.

The human role is interpretation and strategy: validating AI-flagged signals for strategic relevance; interpreting context, tone, and journalist intent; recognizing patterns across time and sources; connecting signals to business priorities and stakeholder needs; making strategic recommendations (the "A" in SIGNAL); and quality-checking for false positives before executive delivery.

Research supports this hybrid approach. Industry implementations consistently show that human review of AI-flagged content catches false positives that would otherwise reach executives and waste organizational attention. The pattern holds across domains: A 2024 study in *npj Digital Medicine* examining clinical text summarization found that human oversight was essential for catching AI errors that could affect patient care, with the researchers noting that "hallucination detection remains challenging" even for state-of-the-art models.

The principle is consistent: Neither AI nor human alone achieves optimal results. The combination outperforms either.

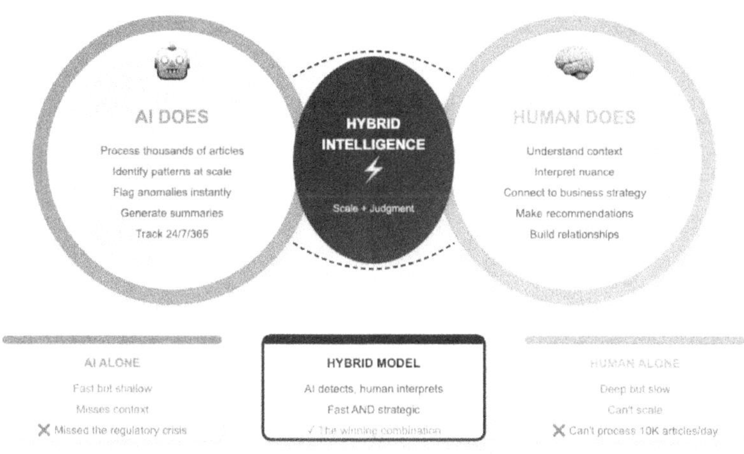

Figure 7.1: The Hybrid Intelligence Model—AI for Scale + Human for Strategy

How This Works in Practice: The Human Tagging Process

Before we get to Henrik's dashboard, let me show you what happens behind the scenes—the actual operational work that makes MRS possible.

Every article that contributes to a Media Reputation Score goes through a human tagging process. This isn't optional. This isn't a "nice to have." This is what separates meaningful intelligence from automated noise.

The Multi-Dimensional Tagging Framework

When an analyst reviews an article, they apply multiple dimensions of classification. While the specific protocols and weightings are calibrated to each organization's industry and competitive context, the core dimensions include sentiment, prominence, salience, and source authority—plus bonuses for voice and key message alignment.

Sentiment is not a simple positive/negative binary, but a nuanced scale that captures degrees of favorability. An article can be strongly positive, slightly positive, neutral, slightly negative, or strongly negative—and importantly, different companies mentioned in the same article can receive different sentiment scores. A piece comparing two competitors might praise one while criticizing the other. AI struggles with this multi-entity sentiment parsing; humans handle it naturally. In MRS calculations, sentiment acts as a multiplier: Positive coverage amplifies the score, negative coverage diminishes it, and neutral coverage falls in between.

Prominence captures how centrally the brand figures in the coverage. There's a meaningful difference between a headline mention, prominent placement in the opening paragraphs, and a passing reference buried in paragraph 12. Prominence affects how much weight an article should carry in overall scoring—and determining true prominence requires reading comprehension, not just keyword location detection. Higher prominence means a higher multiplier.

Salience determines whether this is exclusive coverage of your brand or whether you're one of several companies mentioned. An in-depth profile carries different strategic weight than a roundup where you're one name among many. Exclusive or dominant coverage receives a higher multiplier; shared mentions receive less weight. Salience affects both the score and how you should interpret the coverage strategically.

Source Authority weights the credibility and reach of the publication. A feature in the *Financial Times* or *Wall Street Journal* carries different weight than a trade blog or regional outlet. This isn't snobbery—it's recognition that stakeholder exposure and perceived credibility vary dramatically by source tier. Your PBI discovery process should identify which sources your priority stakeholders actually read and trust, and weight accordingly.

Beyond these core multipliers, two bonuses recognize additional strategic value:

Voice Bonus applies when your executives or credible third parties speak on your behalf. Coverage where your CEO demonstrates thought leadership carries different weight than a straightforward company announcement. When an independent analyst or respected industry figure validates your position, that third-party credibility adds value beyond the base metrics. The voice bonus recognizes that *who says it* affects impact.

Key Message Bonus rewards coverage that advances your priority narratives. An article that reinforces your "innovation leader" positioning or communicates your sustainability commitments delivers more strategic value than neutral coverage of the same prominence. When human taggers identify that an article contains and reinforces a key message from your communications strategy, the bonus applies.

Why Human Judgment Remains Essential

Each of these dimensions requires contextual understanding that current AI cannot reliably provide. Is "ambitious sustainability targets" a compliment or a veiled criticism? It depends on the publication, the journalist's history, and the surrounding context. Is a passing mention in a *Financial Times* deep-dive more valuable than a headline in a trade publication? It depends on who Henrik needs to reach. Is the CEO's quote being used to illustrate thought leadership or to set up criticism in the next paragraph? Only reading comprehension answers that.

The human tagging process takes more time than automated classification. That's the point. The additional time invested in thoughtful human analysis is what produces scores that actually mean something—scores Henrik can trust when he walks into the boardroom.

The Scale Challenge

Here's the practical reality that drives the hybrid model.

In a recent automotive industry analysis, we processed a dataset of 2,500 articles covering five major manufacturers. Each article required assessment across multiple dimensions for each company mentioned. A single article covering four companies might require 15-20 individual tagging decisions—sentiment, prominence, salience, and source authority for each entity, plus potential bonuses for voice and key message alignment.

Across that dataset, nearly 60% of articles were exclusive coverage of a single brand, about 6% mentioned four or more companies (requiring complex multi-entity tagging), and sentiment distributions varied significantly by company, reflecting genuine market perception differences that only careful human analysis could parse.

Multiply this across a large brand generating 3,000-5,000 relevant mentions monthly, and the scale challenge becomes clear. Human analysts cannot tag every article with the care required for accurate scoring. But automated-only analysis produces too many false positives and misses too much nuance.

This is where the hybrid model becomes essential. First, AI processes everything—all 5,000 mentions get automated sentiment scoring, topic classification, and source identification. Second, AI flags the critical subset—tier-1 sources, threshold anomalies, and competitive signals, perhaps 300-500 articles. Third, humans tag the critical subset—analysts apply the full tagging framework to the flagged articles. Fourth, humans validate AI on a sample—regular audits of AI classifications against human judgment.

The result: You get the scale of AI processing with the accuracy of human judgment where it matters most.

What This Means for Your MRS

When you see a Media Reputation Score, that number represents the integration of volume processing by AI across thousands of mentions; human expert analysis of strategically significant coverage; multiple scoring dimensions applied with trained judgment; and continuous calibration between automated and human classifications.

The specific weightings, protocols, and calibration methodologies vary by industry, competitive context, and organizational priorities—which is why implementation requires expertise, not just tools. But the principle is constant: Credible reputation scoring requires human judgment at the core, enabled by AI at scale.

This is the operational reality that makes MRS defensible in executive conversations. It's not a black-box algorithm that no one can explain. It's a disciplined methodology that combines the best of human expertise and technological capability.

Henrik's Dashboard: From Tagged Articles to Strategic Intelligence

Let's return to Henrik, the regional president tracking digital transformation narrative in his markets and being served by Sophia, his measurement analyst.

Henrik's organization generates approximately 3,500 relevant media mentions per month across his priority markets. No human team could manually analyze this volume with consistency. But Henrik also can't trust AI-only analysis—the stakes are too high for false positives or missed signals that could affect his $800M regional business.

Here's how the hybrid model works for Henrik.

Layer 1: AI Processing (All 3,500 mentions). The AI system processes everything: automated sentiment scoring using the MRS methodology; topic classification into Henrik's reputation pillars (Digital Leader,

Platform/Partner, Responsible Corporate Citizen, Performance); source authority weighting based on the Media Weighting Matrix; geographic filtering to Henrik's priority markets; competitive benchmarking against his three key rivals; and velocity and trend detection for week-over-week changes. This layer runs continuously. Henrik's team never sees the raw 3,500 mentions—they see AI-processed data.

Layer 2: AI Filtering (Surfaces ~350 mentions for review). AI flags the top 10% for human review based on predetermined criteria: tier-1 sources (any mention in *Financial Times*, Bloomberg, *Wall Street Journal*, *The Economist*, or his regional business press flagged automatically); threshold breaches (any day where sentiment moves more than 0.5 standard deviations from baseline); anomalies (unusual patterns such as a competitor mentioned at 3x normal rate or a new topic cluster forming); executive mentions (any coverage featuring competitor executives or industry analysts); and competitive signals (coverage where Henrik's company is directly compared to competitors). The 350 flagged mentions represent coverage that might be strategically significant. Human judgment determines if it actually is.

Layer 3: Human Analysis (350 mentions reviewed weekly). Henrik's measurement analyst, Sophia, reviews the AI-flagged content with specific questions in mind: context validation (is the AI sentiment score accurate given the full article context, catching the "ambitious, though..." false positives?); strategic relevance (does this matter for Henrik's Digital Leader priority, or is it noise?); pattern recognition (is this article part of a larger narrative shift, does it connect to other coverage this week?); source credibility (is this journalist influential, what's their track record, are they a known skeptic or advocate?); and false positive elimination (should this have been flagged at all, or is it routine coverage?). Sophia spends approximately 8-10 hours weekly on this review—roughly two minutes per flagged article, with more time on complex pieces.

Layer 4: SIGNAL Development (3-5 weekly insights). From approximately 350 reviewed mentions, Sophia identifies 3-5 items worthy of SIGNAL stories for Henrik. These might include an FT article signaling competitive threat (Pattern: Competitive Threat), a cluster of coverage suggesting momentum opportunity (Pattern: Momentum Opportunity); or an early warning of narrative shift requiring attention (Pattern: Erosion Alert). These become the executive-ready intelligence that Henrik actually receives and acts on.

PRO TIP

> ### THE 90/10 RULE
>
> AI processes 100% of coverage. AI flags the top 10% for human review based on: tier-1 sources, threshold breaches, anomalies, executive mentions, and competitive signals. Humans validate, interpret, and develop strategic intelligence from that 10%. Result: Scale of AI processing + accuracy of human judgment where it matters most.

What Henrik Sees

Henrik doesn't see 3,500 mentions, or 350 flagged articles, or even the analyst's review notes. He sees a weekly dashboard showing MRS trends, competitive positioning, and key metrics; 3-5 SIGNAL stories when something requires his attention or decision; and a monthly brief summarizing progress against his Digital Leader narrative goals.

The entire system—AI processing, human review, SIGNAL development—runs in the background. Henrik is offered intelligence, not measurement.

The Efficiency Math

Without AI, you'd face 3,500 mentions at five minutes each—290 hours per month, impossible to staff. You'd miss patterns across that volume, have inconsistent methodology, and might produce 3-5 SIGNALs if you were lucky.

With the hybrid model, AI processes all 3,500 mentions in minutes. Human review covers 350 mentions at two minutes each—just 12 hours per month. The system catches patterns algorithmically, applies consistent scoring methodology, and produces 3-5 SIGNALs systematically.

Without AI, you couldn't process the volume. Without humans, you'd deliver noise alongside signal and miss the context that makes intelligence actionable. The hybrid model delivers both scale and judgment.

The Critical Discipline: Tuning as You Go

The hybrid model isn't set-and-forget. It requires continuous calibration.

Tune Your AI Thresholds. Start conservative. If your AI flags 500 articles weekly and 400 turn out to be noise after human review, your threshold is too sensitive. Adjust until you're catching genuine signals without overwhelming analysts with false positives.

Build Your Training Feedback Loop. When human analysts override AI classifications, feed that data back into the system. Over time, the AI learns what matters for your specific brand, industry, and stakeholders. Research shows this iterative approach dramatically improves accuracy.

Document Your Decision Patterns. When you act on a signal and it proves valuable (or proves to be noise), document it. These case studies become your pattern library—helping both AI and human analysts recognize similar situations faster.

Monitor for Drift. AI models can degrade over time as language evolves, new topics emerge, and competitive landscapes shift. Regularly audit a sample of AI classifications against human judgment to catch drift early.

Why This Keeps Measurement Professionals Employed

Let me be direct about something: AI is not going to replace communications measurement professionals. But it will transform what we do.

The fear is understandable. When AI can process 50,000 articles while you read 50, it's natural to wonder about your job security. But this fear misunderstands where human value lies.

What AI Can't Do. AI cannot sit in Henrik's shoes and understand that a *Financial Times* article about "ambitious digital transformation" is actually skeptical, not positive—because AI doesn't know Henrik's competitive context, his board's expectations, or the FT journalist's track record. AI cannot recognize that three articles across three weeks in three credible outlets represents a narrative shift requiring strategic response—because AI analyzes articles independently without temporal pattern recognition. AI cannot recommend a $500K intervention with 50:1 expected ROI—because AI doesn't understand business trade-offs, budget constraints, or stakeholder politics. AI cannot write a SIGNAL story that moves an executive to action in two hours— because AI doesn't understand the executive's priorities, decision windows, or communication preferences.

The professionals who thrive will be those who evolve their role.

Become AI trainers, not just analysts. Your expertise in interpreting coverage—understanding journalist intent, recognizing narrative patterns, connecting signals to business stakes—is exactly what AI needs to learn. Every time you override an AI classification with better judgment, you're teaching the system. You're not competing with AI. You're training it.

Focus on the 10% that matters. Let AI handle volume processing. Your value is in the strategic interpretation layer—the context, judgment, and recommendations that AI can't provide. This is actually more valuable work than reading through thousands of articles. You're being promoted, not replaced.

Build the bridge to business. AI can score articles. It can't explain to the CFO why a Trust signal decline matters for the earnings call, or recommend a governance transparency campaign with specific budget, timeline, and expected ROI. That's the SIGNAL work from Chapter 6—and it requires human judgment every step of the way.

Validate before you escalate. Every time you catch a false positive before it reaches an executive, you build credibility. Every time you surface a true signal that AI alone would have missed, you prove your value. The hybrid model creates space for this expertise to shine.

The research backs this up. Gartner's AI research consistently emphasizes the need for human oversight in enterprise AI deployments, noting that governance challenges including hallucinations remain significant barriers to AI ROI. The EU AI Act now legally requires human oversight for high-risk AI applications. Organizations recognize that AI alone isn't sufficient for high-stakes decisions. They're investing in hybrid systems that combine AI scale with human judgment.

Your job isn't disappearing. It's evolving—toward higher-value strategic work and away from volume processing that AI handles better.

KEY CONCEPT

> ### YOUR JOB ISN'T DISAPPEARING—IT'S EVOLVING
>
> AI cannot: Sit in Henrik's shoes and understand that an FT article is actually skeptical. Recognize that three articles across three weeks represents a narrative shift. Recommend a $500K intervention with expected ROI. Write a SIGNAL that moves an executive to action.
>
> You're not being replaced by AI. You're being augmented by it—toward higher-value strategic work.

Practical Implementation: Where to Start

If you're building or refining your hybrid intelligence system, here's a practical sequence based on what we've seen work across implementations.

Phase 1: Establish AI Baseline (Weeks 1-4). Deploy AI-powered monitoring across your coverage universe. Whether you're using Meltwater, Cision, Brandwatch, or another platform, let the system run for 30-60 days to establish baseline volumes (how many mentions do you typically generate?); sentiment distributions (what's your normal positive/negative/neutral mix?); competitive benchmarks (where do you stand relative to peers?); and source patterns (which outlets cover you most frequently?). Don't try to act on this data yet. Just observe. Understand what "normal" looks like before you try to identify anomalies.

Phase 2: Define Your Tier-1 Sources (Week 5). Work with your stakeholders (using PBI conversations from Chapter 4) to identify the 50-100 outlets that matter most. Henrik's Media Weighting Matrix is your guide here—he's already told you which publications influence his thinking. Which publications do your executives read? Which sources do your investors, regulators, and customers trust? Which journalists have influence in your industry? These become your priority human review set. Any coverage from these sources gets human attention regardless of AI classification. Use the Media Weighting Matrix from Chapter 4 to formalize this list.

Phase 3: Build Your Review Protocol (Weeks 6-7). Train analysts on what to look for when reviewing AI-flagged content. Create a checklist covering whether the sentiment classification is accurate given full article context; whether journalist tone matches AI score (watching for professional skepticism); whether this is strategically relevant to current business priorities; whether this is part of a larger pattern forming (checking related coverage); whether this warrants escalation or SIGNAL development; and whether the AI threshold for this source or topic should be adjusted. Document decisions. When an analyst overrides AI, capture the reasoning. This becomes your training data for continuous improvement.

Phase 4: Establish Feedback Loops (Ongoing). Create systematic processes for analyst corrections to improve AI calibration: weekly review of override patterns (are certain topics consistently mis-scored?); monthly accuracy audit (sample 50 AI classifications, verify against human judgment); and quarterly threshold adjustment (are you flagging too much or too little?). The goal is continuous improvement. Your hybrid system should get better every month.

Phase 5: Connect to SIGNAL Workflow (Week 8+). Ensure your human review process feeds directly into SIGNAL development (Chapter 6). Reviewed items that require action flow into SIGNAL story development. SIGNAL stories flow to executive delivery via PBI-defined channels. Executive actions flow to outcome tracking for proof chains. The end-to-end workflow: AI Detection → Human Review → SIGNAL Development → Executive Decision → Outcome Measurement.

This covers the technical implementation of your hybrid system. Chapter 8 addresses the equally important challenge: building the organizational culture that makes intelligence actionable..

Common Implementation Mistakes to Avoid

Over-flagging. If your AI flags 80% of coverage for human review, you've defeated the purpose. Start with conservative thresholds (flag 5-10%) and expand only if you're missing important signals.

Under-investing in humans. The hybrid model requires trained analysts. Don't automate AI processing and then assign one junior analyst to review everything. Match human resources to review volume.

Skipping the feedback loop. If analyst corrections don't improve AI performance over time, you're doing the same work twice. Build systematic feedback processes.

Forgetting the business connection. A perfectly tuned hybrid system is worthless if it doesn't produce intelligence that drives decisions. Always work backward from stakeholder needs (Chapter 5).

Key Takeaways

AI and human intelligence serve different purposes in reputation measurement. Neither is sufficient alone.

AI excels at processing volume (thousands of mentions); detecting velocity and anomalies; applying consistent methodology across time and sources; enabling multilingual and multi-market monitoring; and competitive benchmarking at scale.

Humans excel at interpreting context, tone, and intent; recognizing patterns across time and sources; validating strategic relevance; eliminating false positives; and making recommendations (the SIGNAL "A").

The hybrid model works by having AI process all coverage and flag the top 10% for human review. Humans validate, interpret, and develop strategic intelligence. Continuous feedback loops improve AI accuracy over time. False positive rates decrease while strategic relevance increases.

For measurement professionals, this isn't a threat to your career—it's an evolution. Your expertise in interpretation, context, and strategic judgment becomes more valuable, not less. You're not being replaced by AI. You're being augmented by it.

The organizations that win will be those that build true hybrid intelligence: AI scale with human wisdom. Neither alone. Both together.

What's Next

You now have the complete intelligence system. Chapter 3 showed you how to detect signals. Chapter 4 showed you how to align with PBI—finding your Henrik and mapping his priorities. Chapter 5 showed you how to quantify with MRS against those priorities. Chapter 6 showed you how to communicate with SIGNAL. Chapter 7 showed you how to combine AI and human judgment.

The technical system is in place. But methodology alone doesn't drive change—culture does. Chapter 8 addresses the organizational transformation required: how to build a culture where intelligence actually drives decisions, not just produces reports. Then Chapter 9 provides the implementation playbook—the step-by-step roadmap from pilot to enterprise function.

From framework to adoption.

References

Wankhade, M., Rao, A.C.S., & Kulkarni, C. (2022). A survey on sentiment analysis methods, applications, and challenges. *Artificial Intelligence Review*, 55, 5731–5780. https://link.springer.com/article/10.1007/s10462-022-10144-1

Gartner. (2025, July). The 2025 Hype Cycle for Artificial Intelligence. Gartner, Inc. https://www.gartner.com/en/articles/hype-cycle-for-artificial-intelligence

Gartner. (2025, June 17). Top Data & Analytics Predictions for 2025 and Beyond. Gartner, Inc. https://www.gartner.com/en/newsroom/press-releases/2025-06-17-gartner-announces-top-data-and-analytics-predictions

Helal, N. A., Hassan, A., Badr, N. L., & Afify, Y. M. (2024). A contextual-based approach for sarcasm detection. *Scientific Reports*, 14, Article 15415. https://doi.org/10.1038/s41598-024-65217-8

Vectara. (2024). Hallucination Leaderboard. GitHub/Hugging Face. https://github.com/vectara/hallucination-leaderboard

Asgari, E., et al. (2025). A framework to assess clinical safety and hallucination rates of LLMs for medical text summarisation. *npj Digital Medicine*, 8, Article 274. https://www.nature.com/articles/s41746-025-01670-7

European Union. (2024). Artificial Intelligence Act. Official Journal of the European Union.

Note on Sources

The financial services company case study, automotive industry analysis, and Henrik dashboard illustration are composite examples based on the author's professional experience implementing hybrid AI-human intelligence systems.

Specific metrics and outcomes have been adjusted to protect client confidentiality while preserving the operational principles demonstrated.

CHAPTER 8

BUILDING REPUTATION INTELLIGENCE CULTURE

From Measurement to Action: Creating an Intelligence-Driven Organization

You have the methodology. You have the technology. You have the data.

Six months later, nothing has changed.

The dashboards update weekly, but no one looks at them. The SIGNAL framework sits documented in a shared drive. Persona Canvases were completed during the workshop, then forgotten. Executives still make decisions based on gut feel, competitive pressure, or whoever argues loudest in the room.

This isn't a methodology problem. It's a culture problem.

And here's what I've learned across dozens of implementations: Technology is 20% of the challenge. Culture is 80%.

The best framework in the world fails if executives don't trust the intelligence team; if short-term pressures override strategic measurement; if insights are tolerated rather than valued; and if success isn't celebrated while failures are punished.

Stanford professors Jeffrey Pfeffer and Robert Sutton documented this phenomenon in their seminal research on the "knowing-doing gap"—the challenge of turning knowledge about how to improve performance into actions that produce measurable results. Their work found that organizations consistently struggle to implement what they already know, not because the knowledge is lacking, but because cultural and organizational barriers prevent action.

The same dynamic plagues reputation intelligence. Organizations know they should be more data-driven. They know early warning matters. They know proactive beats reactive. Yet they continue operating the way they always have—until a crisis forces expensive intervention.

This chapter addresses the cultural foundation that makes reputation intelligence sustainable.

Because methodology without culture is theory. Culture with methodology is transformation.

The Knowing-Doing Gap in Reputation Intelligence

Let me show you what the knowing-doing gap looks like in practice.

At Company A in the technology sector, brand tracking showed Trust declining for six consecutive months. Quarterly reports documented the trend with clear visualizations. The executive team received updates and discussed "interesting findings." Action taken: none—until a regulatory investigation forced a reactive response. The cost: significant market cap decline, a 9-month recovery, and executive turnover.

At Company B in financial services, competitive intelligence showed the Innovation narrative gap widening. Analyst reports flagged positioning risk before a major product evaluation. The product team was aware of the data, and the marketing team had seen the coverage analysis. Action taken: delayed—"need more research before committing resources." The cost: a competitor captured the "category leader" narrative, creating an 18-month gap to close.

At Company C, a consumer brand, employee sentiment data predicted Glassdoor decline with 8-week accuracy. The HR dashboard showed the correlation clearly. The recruiting team saw the warning signals. Action taken: discussed in meetings, no budget allocated. The cost: 200+ lost candidates, significant recruiting inefficiency, and employer brand damage.

The pattern is disturbingly consistent: Intelligence → Awareness → Discussion → No Action → Crisis → Expensive Reaction.

The problem isn't lack of information. It's lack of behavioral change.

According to McKinsey research, only 20 percent of organizations excel at decision making, and a majority say much of the time they devote to decision making is used ineffectively. The same research found that just 37 percent of respondents say their organizations' decisions are both high in quality and velocity.

Brand intelligence exists in this same gap. The data is available. The insights are generated. But the connection between intelligence and action remains broken.

KEY CONCEPT

TECHNOLOGY IS 20%. CULTURE IS 80%.

The best framework in the world fails if executives don't trust the intelligence team; if short-term pressures override strategic measurement; if insights are tolerated rather than valued; and if success isn't celebrated while failures are punished.

Methodology without culture is theory. Culture with methodology is transformation.

Why Organizations Stay Stuck

Before we can build an intelligence-driven culture, we need to understand why organizations resist change—even when they have the data telling them change is necessary.

Barrier 1: The Comfort of Retrospective Measurement. Most organizations treat brand measurement as an afterthought. They run a campaign, then pull a report. A product launch wraps, and someone generates a dashboard. Quarterly earnings happen, and the communications team checks sentiment.

Measurement as output = rearview mirror.

This feels safe because retrospective measurement can't be wrong in real-time. No one gets criticized for reporting what happened. The data arrives after decisions are made, so it can't challenge anyone's judgment in the moment.

But this safety is an illusion. By the time you know what happened, it's too late to change outcomes.

Barrier 2: Fear of Being Wrong. Predictive intelligence is uncomfortable because it can be verified. If you say "Trust is eroding and we'll see analyst skepticism in six weeks," you've made a falsifiable claim. If you're wrong, everyone knows.

Pfeffer and Sutton's research found that fear is one of the primary drivers of the knowing-doing gap. Organizations create cultures where it's safer to do nothing than to act on imperfect information—even when inaction is demonstrably more costly than occasional mistakes.

Brand intelligence requires a culture that rewards intelligent risk-taking and treats prediction errors as learning opportunities, not career-limiting moves.

Barrier 3: Siloed Ownership. In most organizations, "brand" lives in marketing or communications. "Reputation" might sit with corporate affairs. "Employee sentiment" belongs to HR. "Customer perception" is owned by insights or CX teams.

No one owns the integrated view. No one connects the signals across silos. And no one has the authority to act on cross-functional intelligence.

McKinsey's State of Organizations research found that two-thirds of leaders see their organizations as "overly complex and inefficient." This complexity creates barriers to integrated intelligence—each function measures what it owns but no one measures what matters to the enterprise.

Barrier 4: The "Smart Talk" Trap. Pfeffer and Sutton identified what they call the "smart talk trap"—organizations that substitute analysis, meetings, and presentations for action. They found that executives often use plans as substitutes for deeds rather than inspirations for action.

In reputation intelligence, this manifests as endless refinement of dashboards, perpetual debates about methodology, and constant requests for "more data before we can decide." The conversation becomes the work, rather than the precursor to work.

The Shift: From Output to Input

The transformation begins with a fundamental reframe: measurement as input, not output.

Instead of asking "What happened last quarter?" intelligence-driven organizations ask: "What signals do we need to watch this week?" "Which narratives are shifting right now?" "What should we do before the pattern hardens?"

This shift changes everything about how intelligence functions within the organization.

Let me show you how this works in practice through Sophia's story—the measurement analyst we met in Chapter 7. When Sophia delivered her first SIGNAL to Henrik (the Innovation Momentum detection that led to the accelerated campaign), it wasn't just a proof point for the methodology. It was the beginning of a cultural transformation.

Building Intelligence Culture: Sophia's Organization as Case Study

That first SIGNAL—Innovation Momentum detected in tech media coverage, with a recommendation to accelerate the digital payments campaign ahead of the Gartner evaluation window—worked. The campaign launched. The "Leader" positioning was achieved. The outcome was documented: significant estimated value from improved market positioning.

But here's what happened next—and it's more important than any single win.

Month 3: The First Cultural Shift

After the Innovation Momentum success, Sophia's CEO started asking a different question in executive meetings. Instead of "How did our coverage look last month?" she began asking "What signals should we be watching?"

This seems like a small change. It was actually everything.

The question shift moved reputation intelligence from retrospective reporting to forward-looking input. The Intelligence team wasn't being asked to justify what happened—they were being asked to inform what should happen next.

Month 4: The Operating Cadence Emerges

Sophia formalized what had been ad hoc into a consistent operating rhythm.

Weekly (Every Monday). The executive team receives a one-page "Brand Pulse" showing Four Signals movement (Trust, Innovation, Perception, Reputation); week-over-week velocity (not just levels—direction and speed); competitive gaps versus two key competitors; and flags for thresholds breached or patterns detected. The CEO reviews this during her Monday executive team meeting. Five minutes, not 50. No one asks "why are we looking at this?" anymore. They ask "what should we do about it?"

As-Needed (When Thresholds Trigger). Full SIGNALs are delivered only when patterns warrant attention. Not weekly reports regardless of relevance—targeted intelligence when action is needed. Each SIGNAL follows the framework from Chapter 6: Signal → Implication → Gap → Narrative → Action → Lift.

Monthly (First Tuesday). The team conducts deeper competitive analysis with trend views. The product team uses the Innovation signal in roadmap prioritization. The marketing team reviews narrative territory ownership.

Quarterly (Before Board Meetings). A full reputation intelligence briefing prepares leadership for board discussions. Jennifer (CFO) presents reputation intelligence ROI alongside financial metrics. Proof chains are documented: Signal → Action → Outcome → Value.

Month 6: The Behavioral Change

Six months in, Sophia noticed something remarkable: Decisions were changing without her team having to push.

The CPO started checking Innovation signals before finalizing product launch timing—not because Sophia asked, but because it had proven valuable.

The CHRO began correlating internal culture initiatives with Workplace signal trends—tracking whether employee programs were translating into external perception improvement.

Marketing shifted campaign timing based on competitive narrative gaps—launching when competitors were quiet rather than following the traditional calendar.

This is what culture change looks like. Not mandated compliance, but voluntary adoption because the value is undeniable.

The Five Principles of Intelligence-Driven Culture

Based on Sophia's experience and implementations across multiple organizations, five principles consistently separate success from failure.

Principle 1: Executive Sponsorship Is Non-Negotiable

You cannot build reputation intelligence culture from middle management. It requires C-suite championship.

Why? Because reputation intelligence challenges existing power structures. Communications, marketing, product—all have established ways of working and territorial ownership. Cross-functional intelligence threatens comfortable silos.

More practically: Senior executives won't take briefings from junior staff. The CFO responds to peer-level insights, not analyst presentations. The CEO needs intelligence positioned as strategic input, not departmental reporting.

Sophia's breakthrough came when Jennifer (CFO) became a champion. Her credibility—built on the Trust Erosion SIGNAL that protected significant market value—opened doors that Sophia's team couldn't have opened alone.

How to secure executive sponsorship. Start with a one-on-one conversation: "You make critical decisions about [investor confidence / competitive positioning / talent strategy] with incomplete information. What if we could detect [relevant risk] six weeks before it becomes visible?" Then propose a limited pilot: "Three months, focused on one signal type you care about. If no value, we stop. If value delivered, we discuss expansion." Finally, deliver undeniable proof—the first SIGNAL must prevent a crisis, capture an opportunity, or improve a decision in ways the sponsor cares about.

Principle 2: Start Small, Prove Value, Scale

The instinct is to build comprehensive capability—all personas, all signals, all markets. Resist it.

Comprehensive implementations overwhelm teams, dilute quality, and delay proof points. By the time you've built everything, executive patience has expired.

Instead: Pick one persona. Deliver one major SIGNAL. Document one proof chain. Use that success to justify expansion.

Sophia started with Henrik—Innovation signals focused on his digital transformation priority. That first proof point gave her credibility. Then Jennifer (CFO) became a champion through the Trust Erosion SIGNAL. David, the Chief Product Officer, and Lisa, the Chief Human Resources Officer, became Sophia's next sponsors. Full C-suite coverage came at month 12—after nine months of demonstrated value.

Principle 3: Quick Wins Are Required, Not Optional

You must deliver significant value within 90 days. Not "interesting insights." Not "useful context." Significant value: prevented a crisis, captured an opportunity, or improved a major decision.

Why 90 days? Because executive attention spans are short. Because competing priorities emerge. Because skeptics will use any delay to argue for cancellation.

McKinsey research on transformation initiatives found that 70 percent fail—often because organizations spend too long building infrastructure before proving worth. The successful 30 percent secure early wins that justify continued investment.

Sophia's 90-day proof: Trust Erosion SIGNAL delivered month two, action approved month three, value realized month six. By the time skeptics could organize opposition, the results were undeniable.

Principle 4: Measure What You Want to Change

What gets measured gets attention. What gets attention gets action.

But here's the trap: Measuring activity (reports delivered, dashboards updated, meetings held) doesn't drive outcome change. You need to measure outcomes.

The intelligence team tracks SIGNALs delivered (with date, persona, and topic); actions taken (budget approved, timing changed, campaign launched); outcomes achieved (crisis prevented, opportunity captured, positioning improved); and value documented (ROI calculated, proof chain complete).

This creates accountability and demonstrates worth. When Sophia reports "significant documented value from 14 SIGNALs over 12 months," no one questions the investment.

Principle 5: Celebrate Wins Publicly

Success breeds success. When intelligence delivers value, make it visible.

This matters for several reasons. It creates organizational permission—when the CFO presents reputation intelligence ROI to the board, the entire organization gets the message. It provides budget justification—public wins create evidence for investment requests. It enables talent attraction—high performers want to work on high-impact initiatives. And it drives cultural shift—intelligence moves from "experiment" to "how we work."

Sophia's turning point: Jennifer presented the Trust Erosion case study to the board in Q2. The CEO mentioned reputation intelligence ROI in the company all-hands. By Q3, internal requests for intelligence support exceeded the intelligence team's capacity—a good problem to have.

PRO TIP

> **THE FIVE PRINCIPLES OF INTELLIGENCE CULTURE**
>
> 1. Executive sponsorship is non-negotiable. You can't build from middle management. 2. Start small, prove value, scale. Comprehensive implementations fail from being overwhelmed. 3. Quick wins are required—deliver significant value within 90 days. 4. Measure outcomes, not activity. Track decisions influenced, not reports produced. 5. Celebrate wins publicly. Success breeds organizational permission.

The Operating Cadence: Making Intelligence Habitual

Culture change requires routine. Not occasional heroics, but consistent habits that embed intelligence into organizational rhythm.

Here's what a mature operating cadence looks like—the system Sophia built over twelve months:

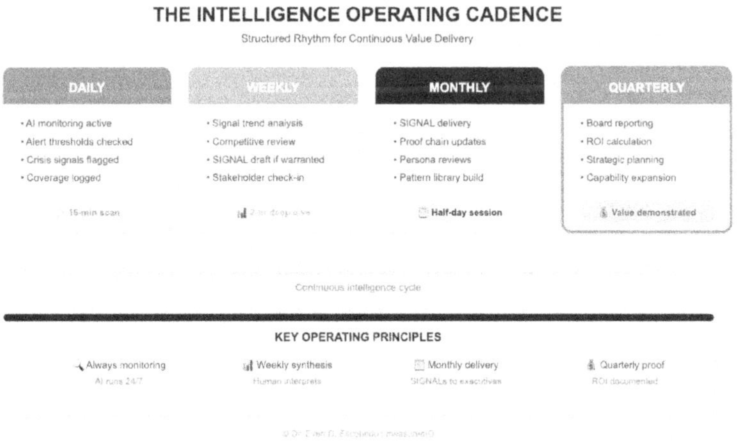

Figure 8.1: The Intelligence Operating Cadence—Structured Rhythm for Continuous Value Delivery

Weekly Rituals

Monday 8 AM: Brand Pulse distributed to executive team. This is a one-page, five-minute read covering Four Signals plus velocity, top three movements flagged by threshold, and a week-ahead preview.

Tuesday 2 PM: Product team reviews Innovation signal in roadmap meeting. The CPO checks competitive Innovation positioning, and feature timing decisions are informed by media momentum.

Friday 10 AM: Intelligence team reviews incoming data for pattern detection. This includes threshold monitoring, emerging narrative identification, and flagging SIGNAL candidates for development.

Monthly Rituals

First Tuesday: Full Competitive Analysis. This involves driver-by-driver comparison with key competitors, identifying territory gaps, and flagging strategic opportunities.

Last Friday: Outcome Brief (if actions were taken previous month). This documents outcomes from SIGNAL-driven decisions, validates ROI, and captures learning.

Quarterly Rituals

Week before quarter end: 90-Day Dashboard update. All active SIGNALs are reviewed, predictions versus actuals are validated, and trend analysis is conducted across quarters.

Board meeting prep: Executive briefing package. This includes a reputation intelligence summary, competitive positioning analysis, and investment recommendations for next quarter.

Annual Rituals

December: Full-year intelligence audit. Total value is documented, methodology refinements are identified, and next-year priorities are established.

This cadence transforms intelligence from event (big quarterly presentation) to habit (integrated into how decisions get made).

QUICK CHECK

> ### THE OPERATING CADENCE
>
> Weekly: Brand Pulse to executive team (one page, five minutes). As-Needed: Full SIGNALs when thresholds trigger. Monthly: Competitive deep-dive and outcome briefs. Quarterly: Board preparation and 90-day review. Annually: Full intelligence audit and methodology refinement. Culture change requires routine. Not occasional heroics—consistent habits.

The Five-Stage Action System

Detecting signals isn't enough. Organizations need a systematic process for moving from detection to action to outcome.

Stage 1: Signal Detection. This is where AI earns its value. Automated monitoring processes thousands of mentions, identifying patterns that human analysts couldn't see at scale. Detection includes threshold alerts when signals breach defined levels; pattern matching against historical precedents; competitive movement tracking; and velocity monitoring (rate of change, not just current level). Sophia's system monitors approximately 15,000 relevant mentions monthly across her markets. AI flags roughly 10 percent for human attention. The rest is processed, scored, and tracked—but does not require manual review.

Stage 2: Human Interpretation. This is where AI reaches its limits and human judgment becomes essential (as we covered in Chapter 7). Analysts assess flagged signals by asking: Is this pattern real or noise? What's the strategic significance? Which persona needs to know? What precedent does this match? What action would make sense? The transformation: "Trust declined 7 points" (observation) becomes "Trust pattern matches pre-downgrade cases with 30 percent probability of analyst action in 6 weeks, recommend governance transparency program, expected substantial protection, strong ROI potential" (actionable intelligence).

Stage 3: Stakeholder Delivery. Right intelligence, right person, right time. The SIGNAL framework (Chapter 6) structures delivery for executive consumption: Signal (what changed, specific and quantified); Implication (business stakes if unaddressed); Gap (what's missing or vulnerable); Narrative (the pattern or story emerging); Action (specific recommendation with owner and timeline); and Lift (expected outcome and value). Sophia routes SIGNALs to specific personas based on topic: Trust to Jennifer (CFO), Innovation to David (CPO), Workplace to Lisa (CHRO).

Stage 4: Action Execution. The SIGNAL includes a recommended action with clear accountability: what specifically to do, who owns the action, when it should happen, what resources are required, and what outcome is expected. Sophia's team doesn't own execution—they enable it. The action owner (usually in communications, marketing, or product) implements. The intelligence team tracks.

Stage 5: Outcome Validation. Did the prediction come true? Did the action work? What did we learn? This stage closes the loop and builds credibility by comparing predicted outcome to actual outcome; documenting value created or protected; capturing methodology refinements; and updating the precedent database for future pattern matching. Sophia's Year 1 validation: 14 SIGNALs delivered, 11 resulted in action, 9 achieved predicted outcomes, total documented value: substantial.

When Intelligence Drives Decisions: Three Stories

Let me show you what happens when this system works.

Story 1: The Campaign That Almost Launched Too Late

Henrik's marketing team had scheduled a major digital payments campaign for Q4—following the traditional annual planning cycle. The creative was approved, media was booked, budget was allocated.

In early Q3, Henrik's Innovation signal detected unusual movement. Tech media coverage of real-time payments was accelerating. Two competitors had announced platform updates. Industry analysts were researching category assessments.

The SIGNAL: Innovation window closing. Gartner evaluation likely in 8-10 weeks. Q4 campaign timing would miss the window.

Traditional response: "The plan is set. We can't change now."

Intelligence-driven response: Marketing reviewed the signal, assessed the risk, and made a call. Campaign accelerated to late Q3. Some media efficiency lost, but timing aligned with analyst evaluation window.

Outcome: Company included in Gartner assessment with "Leader" consideration. Competitors who launched Q4 were evaluated in following year's cycle. Eighteen-month positioning advantage captured.

Value: Not easily quantified, but sales team reported analyst validation as key factor in three enterprise deals worth $40M+ in aggregate.

Story 2: The Crisis That Never Happened

Jennifer (CFO) received a Trust Erosion SIGNAL in February. Governance coverage had turned skeptical in financial media. Pattern matched three historical cases where similar coverage preceded analyst downgrades.

The signal wasn't alarming in isolation—Trust had declined 7 points. But velocity was concerning (600 percent week-over-week increase in governance-focused coverage) and source concentration was high (tier-1 financial media, not general news).

Traditional response: "Trust is still in acceptable range. Monitor and report next month."

Intelligence-driven response: Jennifer approved a proactive governance transparency program. Enhanced disclosures, analyst briefings, regulatory engagement—all before any formal inquiry.

Outcome: No analyst downgrades. Coverage tone stabilized within six weeks. Trust signal recovered to baseline by month three.

Value: Based on comparable cases, estimated substantial market cap protection. Strong positive ROI on the transparency investment.

Story 3: The Talent War Won Before It Started

Lisa (CHRO) received a Workplace Erosion SIGNAL in September. Internal culture metrics were strong, but external perception—tracked through media coverage of workplace topics and industry talent coverage—showed competitors gaining narrative advantage.

Two fintech competitors were dominating "employer of choice" coverage. Tech talent media increasingly positioned Henrik's company as "traditional financial services" rather than "innovative fintech."

The signal: Talent perception gap widening. If unaddressed, recruiting efficiency would decline in Q1, when competition for engineering talent peaks.

Traditional response: "Our Glassdoor scores are fine. HR will keep doing what we're doing."

Intelligence-driven response: Lisa launched an accelerated employer brand campaign in October—engineering blog posts, tech conference presence, developer community engagement. All positioned ahead of Q1 recruiting season.

Outcome: Application rates for engineering roles increased 34 percent year-over-year in Q1. Offer acceptance rate improved from 62 percent to 78 percent. Cost-per-hire decreased despite tight talent market.

Value: Estimated $3M in recruiting efficiency improvement. More importantly: the talent pipeline remained healthy while competitors struggled.

Overcoming Resistance: The Skeptic's Playbook

Every organization has skeptics. Here's how Sophia handled the most common objections.

"We don't have time for another report." Response: "You're right—you don't. That's why we're not sending reports. We're sending alerts only when action is needed. Most weeks, you won't hear from us. When you do, it matters." The key insight: Intelligence culture isn't about adding work. It's about filtering noise so executives see only what requires attention.

"Our existing measurement works fine." Response: "It works for understanding what happened. It doesn't work for understanding what will happen. Keep what you have. Add this one capability—early warning. If it doesn't prove valuable in 90 days, we stop." The key insight: Never attack existing systems. Position intelligence as complementary, not competitive.

"How do we know your predictions are reliable?" Response: "You won't—until we prove it. Let's track predictions explicitly. I'll tell you what I think will happen, document it, and we'll see if I'm right. If I'm consistently wrong, we'll stop. If I'm consistently right, you'll have a valuable capability." The key insight: Embrace accountability. Predictions that can't be verified aren't predictions—they're opinions.

"This seems expensive for uncertain value." Response: "What's the cost of being surprised? Calculate the last crisis that caught you off guard—the recovery cost, the management time, the opportunity cost. Now ask: What would early warning have been worth?" The key insight: Reframe from cost of intelligence to cost of ignorance.

"Our industry is different." Response: "Every industry has stakeholders who form perceptions, competitors who shape narratives, and signals that precede outcomes. The specific signals differ. The principle doesn't." The key insight: Acknowledge industry context while maintaining methodology confidence.

The Integration Challenge: Connecting Intelligence to Decision Systems

Culture change requires more than good intentions. It requires structural integration—embedding intelligence into the systems where decisions actually get made.

Integration Point 1: Executive Meeting Agendas. If intelligence isn't on the agenda, it won't be discussed. Sophia worked with the CEO's chief of staff to add "Reputation Intelligence" as a standing item in the Monday executive meeting—five minutes, every week. Not a presentation. Not a deep dive. Just: "Here's what's moving. Here's what we're watching. Any questions?" The standing agenda item creates accountability. If there's nothing to report, you have to say "nothing to report." That's uncomfortable enough to motivate consistent monitoring.

Integration Point 2: Budget Allocation Processes. Annual planning typically allocates budget based on historical spending and incremental adjustments. Intelligence rarely influences these decisions because it's not part of the process. Sophia inserted intelligence into budget conversations by providing "signal-informed investment recommendations" before each planning cycle. Not replacing financial analysis—augmenting it with reputation context. For example: "Based on current Innovation signal trajectory and competitive positioning, we recommend increasing digital thought leadership budget by 40% and reducing traditional advertising by 20%. Here's the signal data supporting this shift."

Integration Point 3: Crisis Protocols. Every organization has crisis response procedures. Few include intelligence triggers for proactive intervention. Sophia added signal thresholds to the crisis protocol: "When Trust signal declines more than 15% in 30 days AND source concentration exceeds 60% in tier-1 financial media, escalate to CFO within 24 hours regardless of other workload." This transforms crisis response from reactive to proactive. The crisis protocol activates before crisis hits.

Integration Point 4: Performance Reviews. What gets evaluated gets prioritized. Sophia worked with HR to add "evidence-based decision making" as a competency in leadership performance reviews. Not a major weighting—just present. Enough that leaders know their use of intelligence is being observed.

Integration Point 5: New Executive Onboarding. When new executives join, they learn "how we do things here." If intelligence isn't part of onboarding, newcomers won't adopt it. Sophia developed a 30-minute intelligence briefing for new executives: Here's what we monitor, here's how we deliver insights, here's what we expect from you. The briefing ends with: "You'll receive your first Brand Pulse Monday. Your analyst is [name]. They'll reach out to understand your priorities."

COMMON MISTAKE

> ### HANDLING SKEPTICS
>
> "We don't have time for another report." → "That's why we send alerts only when action is needed." "Our existing measurement works fine." → "Keep what you have. Add early warning capability. If no value in 90 days, we stop." "How do we know your predictions are reliable?" → "Let's track them explicitly. If I'm consistently wrong, we'll stop." The antidote to skepticism is demonstrated value.

The One-Year Transformation: What Changes

Let me paint a picture of what organizational change looks like after 12 months of sustained intelligence culture building.

Before (Month 0)

Executive team meeting, Monday. The CFO says: "I saw something in the Journal about our competitor's regulatory issues. Should we be worried about ours?" The CEO responds: "I don't know. Someone check on that." Communications takes a note, unclear what action to take. Meeting moves on.

After (Month 12)

Executive team meeting, Monday. The CEO opens: "I see Trust signal is down 4 points this week. Jennifer, is this the governance coverage Sophia flagged?" The CFO responds: "Yes. Pattern match is 67% to the 2023 situation. Sophia's recommendation is enhanced disclosure in next quarterly report. I've approved the approach." The CEO acknowledges: "Good. David, any Innovation signals we need to discuss?" The CPO reports: "Clean week. Holding 'Leader' position, no competitor movement detected." The CEO concludes: "Alright, let's move to operations."

The difference: Executives speak the language of signals. Intelligence is referenced naturally, not as a separate topic. Action is already in progress before the meeting. Discussion is strategic, not reactive. Meeting is efficient because preparation happened.

This is what cultural transformation looks like. Not dramatic announcements or organizational restructuring. Quiet, systematic change in how conversations happen and decisions get made.

Key Takeaways

The Culture Challenge. Technology is 20% of success; culture is 80%. The knowing-doing gap—organizations know what to do but fail to act—is the primary barrier. Fear, silos, retrospective measurement, and "smart talk" prevent intelligence from driving action.

The Five Principles. First, executive sponsorship is non-negotiable—you can't build culture from middle management. Second, start small, prove value, scale—comprehensive implementations fail from being overwhelmed. Third, quick wins are required—90-day proof points maintain momentum and credibility. Fourth, measure outcomes, not activity—track SIGNALs delivered, actions taken, value created. Fifth, celebrate wins publicly—success breeds organizational permission and investment.

The Operating Cadence. Weekly Brand Pulse to executive team. As-needed SIGNALs when thresholds trigger. Monthly competitive deep-dives. Quarterly board preparation and annual audit.

The Five-Stage Action System. Stage 1 is Signal Detection (AI-enabled monitoring). Stage 2 is Human Interpretation (analyst judgment). Stage 3 is Stakeholder Delivery (persona-specific SIGNALs). Stage 4 is Action Execution (clear accountability). Stage 5 is Outcome Validation (proof chain documentation).

A Personal Reflection: Why Culture Matters Most

I've spent years building measurement systems and developing methodologies. I've created frameworks, designed dashboards, and written reports that—I thought—were brilliant examples of intelligence work.

Most of them failed to change anything.

The frameworks gathered dust. The dashboards went unvisited. The reports were filed and forgotten. Not because they were wrong, but because the culture wasn't ready for them.

It took me longer than I'd like to admit to learn the lesson: The best intelligence in the world is worthless if no one acts on it.

My experience at Western Union taught me this viscerally. We had sophisticated measurement. We had talented analysts. We had executive interest. But the connection between intelligence and action remained fragile—dependent on individual relationships and ad hoc advocacy rather than systematic integration.

The methodology I've shared in this book—MRS, PBI, SIGNAL, the hybrid AI+Human approach—is essential. But it's not sufficient. The cultural foundation determines whether methodology translates to impact.

When I work with organizations now, I spend as much time on culture as on methodology. Who are the potential champions? What are the organizational barriers? Where does intelligence naturally fit in decision processes? How can we create quick wins that build credibility?

These questions matter more than the technical details of scoring algorithms or dashboard design.

Sophia's story isn't just an illustration of methodology. It's a demonstration of what becomes possible when culture and methodology align. The substantial documented value didn't come from better data or smarter algorithms. It came from systematic integration of intelligence into how decisions get made.

That integration is the hard part. It's also the part that matters most.

Becoming Strategic

Building reputation intelligence culture is challenging work. It requires patience, persistence, and political skill. It means navigating skeptics, overcoming inertia, and proving value repeatedly before trust is earned.

I want to acknowledge something directly: for some of you, the culture you're trying to build intelligence within is the same culture that has been actively working against you. Maybe measurement has been treated as a back-office function for so long that the people around you have genuinely stopped seeing its potential. Maybe you've had a leader who, for whatever reason, simply wasn't going to give your team a fair hearing, no matter how good the work was. If that's your situation, the challenge isn't just building the right methodology. It's surviving long enough, and staying visible enough, to find your Henrik.

That's a harder path. But it's a real one. The practitioners I've seen navigate it successfully share one characteristic: they stopped waiting for permission and started building proof. They found one executive — not necessarily the most powerful one, just the most curious — and they delivered something undeniable. One insight. One early warning that turned out to be right. One brief that made a leader's meeting go better than it would have otherwise. Culture doesn't change because you built a perfect measurement system. It changes because the right person saw something they couldn't explain without you.

But it's also some of the most rewarding work a communications professional can do. When intelligence actually drives decisions—when you see executives making better choices because of insights your team provided—the impact is tangible and lasting.

You're not just measuring anymore. You're shaping.

The methodology is here. The framework is proven. The case studies demonstrate what's possible.

The question is: Are you ready to build the culture that makes it real?

Bridge to Chapter 9

You understand the mandate. You see the strategic case.

Now comes the practical question: How do you actually build it?

Chapter 9 provides the implementation playbook—the phase-by-phase roadmap for building reputation intelligence capability from zero to enterprise function.

From mandate to method.

Let's build.

References

Pfeffer, J., & Sutton, R. I. (2000). The Knowing-Doing Gap: How Smart Companies Turn Knowledge into Action. Harvard Business School Press.

McKinsey & Company. (2019). "Decision making in the age of urgency." McKinsey Global Survey.

McKinsey & Company. (2023). "The State of Organizations 2023: Ten shifts transforming organizations."

Harvard Business Review. (2020). "10 Steps to Creating a Data-Driven Culture."

Harvard Business Review. (2023). "What Does It Actually Take to Build a Data-Driven Culture?"

McKinsey & Company. (2018). "Why data culture matters." McKinsey Analytics.

Kahneman, D., & Tversky, A. (1979). "Prospect Theory: An Analysis of Decision under Risk." *Econometrica*, 47(2), 263-291.

Bain & Company. (2023). "RAPID Decision Making Framework."

Note on Sources

The Sophia case study, including the organizational transformation timeline, operating cadence development, and the three outcome stories (Campaign Timing, Crisis Prevention, Talent War), represents a composite illustration based on the author's professional experience implementing reputation intelligence systems across multiple organizations. Company A, B, and C examples in the knowing-doing gap section are similarly anonymized composites. Specific metrics, timelines, and financial outcomes have been adjusted to protect client confidentiality while preserving the operational principles demonstrated.

BUILD YOUR PLAYBOOK

From Vision to Implementation From Inspiration to Action

You've seen the methodology. You understand the mandate. You know what's possible.

Now comes the hardest part: actually building it.

This is where most transformations fail—not from lack of vision, but from lack of execution. Organizations get inspired by case studies, energized by possibilities, then paralyzed by the question: "Where do we even start?"

This chapter is your answer.

It's the implementation roadmap that takes you from zero reputation intelligence capability to enterprise function. Not theory. Not aspiration. Practical guidance you can act on.

We'll cover the phases of implementation, the principles that separate success from failure, the decisions you'll need to make, and the pitfalls to avoid.

Think of this as your construction blueprint. The previous chapters explained WHAT to build and WHY it matters. This chapter shows you HOW to build it—the sequence, the priorities, the critical path.

Let's begin.

Why Most Implementations Fail

Before diving into tactics, let's understand why the majority of reputation intelligence initiatives fail within 18 months.

It's rarely the methodology. It's almost always the approach.

Failure Pattern 1: Boiling the Ocean. Organizations try to implement everything at once—all personas, all signals, all markets, all use cases. The team gets overwhelmed, quality suffers, and nothing ships well. The alternative: Start small, prove value, scale. Pick one executive stakeholder. Deliver one significant proof point. Use that success to justify expansion.

Failure Pattern 2: Perfection Over Progress. Teams spend months building the "perfect" methodology before delivering anything. They wait for ideal technology, complete staffing, and flawless processes. By the time they're ready to launch, executive attention has moved elsewhere. The alternative: Ship fast, learn, improve. Launch a 90-day pilot with "good enough" capability. Deliver intelligence even if imperfect. Refine based on feedback and outcomes.

Failure Pattern 3: Technology-First Thinking. Organizations buy expensive platforms before understanding stakeholder needs. They implement dashboards nobody asked for and build infrastructure without proving business value. The alternative: Stakeholder-first approach. Interview executives to understand their decisions and information gaps. Design intelligence to serve those specific needs. Choose technology that enables the intelligence, not vice versa.

Failure Pattern 4: Analyst-Driven Priorities. The intelligence team decides what's important and delivers insights analysts find interesting—but not what executives actually need. There's no connection to business priorities or decision calendars. The alternative: Executive-driven, analyst-enabled. Executives define priorities. Analysts translate those priorities into signals and deliverables. Intelligence is timed to decision moments.

Failure Pattern 5: No Quick Wins. Implementation takes 12 months before delivering first value. By month six, executives have forgotten why they approved the pilot. The initiative gets cancelled before proving worth. The alternative: 90-day quick win required. You must deliver significant value within the first quarter—a prevented crisis, captured opportunity, or improved major decision. This proof point justifies continued investment.

COMMON MISTAKE

WHY IMPLEMENTATIONS FAIL

1. Boiling the ocean: Trying everything at once. 2. Perfection over progress: Waiting to launch until "ready." 3. Technology-first thinking: Buying tools before understanding needs. 4. Analyst-driven priorities: Delivering what analysts find interesting, not what executives need. 5. No quick wins: Taking 12 months before delivering first value.

The majority of reputation intelligence initiatives fail within 18 months. It's rarely the methodology—it's almost always the approach.

Building on the Five Principles

The Five Principles from Chapter 8—executive sponsorship, starting small, quick wins, measuring outcomes, and celebrating publicly—remain your cultural foundation. This chapter translates those principles into a concrete implementation sequence.

But implementation adds tactical considerations: Who specifically should you target first? What technology do you actually need? How do you structure the executive conversation? What does week-by-week progress look like?

Let's walk through the phases.

The Implementation Phases

Building reputation intelligence capability follows a predictable progression. Here's how to think about the journey.

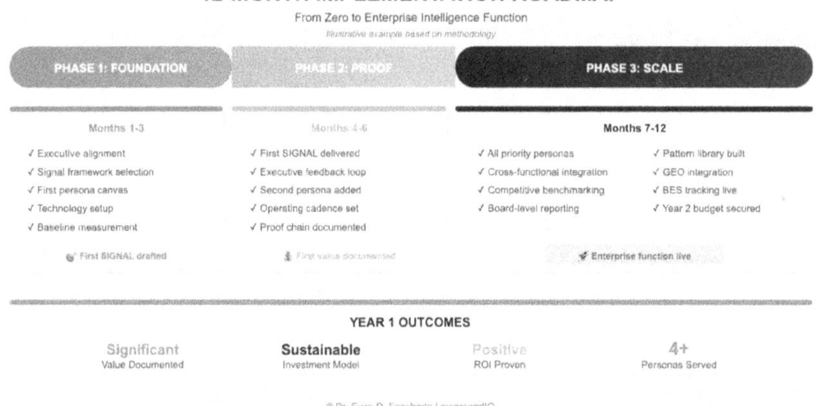

Figure 9.1: 12-Month Implementation Roadmap—From Zero to Enterprise Intelligence Function

Phase 1: Foundation (Months 1-3)

The single most important milestone in Phase 1 is completing your Persona-Based Insights work. Before you build dashboards, before you calculate scores, before you create your first SIGNAL brief—you need to know whom you're serving and what they care about.

Find your Henrik, as Sophia did. Schedule the conversations. Document the priorities. Build the Media Weighting Matrix. This isn't preliminary work you can skip. This is the foundation that determines whether your program succeeds or becomes another ignored reporting function.

Success criteria for this phase are an executive sponsor confirmed and engaged; a first SIGNAL delivered that drives action; value documentation begun; and a go/no-go decision made for Phase 2.

This phase is about proving the concept works in your specific organizational context. Everything else depends on success here.

What Phase 1 Actually Looks Like

Let me make this concrete. In Sophia's implementation, Phase 1 unfolded like this: In Weeks 1-2, Sophia identified Jennifer (CFO) as her best sponsor candidate based on Jennifer's visibility into investor relations challenges and her frustration with being surprised by analyst sentiment shifts. Henrik's success—the Innovation Momentum SIGNAL that had delivered significant value—gave Sophia credibility, but Jennifer needed her own proof point.

In Weeks 3-4, based on Jennifer's input—she wanted to predict governance concerns before they impacted analyst ratings—Sophia designed a Trust-focused pilot. She configured media monitoring to track governance and regulatory coverage, established baseline metrics, and defined what a "signal" would look like.

In Weeks 5-8, the intelligence team processed incoming coverage, identified patterns in governance mentions, and began building analytical frameworks. No major signal emerged yet, but the foundation was solid.

In Weeks 9-11, a pattern emerged. Governance coverage in tier-1 financial media had increased 600% week-over-week. Tone was increasingly skeptical. The pattern matched three historical cases that preceded analyst downgrades.

In Week 12, Sophia delivered her first SIGNAL to Jennifer: Trust Erosion detected, 30% probability of analyst action within 6 weeks, recommended proactive governance transparency program. Jennifer approved the intervention.

In Weeks 16-20, no analyst downgrades occurred. Trust signal recovered. Value documented: substantial protected market cap based on comparable case analysis.

That's Phase 1 success: a single proof point that converts skepticism into championship.

Phase 2: Proof of Concept (Months 4-6)

With initial proof established, you expand carefully while deepening capability.

Key activities include adding a second persona; establishing the operating cadence (weekly pulse, as-needed SIGNALs); refining methodology based on feedback; formalizing ROI documentation; and building team capability.

Success criteria for this phase are two personas receiving regular intelligence; multiple SIGNALs delivered with documented outcomes; a clear ROI case for enterprise expansion; and sponsor advocacy to broader leadership.

What Phase 2 Actually Looks Like

Sophia's Phase 2 expansion unfolded over three months.

In Month 4, based on Jennifer's advocacy, David (CPO) agreed to receive Innovation signals. Sophia's team expanded monitoring to include competitive product coverage, analyst report tracking, and technology media.

In Month 5, the operating cadence was formalized—weekly Brand Pulse to both executives, full SIGNALs when thresholds triggered. Sophia refined the SIGNAL format from 3,000 words (too long) to 1,200 words (executive-appropriate).

In Month 6, the second major SIGNAL was delivered: Innovation Momentum detected, 6-week window before Gartner evaluation, recommended accelerated campaign. David approved. Outcome: "Leader" positioning achieved. Estimated value: Significant.

By end of Phase 2, Sophia had two executive champions, documented value exceeding $200M, and a clear case for enterprise expansion.

Phase 3: Enterprise Expansion (Months 7-12)

With proven value and executive advocacy, you scale to full organizational capability.

Key activities include achieving full C-suite coverage; integrating with decision processes (planning cycles, board prep); formalizing the team (dedicated resources, clear charter); embedding intelligence culturally so it becomes "how we work;" and developing advanced capabilities (BES integration, GEO monitoring).

Success criteria for this phase are an enterprise function established; documented value that justifies ongoing investment; organizational recognition as strategic capability; and foundation laid for Year 2 evolution.

What Phase 3 Actually Looks Like

Sophia's enterprise expansion proceeded systematically.

In Month 7, Lisa (CHRO) was added as third persona. Workplace signals were integrated—employee sentiment correlation with external perception, employer brand tracking, and talent market positioning.

In Months 8-9, intelligence was integrated into the quarterly planning process. Board preparation now includes a reputation intelligence briefing. Jennifer presented ROI to the board—for the first time, reputation metrics appeared in board materials.

In Months 10-11, the team was formalized with dedicated analyst resources. A charter was established positioning reputation intelligence as an enterprise function, reporting to the Chief Communications Officer with C-suite access.

In Month 12, the full-year audit showed 14 SIGNALs delivered, substantial documented value, and strong positive ROI. Budget was approved for Year 2 expansion including BES integration and GEO monitoring capability.

That's the full arc: from skeptical pilot approval to enterprise strategic function in twelve months.

KEY CONCEPT

THE THREE PHASES

Phase 1 (Months 1-3): Foundation: Complete PBI, configure monitoring, deliver first SIGNAL, document value. Phase 2 (Months 4-6): Proof of Concept: Add second persona, establish operating cadence, formalize ROI documentation. Phase 3 (Months 7-12): Enterprise Expansion: Full C-suite coverage, integrate with decision processes, formalize team and charter.

The single most important milestone in Phase 1: completing your Persona-Based Insights work.

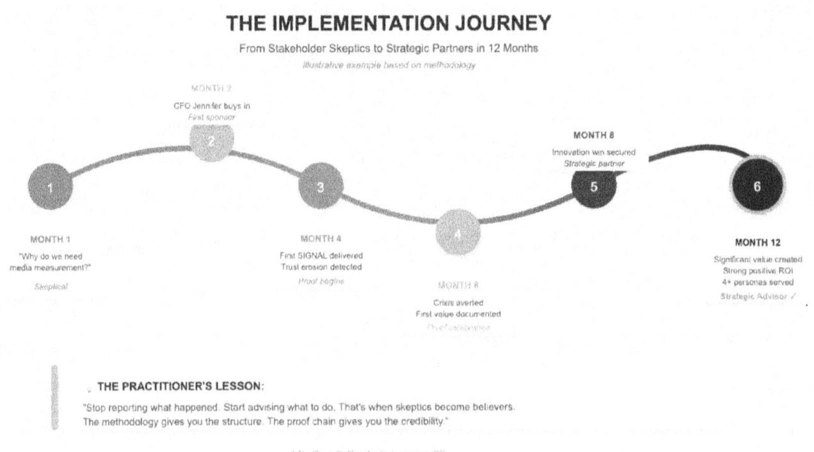

Figure 9.2: The Implementation Journey—From Stakeholder Skeptics to Strategic Partners

Critical Decisions Along the Way

At each phase, you'll face decisions that shape your trajectory. Here's how to think through the most important ones.

Decision 1: Who Should Be Your First Executive Stakeholder?

Consider who has decisions that reputation intelligence can clearly improve; who has budget authority and organizational influence; who is open to new approaches and willing to pilot; and where you can create the most undeniable proof point.

The CFO is often ideal because investor confidence, analyst relations, and trust signals create clear financial value. But context matters—go where you can win.

Decision 2: What Signal Type Should You Lead With?

Match the signal to your stakeholder. For CFO, focus on Trust signals including governance coverage, analyst sentiment, and investor confidence indicators. For CPO, focus on Innovation signals including competitive positioning, product coverage, and category leadership. For CHRO, focus on Workplace signals including employer perception, culture coverage, and talent market positioning.

Start with the signal that most directly serves your sponsor's priorities.

Decision 3: What Technology Do You Actually Need?

For Phase 1, you need less than you think: a media monitoring platform (Meltwater, Cision, or similar); basic analysis and visualization capability; and a delivery mechanism (even email works initially).

Don't over-invest in technology before proving the concept. Sophisticated tools matter more in Phase 3 than Phase 1.

Decision 4: Should You Build Internal Capability or Partner?

Most organizations benefit from a hybrid approach: internal ownership of stakeholder relationships and organizational integration, combined with external expertise for methodology development, advanced analytics, and capability building.

The reputation intelligence methodology is nuanced. Implementation typically benefits from experienced guidance—which is faster and less risky than purely internal development.

Organizations seeking implementation support can explore partnership options through measuredIO and similar specialized firms that bring proven frameworks and implementation experience.

Decision 5: How Do You Handle Organizational Resistance?

Resistance is normal. Common sources include communications teams feeling territorial, marketing concerned about measurement encroachment, skeptics questioning ROI before proof exists, and competing priorities claiming executive attention.

The antidote is demonstrated value. Early wins convert skeptics more effectively than arguments. Focus energy on proving worth rather than debating potential.

The Executive Conversation

Securing executive sponsorship requires a specific kind of conversation. Here's how to structure it.

Before the Meeting

Research your potential sponsor's world. Understand what decisions they make regularly; what information they currently use; what surprises have hurt them (crises they didn't see coming); what opportunities they've missed (moves competitors made first); and what's on their agenda for the next quarter.

This research shapes your pitch. You're not selling a generic capability—you're addressing their specific challenges.

The Meeting Structure (30-45 minutes)

Minutes 0-5: Establish the Problem. "You make critical decisions about [their domain—investor confidence, competitive positioning, talent strategy] with incomplete information. When [specific challenge—analyst sentiment shifts, competitor narrative gains momentum, culture issues surface externally], you often find out too late to respond proactively." Don't lecture. Ask questions that reveal their pain points. Let them articulate the problem.

Minutes 5-15: Show What's Possible. "What if you could see [relevant signal] six weeks before it became visible to everyone else? What would you do differently?" If you have a sample SIGNAL (even using public data), show it. Make the capability concrete, not abstract.

Minutes 15-25: Propose the Pilot. "I'm proposing a 90-day pilot. We'd focus specifically on [signal type relevant to them]. Weekly updates, full analysis when patterns warrant attention. At day 90, we evaluate: Did this help you make better decisions? If yes, we discuss expansion. If no, we stop." The key: Make it low-risk and time-bound. You're not asking for permanent commitment—you're asking for a chance to prove value.

Minutes 25-30: Secure Commitment. "What would need to be true for you to say yes to this pilot?" Listen to their concerns. Address them directly. Ask for conditional commitment: "If we deliver [specific value they care about], will you support expansion?"

After the Meeting

Send a brief follow-up documenting what you discussed, the pilot parameters, and next steps. Make it easy for them to say yes.

PRO TIP

THE EXECUTIVE CONVERSATION

Minutes 0-5: Establish the problem (let them articulate the pain).
Minutes 5-15: Show what's possible (make the capability concrete).
Minutes 15-25: Propose the pilot (low-risk, time-bound, 90 days).
Minutes 25-30: Secure commitment ("What would need to be true for you to say yes?").

You're not asking for permanent commitment. You're asking for a chance to prove value.

The First 90 Days: A Closer Look

The first quarter is make or break. Here's a more detailed view of how to navigate it.

Weeks 1-2: Executive Discovery. Your goal is to understand your potential sponsor's world: What decisions do they make? What information gaps exist? What keeps them up at night? What would early warning look like for their priorities? This isn't a sales pitch—it's genuine discovery. Listen more than you talk. Let their needs shape your pilot design. By end of Week 2: Clear understanding of sponsor priorities and conditional commitment to pilot.

Weeks 3-4: Pilot Design. Based on discovery, design your pilot by determining which signal type you'll focus on, what sources you'll monitor, what format deliverables will take, what success metrics you'll track, and what timeline you'll follow. Keep it simple. You can always add complexity later. The goal is proving value, not building comprehensive capability. By end of Week 4: Pilot plan documented, monitoring initiated, team aligned.

Weeks 5-8: Build and Monitor. Now you're actively building toward your first SIGNAL. Process incoming data, identify patterns and emerging themes, develop analytical frameworks, and build toward a deliverable. You may not have a significant signal emerge in this window—that's okay. Use the time to refine your approach and deepen understanding of the landscape. By end of Week 8: Analysis capability operational, patterns identified, SIGNAL candidate emerging.

Weeks 9-12: Deliver and Document. When a pattern emerges that warrants attention, develop and deliver your first SIGNAL with a clear articulation of what you're seeing, strategic significance for your stakeholder, specific recommendation for action, and expected outcome if recommendation followed. Then track rigorously: Was action taken? What happened? How does the outcome compare to prediction?

By end of Week 12: First SIGNAL delivered, action taken, outcome tracking initiated, value documentation begun.

Measuring Success

How do you know if your implementation is working? Track these indicators.

Leading Indicators (Process Health): Executive Engagement measures whether your sponsor is reading and responding to intelligence. Action Rate measures what percentage of SIGNALs result in organizational action. Feedback Quality measures whether you're getting substantive input that helps you improve. Expansion Interest measures whether other executives are asking for similar capability.

Lagging Indicators (Value Creation): Outcomes Achieved measures whether predictions proved accurate and actions delivered results. Value Documented measures whether you can quantify crises prevented, opportunities captured, and decisions improved. ROI Demonstrated measures whether documented value exceeds investment. Organizational Recognition measures whether reputation intelligence is acknowledged as valuable.

If leading indicators are positive, lagging indicators typically follow. If leading indicators are negative, address them before expecting value creation.

Common Pitfalls and How to Avoid Them

Pitfall: Delivering Reports Instead of Intelligence. Reports describe what happened. Intelligence recommends what to do. If your deliverables lack specific, actionable recommendations, you're not providing intelligence—you're providing data. Solution: Every SIGNAL must include a clear recommendation with expected outcome. No recommendation, no SIGNAL.

Pitfall: Losing Sponsor Attention. Executive attention is scarce. If you're not consistently delivering value, your sponsor will move on to other priorities. Solution: Maintain regular touchpoints even when no major SIGNAL is warranted. Weekly pulse updates keep you visible and demonstrate ongoing value.

Pitfall: Over-Engineering the Methodology. Complexity is seductive. It's tempting to build elaborate scoring systems, sophisticated dashboards, and comprehensive frameworks before proving basic value. Solution: Start simple. Add complexity only when it demonstrably improves outcomes. Let needs drive sophistication, not the reverse.

Pitfall: Ignoring Organizational Politics. Reputation intelligence touches multiple functions with established interests. Ignoring the political landscape invites resistance. Solution: Map stakeholders early. Identify potential allies and skeptics.

Build relationships before you need them. Share credit generously.

Pitfall: Failing to Document Value. If you can't prove the value you've created, it's as if you haven't created any. Undocumented wins don't justify continued investment. Solution: Track everything from day one. Build proof chains systematically. Make ROI documentation a habit, not an afterthought.

The Long View

Building reputation intelligence capability is a multi-year journey, not a one-time project.

Year 1 is about proving value and establishing credibility. Individual wins that demonstrate undeniable impact. Converting skeptics through results.

Year 2 is about scaling and systematizing. From pilot to enterprise function. From ad hoc delivery to consistent operating cadence. From project to permanent capability.

Year 3 and beyond is about integration and evolution. Intelligence embedded in strategic planning, M&A evaluation, market entry decisions. Not a separate capability—a way the organization thinks.

The organizations that start now will have significant advantage over those that wait.

The methodology is proven. The technology exists. The only question is execution.

A Personal Note on Implementation

I've watched organizations build reputation intelligence capability from scratch. I've seen the challenges, the setbacks, and the breakthroughs.

What I can tell you with certainty: The organizations that succeed share common traits.

They start before they're ready. They don't wait for perfect conditions, complete data, or full executive buy-in. They begin with what they have and improve as they go.

They focus on value, not activity. They measure outcomes, not outputs. They track what changed because of their work, not how much work they did.

They persist through skepticism. Early stages are hard. Not everyone believes. The organizations that succeed keep delivering value until results speak louder than doubts.

They celebrate and share wins. Success creates momentum. Public recognition creates organizational permission. They don't hide their light under a bushel.

And they remember why they started. Reputation intelligence isn't about dashboards or data or even methodology. It's about helping organizations make better decisions—decisions that protect value, capture opportunity, and build lasting competitive advantage.

That's something worth building.

Getting Started: Your Next Steps

If you're ready to begin building reputation intelligence capability, here's where to start.

This week: Identify your most promising executive sponsor candidate. Research their priorities, decisions, and information gaps. Draft a one-page pilot proposal.

This month: Secure a discovery conversation with your sponsor candidate. Design a pilot based on their specific needs. Initiate monitoring capability.

This quarter: Deliver your first SIGNAL that drives action. Document outcomes and value. Make a go/no-go decision on expansion.

The framework is in this book. The methodology is proven. The case studies demonstrate what's possible.

What remains is your execution.

A Note on Implementation Support

Building reputation intelligence capability is achievable with internal resources, particularly for organizations with existing communications analytics experience.

However, implementation typically accelerates with experienced guidance. The methodology has nuances that benefit from pattern recognition across multiple implementations. The organizational dynamics have predictable challenges that experienced practitioners can help navigate.

measuredIO offers implementation support for organizations seeking to build reputation intelligence capability—from pilot design through enterprise scaling. The frameworks in this book form the foundation; implementation partnerships provide the acceleration.

Whether you build independently or with support, the mandate is clear: Organizations that develop reputation intelligence capability will outperform those that don't.

The question is when to start—not whether you should.

Building Your Team

A common question: What team structure does reputation intelligence require?

The answer evolves with implementation phase.

Phase 1 (Pilot) requires 0.5-1 FTE dedicated analyst time, part-time executive sponsor engagement, and access to a media monitoring platform. Total investment: $50-100K.

Phase 2 (Proof of Concept) requires 1-2 FTE analysts, defined stakeholder relationships, and an established technology stack. Total investment: $150-300K annually.

Phase 3 (Enterprise Function) requires a 2-4 FTE team (lead plus analysts), a clear organizational charter, a full technology suite, and integration with decision processes. Total investment: $500K-1M annually.

The team structure should follow value creation, not precede it. Don't build a large team before proving the capability works. Let demonstrated ROI justify investment.

Key Roles

The Reputation Intelligence Lead owns stakeholder relationships, methodology integrity, and strategic direction. This person must combine analytical capability with executive communication skills.

Analysts process data, identify patterns, develop SIGNALs, and track outcomes.

They need both quantitative skills and judgment about what matters strategically.

Technology/Data Support may be dedicated or shared. This function ensures platforms function, data flows correctly, and visualizations serve analytical needs.

Skills to Prioritize

The most important skills are strategic thinking (connecting data to business implications); executive communication (translating analysis into action); pattern recognition (seeing signals in noise); intellectual curiosity (constantly learning and improving); and organizational savvy (navigating politics and building relationships).

Technical skills matter, but judgment and communication matter more. You can teach tools; strategic thinking is harder to develop.

Technology Considerations

A brief word on technology, because it's often where organizations over-invest early and under-invest later.

What You Need in Phase 1: A media monitoring platform with decent coverage (Meltwater, Cision, Brandwatch, or similar); basic analysis capability (even Excel works initially); and a delivery mechanism (email, shared documents). That's it. Don't go enterprise-platform shopping before proving the concept.

What You'll Add in Phase 2-3: More sophisticated analysis and visualization tools; perception data integration (survey platforms, social listening); competitive benchmarking capability; and dashboard and reporting infrastructure.

What's Emerging: GEO monitoring (AI visibility tracking); BES integration (media + perception dual-lens); predictive modeling (pattern-based forecasting); and real-time alerting (threshold-triggered notifications).

The key principle: Let analytical needs drive technology investment. The best platform in the world creates no value if you don't have the methodology to use it effectively.

Where Should Reputation Intelligence Live?

A common question as the function matures: Where does reputation intelligence sit in the organization?

There's no single right answer, but there are patterns that work—and patterns that don't.

Common Models

Communications/Corporate Affairs. The most natural home for many organizations. Reputation is already in the communications mandate, media relationships exist, and crisis response typically lives here.

The risk: communications is sometimes seen as tactical rather than strategic, which can limit C-suite access.

Marketing. Works well when brand and marketing are tightly integrated. Marketing often has budget, analytical capability, and executive attention.

The risk: reputation intelligence can get absorbed into campaign measurement rather than maintaining its strategic, cross-functional role.

Strategy/Chief of Staff. Positions intelligence as enterprise capability from day one. Direct C-suite access, cross-functional authority, strategic framing.

The risk: may lack the operational infrastructure and media expertise that communications provides.

Standalone Function. Some organizations create dedicated reputation intelligence teams reporting directly to the CEO or COO. Maximum independence and authority.

The risk: requires significant investment and executive commitment before proving value—the opposite of our "start small" principle.

What Actually Matters

More important than reporting line is ensuring three things:

First, **C-suite access.** Wherever intelligence lives, it must have direct channels to executive decision-makers. If SIGNALs have to travel through multiple layers before reaching the CFO, they'll arrive too late—or not at all.

Second, **cross-functional authority**. Reputation intelligence touches communications, marketing, HR, investor relations, and product. The function needs permission to work across silos, regardless of where it's housed.

Third, **analytical credibility**. The team needs to be seen as rigorous and objective, not as advocates for any particular function's agenda. This credibility comes from methodology and track record, not org chart position.

The Practical Path

In Phase 1, don't worry about organizational positioning. Run the pilot from wherever you currently sit. Prove value first.

In Phase 2, as you expand to multiple stakeholders, positioning questions naturally arise. Use your proof points to negotiate the access and authority you need.

In Phase 3, formalize the function with a charter that codifies C-suite access, cross-functional scope, and reporting relationships. By then, your track record justifies the positioning you need.

Sophia's function ultimately reported to the Chief Communications Officer with a dotted line to the CEO's chief of staff—a hybrid that provided both operational home and strategic access. Your organization's right answer will depend on your specific context, relationships, and where your initial champions sit.

QUICK CHECK

> ### YOUR FIRST 90 DAYS
>
> This week: Identify your Henrik. Research their priorities. Next week: Have the discovery conversation. Complete the Persona Canvas. This month: Design and launch the pilot. One stakeholder, one signal type. This quarter: Deliver value. One SIGNAL that drives action. Document the outcome.
>
> By day 90, you need a proof point that converts skepticism into championship.

Key Takeaways

Why Implementations Fail. The most common failure patterns are boiling the ocean (trying everything at once); perfection over progress (waiting too long to deliver); technology-first thinking (buying tools before understanding needs); analyst-driven priorities (delivering what's interesting, not what's needed); and no quick wins (failing to prove value early).

The Five Principles. First, executive sponsorship is non-negotiable. Second, start with one persona, not all. Third, prove ROI before scaling. Fourth, iterate based on outcomes. Fifth, celebrate wins publicly.

The Three Phases. Phase 1 (Months 1-3) focuses on foundation and first proof point. Phase 2 (Months 4-6) focuses on proof of concept and expansion. Phase 3 (Months 7-12) focuses on enterprise capability.

Success Metrics. Leading indicators include engagement, action rate, feedback quality, and expansion interest. Lagging indicators include outcomes achieved, value documented, ROI demonstrated, and organizational recognition.

Bridge to Conclusion

You now have the implementation roadmap—the phases, principles, decisions, and pitfalls that will shape your journey from vision to capability.

The final chapter brings everything together: the personal journey that led to this methodology, the transformation we've witnessed in organizations that embrace reputation intelligence, and the future that awaits those who build this capability.

From playbook to perspective.

Let's conclude.

Note on Sources

The implementation roadmap, five principles, and three-phase framework presented in this chapter represent original methodology developed by the author based on experience implementing reputation intelligence systems across multiple organizations.

Sophia's implementation timeline, including the Phase 1-3 progression and specific week-by-week activities, continues the composite illustration introduced in earlier chapters. Specific metrics, timelines, and outcomes have been adjusted to protect client confidentiality while preserving the operational principles demonstrated.

The executive conversation structure, 90-day pilot framework, and team-building guidance are original frameworks developed through the author's professional practice.

Investment ranges and team structures reflect patterns observed across implementations of varying scale and are intended as directional guidance rather than precise specifications.

CHAPTER 10

THE FUTURE OF REPUTATION INTELLIGENCE

Bringing It All Together

"**W**e have dashboards. We have sentiment tracking. I'm still trying to find the action."

The Chief Communications Officer wasn't being dismissive. Her team had invested in the tools, built the infrastructure, delivered the reports. Every month, executives received comprehensive media analysis—volume trends, sentiment scores, competitive benchmarks, share of voice.

None of it told her what to *do*.

The dashboards described what happened. They didn't prescribe what should happen next. They reported the past without predicting the future. They measured activity without connecting to outcomes.

She had data. What she needed was intelligence.

That conversation crystallized something I'd been feeling for years: Despite all our measurement sophistication—the platforms, the analytics, the monthly reports—we couldn't connect what we were tracking to what the business actually cared about.

We counted mentions but couldn't quantify value.

The CCO wasn't wrong, and at the time, I didn't have a good answer.

That conversation—and my inability to respond convincingly—launched the work that eventually became this book.

The Journey to This Book

Let me tell you about the path that brought me here, because the methodology in these pages didn't emerge from academic theory. It emerged from decades of trial, error, and hard-won lessons across some of the world's most demanding organizations.

I spent thirteen years at Cisco Systems, leading market intelligence strategies and pioneering the integration of social media listening with advanced analytics. It was at Cisco where I first recognized the gap between what we could measure and what actually mattered—the disconnect between data abundance and strategic insight.

From there, I moved to Western Union as Global Lead of Media Analytics and Insight, where I built a Media Monitoring and Analytics Center of Excellence from scratch. Western Union was a different challenge: a 170-year-old financial services company navigating digital transformation while managing reputation across 200 countries and territories.

At Western Union, I inherited what many communications leaders inherit: a measurement approach that generated reports nobody read about metrics nobody acted on. We tracked volume, sentiment, share of voice. We produced monthly decks and quarterly analyses. And nothing changed.

The business made decisions without consulting our data. Crises caught us off guard despite our monitoring. Competitive threats emerged in markets where we had plenty of coverage but no insight. We were measuring everything and understanding nothing.

The breaking point came during a particularly painful episode when analyst sentiment shifted against us—a shift that was clearly visible in hindsight but that our measurement approach completely failed to flag in real time. We had the data. We had the coverage. What we lacked was the methodology to translate information into intelligence.

I've also had the privilege of working with organizations across sectors: the Denver Broncos, the U.S. Olympic Committee, Peet's Coffee, HP. Each engagement reinforced the same lesson: The gap between measurement and intelligence is where value is lost, and bridging that gap is where competitive advantage is created.

That accumulation of experience—across technology, financial services, sports, consumer brands—is what eventually crystallized into the methodology you've found in this book.

I started asking different questions. Not "how much coverage did we get?" but "what does this coverage mean for our business?" Not "what's our sentiment score?" but "what patterns in coverage predict outcomes we care about?" Not "how do we compare to competitors on volume?" but "where are we winning and losing the narrative battles that matter?"

The methodology evolved through experimentation. Some approaches worked; many didn't. MRS emerged from attempts to create a scoring system that actually correlated with business outcomes. Persona-Based Insights came from realizing that different executives needed different signals delivered in different ways. The SIGNAL framework crystallized when I recognized that the gap between insight and action was where most value was lost.

None of this was elegant or linear. It was messy, iterative, and often frustrating. But piece by piece, a coherent methodology emerged—one that transforms reputation measurement from backward-looking reporting into forward-looking intelligence.

Dino Delic (Meltwater), whose DDC research helped form some of the empirical foundation for this book's maturity framework, summarizes the opportunity: "We've assessed over 500 communications teams. The 8% operating at Level 3 or above aren't using better tools—they're using different thinking. This book gives the other 92% a roadmap to join them."

What We've Covered

Let me bring together the core elements of what you've learned.

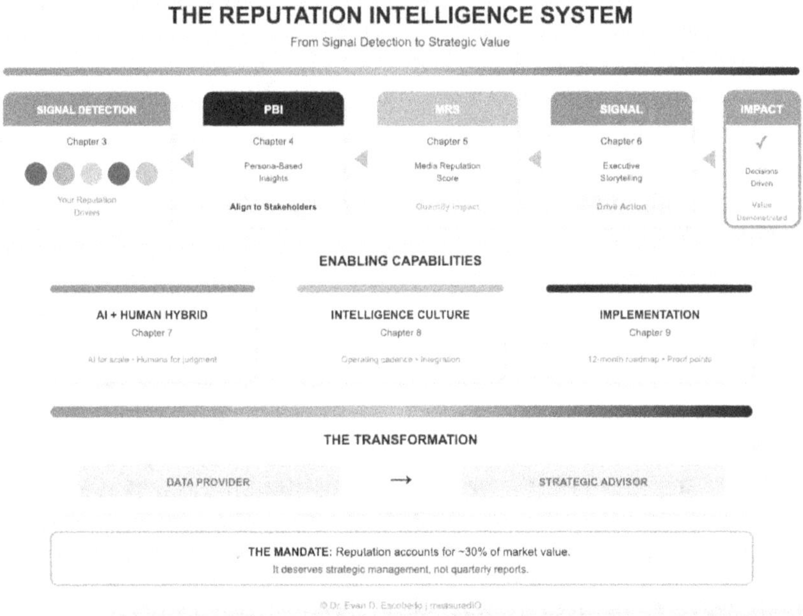

Figure 10.1: The Reputation Intelligence System—From Signal Detection to Strategic Value

The Foundation: Understanding What Reputation Really Is

Reputation isn't what you say about yourself. It's the aggregate perception held by stakeholders based on everything they see, hear, and experience related to your organization. It's constructed through narrative—the stories that media, analysts, employees, and customers tell about who you are and what you stand for.

This understanding changes everything about how we measure. We're not counting mentions; we're tracking narrative formation. We're not scoring sentiment; we're mapping perception drivers. We're not comparing volume; we're assessing competitive positioning in the battles that determine how stakeholders think about our category.

The Four Signals: A Framework for What Matters

Not everything that can be measured should be measured. The pillars you select—whether Trust, Innovation, Perception, and Reputation, or something entirely different—provide focus. These dimensions must capture what your stakeholders actually care about and what actually drives your business outcomes.

For organizations using Trust, Innovation, Perception, and Reputation: Trust signals predict investor confidence and regulatory standing. Innovation signals predict competitive positioning and market leadership. Perception signals predict customer consideration and preference. Reputation signals predict overall stakeholder support and organizational resilience.

But remember Henrik. His pillars were Platform/Partner, Digital Leader, Responsible Corporate Citizen, Employer of Choice, and Performance. For him, Platform/Partner signals predicted partnership opportunities and B2B growth. Digital Leader signals predicted competitive positioning in fintech. Different pillars, same principle: Measure what matters to your business.

By organizing measurement around the dimensions that emerged from your PBI work, you move from comprehensive-but-useless data collection to focused-and-actionable intelligence.

Persona-Based Insights: Delivering What Each Stakeholder Needs

Different executives need different things. The CFO cares about investor confidence and analyst sentiment. The CPO cares about competitive positioning and innovation perception. The CHRO cares about employer brand and talent market standing.

Persona-Based Insights ensures that the right insights reach the right people in the right format at the right time. It's the difference between producing reports and enabling decisions.

Media Reputation Score: Making Measurement Meaningful

MRS transforms raw coverage data into strategic insight. It's not about counting articles; it's about understanding what those articles mean for your business.

The methodology incorporates what matters: source credibility, message alignment, prominence, sentiment nuance, competitive context. It weights and scores in ways that correlate with actual business outcomes. And it produces intelligence that executives can act on—not just data they can file.

The SIGNAL Framework: From Insight to Action

Detection without action is pointless. The SIGNAL framework bridges the gap—providing a structure for translating analytical findings into executive-ready intelligence that drives organizational response.

Signal, Implication, Gap, Narrative, Action, Lift. Each element serves a purpose. Together, they ensure that intelligence doesn't just inform but transforms.

AI + Human Intelligence: The Hybrid Advantage

AI enables scale. Humans provide judgment. The future belongs to organizations that combine both effectively.

AI can process thousands of mentions, detect patterns, and flag anomalies. What it cannot do is interpret strategic significance, navigate organizational context, or build the relationships that turn insight into action. The hybrid approach leverages AI for what it does well while preserving human judgment for what only humans can do.

Building Culture: From Measurement to Operating System

Methodology alone changes nothing. Culture determines whether intelligence actually informs decisions or gathers dust on shared drives.

Building reputation intelligence culture requires executive sponsorship, quick wins, documented ROI, and systematic integration into how organizations actually work. It's the 80% of success that has nothing to do with data or methodology.

The Mandate: Reputation Intelligence as Strategic Function

According to Echo Research's 2024 U.S. Reputation Dividend report, corporate reputation accounts for 28% of total market capitalization across S&P 500 companies — equivalent to $11.9 trillion in value. For companies like Nvidia, Amazon, and Apple, that figure exceeds 50%. An asset of that magnitude is too valuable to manage with quarterly surveys and monthly reports.

Reputation Intelligence must become an enterprise function — not a communications service, not a marketing capability, but a strategic competency that sits alongside finance and strategy in informing the most important decisions organizations make.

KEY CONCEPT

> ### THE COMPLETE SYSTEM
>
> PBI: Discover who needs intelligence and what they care about. MRS: Quantify reputation against those discovered priorities. SIGNAL: Communicate intelligence in a format that drives action. AI + Human: Combine scale with judgment. Culture: Build the organizational foundation that makes it sustainable. Playbook: Execute in phases that prove value before scaling.
>
> Each piece depends on the others. Skip one, and the system fails.

What I've Witnessed

Let me share what becomes possible when organizations embrace reputation intelligence.

CFOs can change how they prepare for earnings calls. Instead of being surprised by analyst questions about governance or competitive positioning, they arrive armed with intelligence about emerging narratives and proactive responses. The dynamic shifts from reactive defense to strategic engagement.

Product leaders can time launches to narrative windows. Instead of shipping when engineering is ready, they ship when the market is ready to receive their message—when competitive noise is low, analyst attention is high, and the narrative environment is receptive. The same product, better outcome.

HR leaders can prevent employer-brand crises. Instead of discovering Glassdoor problems after they've damaged recruiting pipelines, they detect internal-to-external perception correlations early and intervene before external perception declines. Prevention, not recovery.

Communications teams can transform their organizational standing. Instead of being seen as the people who write press releases and handle media calls, they become strategic advisors who inform major decisions with intelligence that no one else provides. Career transformation follows functional transformation.

Organizations can build sustainable competitive advantage. Early adopters develop pattern recognition, predictive accuracy, and organizational capability that late entrants can't easily replicate. The gap widens over time.

These aren't hypothetical possibilities. They're patterns I've observed when organizations commit to building reputation intelligence capability—and outcomes that become increasingly achievable as the methodology matures within an organization.

What Comes Next

The evolution continues. Here's what I see on the horizon.

Integration Deepens

The future isn't three separate views—media intelligence, perception data, AI visibility. It's one integrated intelligence system that connects all inputs into coherent understanding.

Brand Equity Score represents an early version of this integration: MRS plus survey data creating a dual-lens view. Add GEO monitoring, voice of customer data, employee sentiment, and investor perception tracking, and you have something approaching comprehensive reputation intelligence.

The organizations that build integration capability first will see farther than competitors who rely on siloed data sources.

Prediction Improves

As organizations accumulate outcome data—which signals predicted which results, which interventions worked, which patterns repeated— prediction accuracy improves.

Early implementations make educated guesses based on limited precedent. Mature implementations make refined predictions based on extensive pattern matching. The difference in value is substantial.

AI Capability Expands

Today's AI handles pattern detection and anomaly flagging. Tomorrow's AI will handle more sophisticated analysis—connecting disparate signals, identifying complex patterns, generating draft interpretations for human review.

The human role doesn't diminish; it elevates. As AI handles routine analysis, humans focus on strategic interpretation, stakeholder relationships, and organizational integration. The hybrid model evolves but doesn't disappear.

The Standard Rises

What seems like advanced capability today becomes the bare minimum tomorrow. Organizations that don't measure reputation effectively will be at increasing disadvantage as competitors who do measure effectively capture value they leave on the table.

The question isn't whether your organization will eventually build reputation intelligence capability. The question is whether you'll build it early enough to capture the advantage—or late enough to simply play catch-up.

Looking Ahead: The Next Evolution

The methodology in this book represents where reputation intelligence stands today. But the field continues to evolve, and two emerging capabilities point toward where it's heading.

From MRS to Brand Equity Score

In Chapter 3, I introduced Brand Equity Score—the dual-lens approach that integrates media narrative (MRS) with stakeholder perception (survey data). The combination reveals the Public Signal Gap Index (PSGI): the misalignment between what people believe and what narratives are being told.

That gap is where strategic opportunity lives. Under-leveraged goodwill. Over-indexed narrative. Alignment or misalignment between story and reality.

For organizations ready to move beyond media-only measurement, BES represents the next capability layer. It requires more infrastructure—survey data, integration methodology, additional analytical capability—but the strategic insight justifies the investment. You're no longer asking just "What are they saying about us?" but "Is what they're saying aligned with what people actually believe?"

Master MRS first. Then evolve to BES when your organization's readiness allows.

Generative Engine Optimization: The New Discovery Frontier

There's another shift underway that will reshape reputation management entirely: AI is becoming a primary discovery platform.

When a procurement officer asks ChatGPT to recommend enterprise software vendors; when a job candidate asks Claude about company culture; when an investor asks Gemini to summarize a company's competitive position—these AI responses shape perception just as powerfully as traditional media coverage.

But here's the challenge: AI responses are shaped by training data, retrieval sources, and algorithmic synthesis in ways that are opaque and difficult to influence. Your brand's representation in AI-generated responses isn't something you directly control—and most organizations aren't even monitoring it.

Generative Engine Optimization (GEO) is the emerging discipline of understanding and improving how brands appear in AI-generated content. It encompasses monitoring (what do AI systems say about you?); analysis (where do AI responses align or conflict with your desired positioning?); and optimization (what content and signals improve your AI visibility?).

The integration of GEO monitoring with MRS creates yet another dual-lens: narrative quality (how media covers you) plus AI visibility (how AI systems represent you). Organizations building this capability now—while the field is nascent and competitive advantage is available—will be best positioned as AI-driven discovery becomes mainstream.

Early indicators suggest AI visibility correlates with, but doesn't mirror, traditional media coverage. Brands with strong, consistent narratives across authoritative sources tend to be represented more favorably in AI responses. Brands with fragmented, inconsistent, or thin media presence tend to be represented poorly—or not at all.

The implications for reputation strategy are significant. The content you create, the sources you're cited in, the consistency of your narrative across touchpoints—all of these influence not just human readers but the AI systems that increasingly mediate how stakeholders encounter your brand.

The Road Ahead

BES and GEO represent the next frontier of reputation intelligence. Neither is fully mature today, but both are advancing rapidly. Organizations that begin building capability now—even experimentally—will develop pattern recognition and organizational muscle that late entrants will struggle to replicate.

The methodology in this book provides the foundation. MRS, PBI, SIGNAL, the hybrid AI+Human model—these remain essential regardless of what additional capabilities you layer on top. Master them first. Then extend into BES and GEO as your organization's readiness and the field's maturity allow.

The future of reputation intelligence is integration: media narrative plus stakeholder perception plus AI visibility, unified into comprehensive understanding that informs strategic decisions.

That future is closer than most organizations realize.

PRO TIP

> **THE NEXT FRONTIER: BES AND GEO**
>
> Brand Equity Score (BES): Integrates media narrative (MRS) with stakeholder perception (survey data), revealing the gap between what people believe and what narratives are being told. Generative Engine Optimization (GEO): Monitors how AI systems represent your brand. As AI becomes a primary discovery platform, your visibility in AI responses shapes perception.
>
> Master MRS first. Then evolve to BES and GEO when your organization's readiness allows.

The Invitation

I wrote this book because I believe reputation intelligence represents a genuine opportunity for communications professionals to reinvent their role by creating strategic value.

For too long, our field has struggled with the perception—sometimes deserved—that we can't prove our worth. We've measured what's easy rather than what matters. We've produced reports rather than intelligence. We've described what happened rather than predicting what will happen.

Reputation Intelligence changes that equation.

With the right methodology, communications becomes a strategic function. With the right integration, reputation data informs major decisions. With the right culture, intelligence drives action that creates measurable value.

The tools exist. The methodology is proven. The business case is clear.

What remains is execution. Your execution.

Starting Monday

If you've read this far, you're not looking for more theory. You're looking for action.

Here's what I want you to do.

This week: Identify one executive in your organization who makes decisions that reputation intelligence could improve. Research their priorities, their challenges, their information gaps.

Next week: Have a conversation. Not a pitch—a discovery. Learn what they need, what they're missing, what would make their decisions better.

This month: Design a pilot. Small, focused, time-bound. One stakeholder, one signal type, one proof point.

This quarter: Deliver value. Not reports—value. Something that prevents a problem, captures an opportunity, or improves a decision. Document it rigorously.

This year: Build from success. Add stakeholders, expand capability, formalize function. Let demonstrated value justify continued investment.

The path from here to organizational capability runs through those steps. Not all at once—one step at a time. Not perfectly—learning as you go. Not alone—building relationships and partnerships that accelerate progress.

QUICK CHECK

YOUR ACTION PLAN

This week: Identify one executive whose decisions reputation intelligence could improve. This month: Have the discovery conversation. Design a pilot based on their needs. This quarter: Deliver your first SIGNAL that drives action. Document the outcome. This year: Build from success. Add stakeholders, expand capability, formalize function.

The framework is in this book. The methodology is proven. What remains is your execution.

Why Am I in This Meeting? (Revisited)

Remember Marcus? The Regional President who interrupted my share-of-voice presentation to ask about digital transformation in his markets? The one whose eyes pleaded, "Why am I in this meeting?"

That moment was a turning point.

It forced me to do the work I should have done from the start. I documented his priorities—digital transformation narrative, competitive positioning in key markets, analyst perception of innovation. I built measurement around pillars that matched his strategic plan. I created intelligence briefs focused on exactly what he needed to know.

The shift wasn't instant, and it wasn't magic. But over time, the dynamic changed. Instead of polite tolerance, there was genuine engagement. Instead of reports he filed away, there was intelligence he actually used.

The question shifted from "Why am I in this meeting?" to "What are you seeing?"

That's the transformation this book makes possible. From data provider to strategic advisor. From polite dismissal to active partnership. From "Why am I in this meeting?" to "I need you in this meeting."

Your Marcus is out there. Maybe it's your CEO, your CFO, your Chief Communications Officer, or a Regional President frustrated by generic reports. They have questions. They have decisions to make. They're waiting for someone to connect the dots between media data and business outcomes.

Now you know how.

When I started in this field, I was a data provider. I built dashboards. I tracked metrics. I produced reports that looked impressive but changed nothing. I was throwing information over the fence and hoping someone would find it useful.

Marcus changed that.

Not Marcus specifically—but the dozens of executives like him who taught me, sometimes painfully, that measurement without context is just noise. The CEO who asked why he needed media measurement when he read the Wall Street Journal every morning. The Regional President who interrupted my share-of-voice presentation to ask about digital transformation in his markets. The Chief Communications Officer who looked at my seven-pillar framework and said, "These aren't our priorities."

Each of them was telling me the same thing: Start with us. Understand what we need. Then build measurement that serves those needs.

That's the journey this book has taken you through. You've learned to detect signals (Chapter 3). You've learned to discover priorities through Persona-Based Insights (Chapter 4). You've learned to quantify reputation with MRS against those priorities (Chapter 5). You've learned to communicate with SIGNAL (Chapter 6) and combine AI with human judgment (Chapter 7). You've learned to build the culture that makes intelligence actionable (Chapter 8) and the implementation playbook to get there (Chapter 9).

But none of it matters if you skip the discovery work. None of it matters if you don't find your Henrik.

KEY CONCEPT

> **THE TRANSFORMATION**
>
> From: "Why am I in this meeting?" To: "I need you in this meeting." From: Data provider To: Strategic advisor. From: Reporting what happened To: Shaping what happens next. Your Henrik is out there. They have questions. They have decisions to make.
>
> They're waiting for someone to connect the dots. Now you know how.

A Final Word

I've spent over 20 years in communications and marketing—navigating the evolution from basic media monitoring to reputation intelligence, from tactical reporting to strategic function.

What I've learned is This: the gap between where communications measurement has been and where it can go is immense. Most organizations are operating with methodologies designed for a world that no longer exists. They're measuring the wrong things in the wrong ways and failing to connect measurement to decision-making.

This represents both a challenge and an opportunity.

The challenge is that changing how organizations think about reputation measurement requires sustained effort. It means challenging established practices, building new capabilities, and demonstrating value repeatedly until skepticism transforms into championship.

The opportunity is that those who do this work create genuine competitive advantage. They see what others miss. They act while others react. They build organizational capability that compounds over time.

Remember that CEO who asked me "Why do we need Meltwater? Why do we need media measurement at all?"

Today, I have an answer.

We need media measurement—real measurement, reputation intelligence—because reputation represents 30% of market capitalization. Because narrative shapes stakeholder perception before perception shapes behavior. Because the organizations that detect signals early and act on them decisively outperform those that react to crises after they've already caused damage.

We need it because the alternative is flying blind in a world where reputation has never been more valuable or more vulnerable.

Reputation Intelligence isn't just a methodology. It's a strategic choice—a decision to treat reputation as the valuable asset it is and to build the capability to manage it accordingly.

I hope this book has given you the frameworks, the examples, and the confidence to make that choice.

The future belongs to organizations that understand what reputation measurement can become.

Build it.

To continue the conversation and access
implementation resources:
measuredio.com
I'm excited to see what you build!

References

Echo Research. (2024). *U.S. Reputation Dividend Report 2024*. Echo Research.   https://www.echoresearch.com/news-events/119-trillion-in-sp-500-firms-attributed-to-reputation/

Note on Sources

This concluding chapter synthesizes the original methodology presented throughout the book, drawing on the author's professional experience at Cisco Systems, Western Union, and other organizations referenced in the narrative.

The Dino Delic quote regarding DDC research and the 8% of communications teams operating at Level 3 or above is used with permission. The DDC (Data-Driven Communications) research methodology and findings that inform this book's maturity framework are detailed in Delic's whitepaper, "Making the Case for Comms," published by Meltwater.

The outcomes described in "What I've Witnessed"—including CFO preparation changes, product launch timing optimization, employer brand crisis prevention, and communications team transformation—represent patterns observed across the author's professional practice rather than specific client engagements.

All methodology frameworks presented in this chapter (Four Signals, MRS, PBI, SIGNAL, hybrid AI+Human model) are original to this work, developed through the author's experience as described in "The Journey to This Book."

ACKNOWLEDGMENTS

No methodology develops in isolation. This work reflects the contributions of countless colleagues, clients, mentors, and partners who shaped my thinking over more than two decades.

I'm grateful to the teams at Cisco Systems, where I spent 13 formative years learning how to integrate intelligence into strategic decision-making. I'm grateful to my colleagues at Western Union, who trusted me to build something new and gave me the latitude to experiment, fail, and ultimately succeed.

I'm grateful to the organizations that invited me into their challenges—the Denver Broncos, the U.S. Olympic Committee, Peet's Coffee, HP, and many others—each of which taught me something about how different contexts demand different approaches while the underlying principles remain constant.

I'm grateful to my academic colleagues and students. My doctoral work in computer science, focused on the strategic use of social media to drive business advantage, provided the theoretical foundation for much of what became practical methodology. Teaching continues to sharpen my thinking; there's no better test of whether you truly understand something than trying to explain it to someone learning it for the first time.

I owe special thanks to Meltwater and to Dino Delic, the leader who brought the important work of Data-Driven Communications to life.

Dino's vision created a space for innovation and experimentation — and it was within that space that the Media Reputation Score methodology took shape. Michael Samuels in Meltwater's Customer Success team was the critical partner in that development, translating theoretical frameworks into practical implementation and pushing the methodology further than I could have taken it alone. As Michael put it: "What began as an effort to understand coverage became a system for driving strategic action." That captures it better than I could.

I'm grateful to the team at measuredIO for the partnership in bringing these ideas to life and to market. Building a company around these principles has meant the freedom to trial, error, and innovate—to test ideas in the real world and refine them based on what actually works. That environment of continuous learning is where methodology becomes practice.

And I'm grateful to you, the reader, for investing the time to engage with these ideas. I hope they serve you well.

ABOUT THE AUTHOR

Dr. Evan D. Escobedo is a pioneering leader in reputation intelligence and media analytics, with over two decades of experience transforming how organizations measure, manage, and leverage reputation as a strategic asset.

As the founder of measuredIO (measuredio.com) and former Global Lead of Media Analytics & Insight at Western Union, Evan has redefined the field of communications measurement—helping organizations move beyond vanity metrics to signal-based intelligence that informs corporate strategy, protects brand equity, and drives measurable business impact.

The Innovation Behind This Book

Evan's career took a pivotal turn when he developed the Media Reputation Score (MRS) framework—a breakthrough methodology designed to assess not just the volume of media coverage, but its true impact on brand reputation. Central to his approach is the conviction that measurement must be grounded in business priorities: The pillars you measure should reflect what your organization actually cares about, not generic industry categories.

Frustrated by the limitations of traditional PR metrics—Share of Voice, Advertising Value Equivalency, basic sentiment analysis—Evan pioneered a new approach that incorporates AI-driven signal detection to identify reputation shifts before they become crises; human-validated analysis to ensure contextual accuracy beyond automated tools; weighted scoring models that assess the influence, prominence, and credibility of media narratives; Persona-Based Insights (PBI) to discover what stakeholders actually care about before building measurement systems; and the SIGNAL framework to translate data into executive action. The characters of Marcus, Henrik, and Sophia in this book are composites drawn from the many executives Evan has partnered with over two decades—leaders who pushed him to move beyond vanity metrics and deliver intelligence that actually drives decisions.

This methodology has been tested across Fortune 500 companies, professional sports organizations, and global brands—consistently demonstrating that communications teams can evolve from data providers to strategic advisors.

Professional Background

Evan's expertise spans corporate communications, business intelligence, predictive analytics, and AI-driven reputation management. His career includes:

- Thirteen years at Cisco Systems, where he learned to integrate intelligence into strategic decision-making at enterprise scale
- Leadership at Western Union, building the global media analytics and reputation intelligence function
- Consulting engagements with organizations including the Denver Broncos, U.S. Olympic Committee, Peet's Coffee, and HP

Today, Evan partners with Meltwater to bring the methodology in this book to market, delivering reputation intelligence solutions to enterprise clients, and co-leads the Data-Driven Communications (DDC) workshop series worldwide. The DDC research underlying this partnership, led by Meltwater's Dino Delic, assessed 500+ organizations and provides the empirical foundation for this book's maturity framework.

Academic Credentials

Evan holds a Doctorate in Computer Science specializing in the strategic impact of social media and AI-driven analytics in corporate communications. He serves as Adjunct Professor at Colorado Christian University, teaching courses on data-driven marketing, corporate communications, and media intelligence. His doctoral research provided the theoretical foundation for the practical methodologies in this book—bridging academic rigor with real-world application.

Philosophy

Evan's work is guided by a simple principle: "The best intelligence in the world is worthless if no one acts on it."

This belief drives everything in *Reputation Intelligence*—from the SIGNAL framework designed for executive action, to the proof chain methodology that demonstrates tangible ROI, to the cultural guidance that ensures intelligence becomes embedded in organizational decision-making.

His approach transforms communications professionals from reporters of what happened into advisors on what to do—the shift from data provider to strategic advisor that defines the future of the field.

Connect

measuredIO: measuredio.com | LinkedIn: linkedin.com/in/evanescobedo

Speaking & Consulting: Available for keynotes, workshops, and implementation partnerships.

Dr. Escobedo lives in Colorado with his family. When not building reputation intelligence systems, he can be found on the golf course or on a run, pursuing his philosophy: "Everything in Pursuit of Better."

THE REPUTATION INTELLIGENCE TOOLKIT

This appendix provides nine ready-to-use tools to implement the frameworks in this book. Each tool is available as a free interactive application at measuredio.com/book/tools — no software installation required. Open any tool in your browser, fill it in, and print or export your results.

The tools map to four phases of reputation intelligence work:

DISCOVER	MEASURE	COMMUNICATE	PROVE
Tools 1–4	Tools 5 & 9	Tool 6	Tools 7 & 8
Build the foundation: Who needs what intelligence and why?	**Quantify the reputation:** Score, aggregate, and track over time.	Brief the executive: SIGNAL format, acted on in hours.	Show the ROI: Document decisions. Build the career case.

Work through the tools in order the first time. After that, use them as your ongoing operating system — the PBI Builder informs your scoring setup, the scoring tools feed your SIGNAL Briefs, and the Proof Chain captures the impact.

All tools are free to access and use. No account required. Available at measuredio.com/book/tools.

DISCOVER: Tools 1-4

The discovery tools answer one question before anything else: who needs what intelligence, and why? Without this foundation, everything downstream is guesswork. These four tools represent the PBI methodology in practice — structured conversation translated into operational inputs.

Tool 1	Persona-Based Insights™ Builder		
Chapter	Chapter 4: Persona-Based Insights	Phase	Discover
Purpose	The digital implementation of the PBI methodology. Walk through four structured steps — Business Priority, Persona Canvas, Signal Definition, and Agile Statement — to capture everything you need before building your intelligence program. Replaces the PDF worksheet with an interactive, printable application.		
What's Inside	• Step-by-step guided flow from business priority to completed Agile Persona Statement • Persona Canvas capturing mandate, KPIs, decision cadence, trusted sources, and proof requirements • Signal Definition separating mentions, metrics, and true signals • Mention → Metric → Signal ladder to sharpen your thinking • Live preview of your Agile Statement as you type		
	• The So What Test: What's changing / Why it matters / What to do • Reality Check: Does your current reporting answer this need? • Print-ready summary page and plain-text export		
Download	measuredio.com/book/tools/pbi-builder		

Tool 2	Priority Markets Map		
Chapter	Chapter 4: Persona-Based Insights	Phase	Discover
Purpose	When your organization operates across multiple regions or markets, not all of them deserve equal intelligence resources. This tool scores and tiers your markets based on strategic value, narrative priority, risk level, and media ecosystem quality — producing a clear, defensible resource allocation.		
What's Inside	• Score markets across four dimensions on a 1–5 scale • Weighted scoring produces a Priority Index with automatic tier assignment • Critical (Tier 1): Weekly monitoring and dedicated coverage • Important (Tier 2): Bi-weekly monitoring and shared coverage • Monitor (Tier 3): Monthly check-ins and exception-based alerts • Notes field for context, rationale, and regional considerations • Export to Excel for quarterly review and stakeholder alignment		
Download	measuredio.com/book/tools/priority-markets-map		

Tool 3	Media Weighting Matrix		
Chapter	Chapter 4: Persona-Based Insights	Phase	Discover
Purpose	Not all outlets carry equal influence for your stakeholder. Henrik's trusted sources are not the same as the CFO's. This tool translates your PBI conversation into a ranked, tiered outlet list that feeds directly into your MRS Source Authority scores. Build one matrix per persona.		
What's Inside	<ul><li>Score outlets across Reach, Relevance, Relationship quality, and Executive Attention (each 1–5)</li><li>Automatic tier assignment: Tier 1 (3x weight), Tier 2 (2x weight), Tier 3 (1x weight)</li><li>Load a pre-populated Henrik example to see the tool in action</li><li>Tier distribution summary showing your outlet portfolio at a glance</li><li>Sorts automatically by average score — highest influence outlets surface to the top</li><li>Export to Excel for documentation and team alignment</li></ul>		
Download	measuredio.com/book/tools/media-weighting-matrix		

Tool 4	**Competitor Influence Scorecard**		
Chapter	Chapter 4: Persona-Based Insights	Phase	Discover
Purpose	Not all competitors matter equally to your reputation. Some directly threaten your primary narrative; others are noise. This scorecard identifies which competitors most strongly shape the conversation in your space and calibrates monitoring intensity accordingly — so you're watching the right battles.		
What's Inside	<ul><li>Score competitors across five dimensions: Strategic Importance, Innovation Strength, Executive Voice, Market Overlap, and Narrative Authority</li><li>Weighted scoring produces an Influence Index with automatic monitoring tier</li><li>Close Watch: Weekly monitoring for top competitors</li><li>Monitor: Bi-weekly tracking for secondary competitors</li><li>Awareness: Monthly check for lower-priority competitors</li><li>Recommendation field for specific monitoring actions</li><li>Export to Excel for program documentation</li></ul>		
Download	measuredio.com/book/tools/ competitor-influence-scorecard		

MEASURE: Tools 5 & 9

The measurement tools turn your PBI inputs into scored, quantified, trackable reputation data. Tool 5 handles the article-level scoring that is the engine of the MRS. Tool 9 aggregates those scores into the pillar MRS, overall MRS, and competitive benchmarks that go to Henrik. These two tools work together — one scores, the other rolls up.

Tool 5	MRS Scoring Guide		
Chapter	Chapter 5: Media Reputation Score	Phase	Measure
Purpose	The operational manual for scoring articles and calculating your Media Reputation Score. This is the most detailed tool in the toolkit — because execution is where most programs fail. Covers pillar definitions, all six scoring dimensions with rubrics, a live article scorer, and the tagging workflow that keeps the system running.		
What's Inside	• Complete scoring rubrics for all six dimensions: Source Authority (0–100), Prominence (1.0–1.5×), Salience (0.8–1.5×), Sentiment (0.5–1.5×), Key Message Bonus (−20 to +30), Voice Bonus (−15 to +25) • Live Article Scorer: enter dimensions, calculate score instantly, log to a running article library • Pillar Definitions tab: document each pillar's name, keywords, example headlines, and MRS weight • Tagging Workflow tab: daily, weekly, monthly, and quarterly cadence guidance • Formula reference: Article Score, Normalized Score, Pillar Score, Overall MRS • Export article log to Excel for MRS roll-up calculations		
Download	measuredio.com/book/tools/mrs-scoring-guide		

Tool 9	MRS Roll-up Calculator		
Chapter	Chapter 5: Media Reputation Score	Phase	Measure
Purpose	Tool 5 scores individual articles. This tool aggregates those scores into the numbers that go to Henrik — a weighted overall MRS, pillar-by-pillar breakdowns, month-over-month trends, and competitive benchmarks. These three numbers — overall MRS, pillar scores, and competitive delta — are the core of every SIGNAL Brief.		
What's Inside	• Set up 3–5 reputation pillars with custom weights (must total 100%) • Enter monthly pillar averages from your Tool 5 article log; overall MRS calculates automatically • Live pillar bar chart showing each pillar's contribution to overall score • MRS interpretation guide: Strong (70–100), Moderate (50–69), Weak (30–49), Critical (below 30) • Monthly Trend tab: build a running history, see month-over-month movement • Competitive tab: enter competitor MRS by pillar, see delta vs. your brand instantly • Export pillar scores, trend data, and competitive comparison to Excel		
Download	measuredio.com/book/tools/mrs-rollup-calculator		

COMMUNICATE: Tool 6

Intelligence that doesn't reach the executive in a format they can act on is just data with better packaging. The SIGNAL Brief is how reputation intelligence crosses the desk of a Henrik and produces a decision within hours, not weeks.

Tool 6	SIGNAL Brief Template		
Chapter	Chapter 6: The SIGNAL Framework	Phase	Communicate
Purpose	The SIGNAL Brief is how reputation intelligence reaches the executive suite in a format that produces action. This tool walks through all six components of the SIGNAL framework, generates a live preview of your completed brief, and produces a print-ready document for delivery. Write the Executive Summary last; place it first.		
What's Inside	• Signal Detected (S): What changed — specific, quantified, with timeframe • Implications for Business (I): Why it matters — connected to Henrik's outcomes, not comms metrics • Gap Analysis (G): Where you stand — competitive context from your MRS data • Narrative Recommendation (N): What story to tell — strategic, specific, actionable • Action Required (A): Who does what by when — named owners and specific deadlines		
	• Lift Expected (L): Anticipated ROI — quantified where possible • Urgency level selector: Critical (same-day), High (this week), Medium (weekly report), Low (monthly) • Live preview tab and print/PDF export for direct delivery to stakeholders		
Download	measuredio.com/book/tools/ signal-brief-template		

PROVE: Tools 7 & 8

Proof is what separates a strategic advisor from a service provider. These two tools document the evidence that your intelligence drove decisions, and give you a concrete implementation path from first conversation to first SIGNAL Brief.

Tool 7	Proof Chain Builder		
Chapter	Chapter 6: The SIGNAL Framework	Phase	Prove
Purpose	The Proof Chain is your career artifact. One documented Proof Chain is worth more than a year of dashboards. This tool captures the complete signal-to-outcome sequence — what you detected, what you recommended, what decision was made, and what happened — building the ROI library you'll use in every budget conversation and performance review.		
What's Inside	• Four-step structure: Signal Detected → Brief Delivered → Decision Made → Outcome & ROI • Captures MRS pillar score before and after for each chain • Decision status tracking: Full action, Partial action, Pending, No action • ROI fields: estimated value protected or created, signal-to-decision time, MRS change • Impact rating: High (clear causal link), Medium (likely contribution), Low (correlation only) • Chain Library tab: browse, manage, and review your complete proof portfolio • Portfolio summary: total chains, decisions influenced, high-impact chains • Export full library to Excel for QBR presentations and budget conversations		
Download	measuredio.com/book/tools/proof-chain-builder		

Tool 8	90-Day Implementation Roadmap		
Chapter	All Chapters	Phase	Prove
Purpose	The Roadmap translates the methodology in this book into a week-by-week implementation plan. It answers the question every practitioner asks after finishing a framework book: okay, but where do I actually start? The sequence matters as much as the content — and the Go/No-Go checkpoints at the end of each month ensure you build the foundation before you build the intelligence.		
What's Inside	• Month 1 — Foundation (Weeks 1–4): Identify your Henrik, complete PBI conversation, build Media Matrix, Competitor Scorecard, and Priority Markets Map; define pillars and establish tagging workflow • Month 2 — Build (Weeks 5–8): Score first 100 articles manually, calibrate, calculate baseline MRS by pillar; add competitors and build first Competitive Scorecard • Month 3 — Deliver (Weeks 9–12): Create first SIGNAL Brief, deliver to Henrik for feedback, document one influenced decision, build first Proof Chain • Interactive checkbox tracking with overall progress bar • Go/No-Go checkpoint at the end of each month — don't advance until you can honestly say yes • Notes fields for each month to capture context, decisions, and lessons • Export full checklist to Excel for team tracking and manager reporting		
Download	measuredio.com/book/tools/ implementation-roadmap		

A Note on Getting Started

The most common mistake practitioners make with a toolkit like this is trying to use all of it at once. Don't. Start with Tool 1. Have one PBI conversation. Fill in one canvas. Then pick up Tool 3 and score ten outlets. Then score twenty articles with Tool 5. Let the work build naturally.

The practitioners who succeed with this methodology are not the ones who implement it perfectly on day one. They're the ones who implement it incrementally and keep going. A rough PBI canvas and twenty manually scored articles is infinitely more valuable than a perfect system you never actually ran.

Your Henrik is out there. They have questions. They have decisions to make. They're waiting for someone to connect the dots between what's happening in the media landscape and what it means for their business. These tools give you the system to become that person.

All tools available free at measuredio.com/book/tools

INDEX

A

Activation Gap 64
AI (Artificial Intelligence)
  governance challenges 185, 200
  human hybrid model 155
  limitations of 184, 277
AMEC 33, 52, 60, 62, 157
Ansoff, Igor, 60
AVE 23, 25, 32, 51

B

Barcelona Principles xiii, 19, 33, 51, 52,
      53, 55, 56, 57, 59, 60, 62, 157
Brand Equity Score (BES) vi, 267

C

Case studies xviii
  QuickServe (composite) vi, 25, 28, 62
  TechFinance (composite) vi, xvii, xviii,
      xxii, xxiv, xxviii, 98, 169
  YesMadam (2024) 8, 9, 20, 21, 65, 66
Cision 3, 19, 126, 147, 189, 201, 239,
      249
Crisis management 25, 26, 62

D

Data-Driven Communications (DDC)
      13, 21, 278

Delic, Dino 13, 21, 87, 96, 258, 273,
      275, 279

E

Edelman Trust Barometer 37, 61
Edward Bernays 30

F

Four Signals Framework 71
  Innovation 96, 100, 108, 109, 112,
      116, 117, 121, 124, 133, 134,
      135, 136, 138, 139, 157, 161,
      162, 167, 173,
  Perception 36, 48, 49, 58, 60, 61, 69,
      70, 71, 74, 75, 77, 78, 79, 80, 81,
      82, 83, 87, 96, 121, 134, 135,
      157, 213, 259
  Reputation i, ii, iii, vi, ix, x, xiii, xiv, xv,
      xix, xxi, xxiv, xxvi, xxviii, xxix, 7, 8,
      16, 23, 36, 37, 38, 121, 122, 123,
      125, 126, 128, 132, 151, 154,
      156, 287
  Trust 71

G

Generation 19
Generation 1/2/3 measurement 19
GEO (Generative Engine Optimization)
      237, 238, 249, 263, 266, 267

H

Henrik (Regional President persona)
xvii, xviii, xxiv, 17, 18, 98, 99, 114,
115, 116, 117, 123, 130, 131,
142, 143, 147, 151, 200, 201,
204, 205, 212, 235, 252, 259,
271, 278, 284, 286, 287, 288,
290, 291
Human-AI hybrid model xiv, 89, 133,
137, 149, 155, 157, 183, 184,
186, 187, 188, 215, 219, 227,
228, 261, 262, 267, 273

I

Implementation roadmap xxvii, 231,
253
Innovation signal 5, 50, 83, 138, 161,
167, 213, 218, 221, 224

M

Maturity Levels 12, 17
McKinsey & Company 230
measuredIO v, vi, 152, 240, 247, 276,
277, 279
Media Reputation Score (MRS) vi, xxi,
16, 86, 157, 277
Meltwater ix, x, xi, 3, 13, 19, 20, 21, 36,
60, 61, 63, 87, 95, 96, 123, 126,
127, 137, 147, 156, 188, 189,
201, 239, 249, 258, 272, 273,
275, 276, 278, 279
Monday Morning Test xiii, 3, 20, 23,
64, 83

O

Operating Cadence xv, 212, 217, 227

P

Persona-Based Insights (PBI) vi, xiv, xxi,
16, 86, 122, 278

R

RepTrak 23, 25, 36, 37, 43, 44, 48, 57,
61, 69, 76, 112, 122, 126, 127,
132, 139, 156

S

Share of Voice (SOV) 34, 35, 56, 277
SIGNAL Framework xiv, 16, 162, 163,
180, 260, 288, 289
Source authority weighting 66

T

TechFinance case study vi, xvii, xviii,
xxii, xxiv, xxviii, 98, 169
Trust signal 27, 46, 73, 90, 100, 109,
162, 164, 169, 171, 172, 200,
222, 224, 226, 236

W

Western Union i, iii, ix, 227, 256, 273,
275, 277, 278

Y

YesMadam case study 21